SYDENHAM AND FOREST HILL PAST

For
STEVE GRINDLAY
to whom I pass the baton

First published 1999
by Historical Publications Ltd
32 Ellington Street, London N7 8PL
(Tel: 020-7607 1628)

ISBN 0 948667 61 3
British Library Cataloguing-in-Publication Data
A catalogue record for this book is available from the British Library.

Typeset in Palatino by Historical Publications
Reproduction by G & J Graphics
Printed in Zaragoza, Spain by Edelvives

SYDENHAM AND FOREST HILL PAST

John Coulter

historical PUBLICATIONS

1. *Robert Morden's 1686 map shows Sidnum Place (Place House), Perry Street, and Sidnum as the three local place names.*

Contents

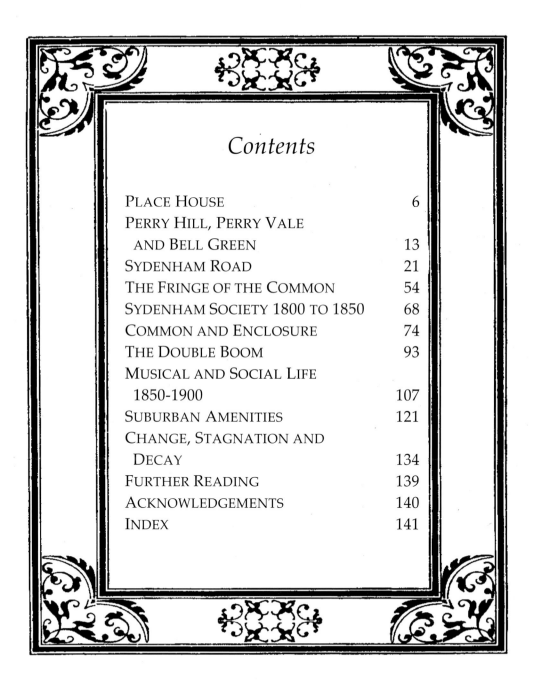

PLACE HOUSE 6

PERRY HILL, PERRY VALE
  AND BELL GREEN 13

SYDENHAM ROAD 21

THE FRINGE OF THE COMMON 54

SYDENHAM SOCIETY 1800 TO 1850 68

COMMON AND ENCLOSURE 74

THE DOUBLE BOOM 93

MUSICAL AND SOCIAL LIFE
  1850-1900 107

SUBURBAN AMENITIES 121

CHANGE, STAGNATION AND
  DECAY 134

FURTHER READING 139

ACKNOWLEDGEMENTS 140

INDEX 141

2. *Place House in 1791, after the demolition of the southern half, from the drawing by J. C. Barrow.*

Place House

THE MANOR OF SYDENHAM

It would be difficult to write a political history of Sydenham, as the village has been the seat of only the most evanescent authorities. From the fifteenth to the seventeenth century there was a 'manor' of Sydenham, but that word was capable of a wide variety of meanings, and in this case probably signified little more than a large estate. There is no evidence that the lords held courts or exercised other manorial prerogatives. The ministers and officials of St Bartholomew's Church gave some moral leadership to the district for twenty-five years in the nineteenth century, before the creation of new parishes diluted their influence. With these flimsy exceptions Sydenham has always been immediately subject to larger outside authorities, most notably the manor, the parish, the board of works, and the council of Lewisham.

If Sydenham, as one place-name scholar has suggested, means the drunkard's settlement, the modern inhabitants can take comfort from the thought that Sipa (the drunkard) would almost certainly have lived at what we now call Catford. For the history of Sydenham begins with Place House, which stood between the Pool River and Catford Hill. In many early references it is called Sydenham Place, Sydenham Place House, or Sydenham House. The first development of the district was as closely dependent upon the Pool as that of Lewisham was upon the Ravensbourne. The Saxon or Jutish invaders who founded Lewisham, probably in the sixth century, penetrated this heavily forested country by following the course of the Ravensbourne south from the Thames and Deptford. After the original settlement in the centre of Lewisham was established it was natural for expansion to follow the same lines, further up the Ravensbourne to Bellingham, and along the tributary known as the Pool to Sydenham. The fact that the Roman road known as the London to Lewes Way ran across the site later occupied by Place House is probably just coincidence, as there is no record of settlement nearby for many centuries after the departure of the Romans.

The earliest record of Place House finds it occupied by John Abel, members of whose family have been described, rather doubtfully, as lords of Catford. At the beginning of the fourteenth century there were two large estates in the area, each regarded by its owners as a manor. It was perhaps when the other, which stretched away eastwards towards Hither Green, was confirmed as the Manor

3. *Place House and Perry Hill in 1799.*

(arable land, a carucate being the amount a team of oxen could plough in a season), thirty acres of mead, 300 acres of wood, plus rents of forty shillings, two ounces of pepper, two cocks, and three hens, all in the parish of Lewisham. Welles had possessed the property since at least 1417-18, when he and his wife Margery conveyed precisely the same houses, lands, and rents to trustees, perhaps as part of a marriage settlememt.

The manor of Sydenham is next heard of in 1498, when Robert Cheseman left "my manor of Shyppynham, and Perystrete" to his wife Johan for life, and then to his son John. The Chesemans were holders of numerous court appointments under the Tudors, major landowners in Lewisham and the adjoining parishes, and timber merchants on a grand scale. The bequest to Johan Cheseman was burdened with the proviso "that the woods now growing upon the lands go to the marrying of my daughters". If Robert Cheseman bought his manor of Sydenham from Richard Foster the three hundred acres of wood were surely the main attraction.

It is not quite certain that the manors of Sydenham left by Sir John Welles and Robert Cheseman were identical, but there can be no question that the Chesemans owned Place House and the surrounding farmland. The linking of the manor of Sydenham with Perry Street (now Perry Hill) strongly suggests the connection, and it is confirmed by the ease with which the descent of Place House can be traced from the Cheseman to the Edmonds family. With them we reach the seventeenth century, and an unbroken chain of documentary evidence.

RICHARD HOWLET

Place House was inherited by John Cheseman, and from him it passed to his daughter Joan, who married Edmund Ford. In 1547 Edmund and Joan Ford sold the "manor of Sippenham, thirteen messuages, gardens, and orchards, 200 acres of land, forty acres of mead, forty acres of pasture, forty acres of wood", plus various rents, to Richard Howlet. (The reduction of the woodland from three hundred to forty acres is testimony to the energy of the Chesemans.) The purchaser was Richard Howlet, Clerk to the Navy, and the owner of estates at Deptford, but he seems to have made Place House his principal home. "Richard Howlett of Sidnam, Kent, Esq., son of John, son of Richard of Newton, Yorks." was granted a coat of arms in 1559.

The Place House extended by John Abel in 1318-19 was certainly not the one shown in the surviving engravings. They depict a Tudor mansion, and

of Catford by a royal grant in 1331, that the Abel estate, which lay to the west, began to be called the Manor of Sydenham. In 1318 or 1319 Abel, "for the purpose of enlarging his mansion at Cipenham, enclosed part of the road between Cadford and Begenham, and gave the public another, 70 perches long and 24 feet wide, equally near, ample, and fit." On the road from Catford to Beckenham there is still a pronounced deviation from the direct line at the point where Catford Hill becomes Perry Hill, which is precisely where Place House stood. If the road were straightened it would run across the site of the mansion.

The first surviving reference to a manor of Sydenham was made by Sir John Welles, who served as Lord Mayor of London in 1431. In his will he left his "manor of Sippenham in the parish of Leuesham in Kent to be sold for pious and charitable uses". Welles died in 1442, and in the next year his executors, in a document dated from Sydenham, sold to Richard Foster, a Bristol merchant, four messuages, three carucates of land

4. *The west facing side of Place House, probably sketched between 1808 and 1810.*

most probably one dating from the middle of the sixteenth century. Such a lavish rebuilding is unlikely to have been carried out by any of the fleeting tenants of the house, and of the owners the most probable candidate is the ambitious and wealthy Howlet. He lived in some state at Sydenham, with numerous servants in livery. The house had "spacious and lofty apartments, richly wainscotted, and adorned with laboriously carved work", and bow windows "ornamented with the best painted glass of the times". The gardens ran down to a terrace overlooking the river.

But which river was it? Today the Pool runs close to the site of Place House, but the mid eighteenth century maps all show the confluence of the Pool and Ravensbourne much further south than is now the case. This could simply mean that the other cartographers were copying one of John Rocque's frequent mistakes, but if he was right in this instance it was the Ravensbourne that bounded the garden of Place House until its course was altered late in the eighteenth century. The road that ran past Place House, now represented by the cul-de-sac known as Elm Lane, was then of some importance, because it led, via a bridge across the river, to Bromley Road.

Howlet's funeral in 1560 was of professional interest to the London undertaker Henry Machyn, who described it in his diary. "The XX day of September was bered in Kent Master Recherd Howllett of Sydnam, squyre, in the parryche of Lussam, with a pennon of armes and a cote armur and a ii dosen of skochyons of armes and a d[emi] of buckram and Master West dyd pryche, and after to Sydnam to dener, the wyche was a fyse dener and the godlest dener that has bene in Kentt for all kindes of fysse both fresse and salt..." Probably in 1560 some at least of the fresh fish was available from the river at the foot of the garden.

In his will Richard Howlet left the manor to his wife Anne for life, and then to his daughter Rachel and her husband Robert Edmunds, with a special injunction that they should "kepe and maintaine the mansion howse". This may suggest the anxious pride of the builder. One incident in the history of Place House is recorded from this period. "On 6 September 1568 Richard Chamber of Lewisham, yeoman, broke into the house of Robert Edmonds at Lewisham, while John Morris was there, and stole 2 blue coats (8s.), a pair of hose (5s.), a striped canvas doublet (2s.), a pair of yellow upper-stocks (3s.) and a shirt (12d.) belonging to Morris." Chamber was found guilty and sentenced to be hanged. The Edmondses, a Lewisham yeoman family, continued to own the manor and Place House, or parts of them, for two hundred years; but their main interest was probably in the farmland. They did not necessarily occupy Place House for all, or even most of that time.

COURTIERS

As long as Greenwich remained popular with our kings and queens the adjoining parishes were favourite places of residence for their courtiers, who had to be constantly on hand to carry out their duties and to claim any office or estate that might become available. This is doubtless what attracted Howlet to Place House, and it is likely that the other royal officials associated with Sydenham also lived there as tenants of the Edmunds family. The first of these may have been Francis Throckmorton (son of Sir John Throckmorton, Justice of Chester) who was executed for treason in 1584. Lady Margery Throckmorton, mother of Francis, was certainly living in Lewisham (possibly at Place House) in 1583, and in 1586 Queen Elizabeth confirmed a lease that Throckmorton had granted to Francis and Edward Bryges of "the capital messuage called Sydenham alias Sepnam and lands in Lewisham".

The next tenant of Place House was probably Doctor William Aubrey (1529-1595), an eminent lawyer, and great-grandfather of John Aubrey the antiquary. He was Regius Professor of Civil Law at Oxford, MP for various boroughs, and a great favourite with Queen Elizabeth, who called him her 'little doctor'. "A person he was of exquisite learning and singular prudence", says Anthony Wood. The Queen visited him at least twice on her progresses, making 'Sydenham House' a resting place on journeys between Greenwich and Beddington in 1590 and 1592. In his will Aubrey left to his wife Wilgiford, "all my interest in my house and lande at Sidenham in the Countie of Kent, and all my kyne and cart horses there beinge and furniture of household of the same house and all my goods and chattells beinge at Sidenham other than my rydinge horses and geldinge". He also gave half a year's wages to "Alice my maide at Sidenham".

The phrase 'all my interest' indicates that Aubrey held his house at Sydenham on a lease. Wilgiford Aubrey, who soon re-married, disposed of the remainder quite quickly. The purchaser may have been Sir Richard Bulkeley of Beaumaris (1533-1621), another favourite of Queen Elizabeth. John Chamberlain relates that in 1602, "on Mayday the Queen went a mayenge to Sir Richard Buckley's at Lewisham, some three or fowre miles of Greenwich" The spot where the maying party picnicked has been identified since at least 1719 with Honor Oak Hill, so named in commemoration of the event. Bulkeley is known to have lived at Sydenham. In 1607 Lady Mary Bulkeley wrote a piteous letter to the Earl of Salisbury from 'Sepnam' about an affray at Greenwich in which the servant of her scapegrace son, Sir Richard Bulkeley the Younger, had, she believed, murdered the Under Sheriff of Kent. According to a more authoritative account the servant, Edward Ryle, attacked a witness named John Note, "felled him to the ground with his cudgel and then threw him into the ditch, where he died". Young Bulkeley had been disowned by his father for marrying "a poor cottager's daughter". It seems fair to assume that the Bulkeleys lived at Place House. History, cartography, archaeology, even legend, have failed to record any other mansion at Sydenham of a fit size and grandeur to entertain Queen Elizabeth. The Bulkeleys continued to figure in the Lewisham parish registers until at least 1611.

THE EDMONDS FAMILY

Meanwhile the Edmonds family continued to own the manor and manor house of Sydenham. Robert Edmonds had died in 1574, which may have been the point at which Place House became available for letting, but his widow Rachel (the daughter of Richard Howlet) lived on until c.1611. Another result of the death of Richard may have been an inquisition that was held at Deptford in 1577, which determined that the manor of Sydenham was gavelkind land. This meant that it should not descend to the eldest son, but be divided equally between all. The ruling made no difference in the next generation, as Robert and Rachel had only one son, but was to prove fatal to Place House in the future.

In 1609 a survey of the manor of Lewisham, to which Sydenham continued to be subject despite its quasi-manorial status, recorded that Rachel Edmonds held "the manor house of Sipenham, one farme house, vi tenements, one mansion house, and of land ccxxix acres". From Rachel the manor passed to her son George (the Elder), who lived for some time at Woodford in Essex before returning to Lewisham. In 1621 his lands in the manor of 'Sitnam' were listed as eleven acres attached to the manor house; pasture called Parkfield fourteen acres, Peartreefield ten acres, Newlands twenty acres, Newlands spring six acres, and Ozi lands thirty acres; arable land called Rowlands ten acres, Cleys nine acres, Herberts Croft four acres, Bridgfield (in occupation of William Symons) eight acres, Walhawes three acres; a tenement called the Tile kill and sixteen acres of land adjoining; one acre and three rods of wood; three closes called Rindells downes fourteen acres; and a tenement and thirteen acres near Rushey Green. This comes to about 180 acres.

George Edmonds began the break up of the Sydenham manorial lands. In 1626 he sold about fifteen acres of Randelsdownes to Jeffrey Howland, a London grocer, who a few years later resold them to Abraham Colfe, the Vicar of Lewisham. Colfe was eagerly buying land to endow his charities, and in 1634 he acquired from Edmonds and his daughter Anne (for whom it served as a dowry on her marriage to William Shawe) the field known as Longmead. The process continued in the next generation, when Colfe made numerous loans to the hard-up sons of George Edmonds, and bought several more pieces of land from them.

It was at the death of George Edmonds the Elder in 1640 that gavelkind came into play. His eldest son Bernard had died young. That left George the Younger, Abraham, and Robert to each inherit a third of the manor. It would have been most sensible, perhaps, to make Place House and its garden equivalent to one third, but the brothers decided instead to physically partition Place House into three dwellings. Lysons reports that "the house, by the partition deed between the Edmondses, was inconveniently divided; rooms belonging to one share were over those belonging to another. By a covenant between the joint-owners, the party pulling down one moiety was to put the other in repair". Robert Edmonds (or his heirs) sold his third to his brothers, briefly reducing the parts to two, but Place House was never to be occupied again as a single house.

The Edmonds brothers did not often use Place House themselves. In 1664 George had a medium sized house near St Mary's church, possibly on the site now occupied by the Lewisham Leisure Centre, and Robert Edmonds was living between Catford and Southend. Abraham was apparently not then a Lewisham resident, though when he

5. *The caption of this drawing is 'View of Beckenham Place', but it is obviously the east facing side of Place House c.1809.*

made his will in 1670 he described himself as "of Itnaham Place in the parish of Lewisham". This was presumably an eccentric spelling of Sydenham. Elsewhere in the will he left land in 'Sitnaham' to his sister Rose. In 1664 it seems likely that Abraham's half of Place House was let to Mr James Symms, while George's had been divided again between Christopher and Robert Brookhowse. Mr Symms had ten hearths in his portion, while the two Brookhouses had four and two. Unless there were other large houses in shared occupation, this total of sixteen hearths would make Place House the fourth largest mansion in the parish after the Rookery, Lewisham House, and the Manor House, Riverdale, all in Lewisham High Street.

The Brookhouse (or Brockhouse) family, who had been active in Lewisham, at Bellingham farm and elsewhere, since the middle of the sixteenth century or earlier, had a close association with their landlords. Richard Brockhouse the Elder was described as a tilemaker in a deed of 1603. He was probably the tenant of the tile kiln that formed part of Sydenham manor in the 1621 list. Charles Brockhouse witnessed the will of George Edmonds in 1667, and Abraham Edmonds witnessed that of

Rachel Brookehouse in 1671. The family was to continue in the southern half of Place House until 1735, when Robert Brookhouse was the tenant.

The Edmonds family vanishes from Lewisham's history late in the seventeenth century. In 1679, either just before his death or as a result of it, Abraham's half was sold to William Grimett. It was sub-divided among his heirs, mostly women who married as often as the wife of Bath, and not re-united until Richard Brooke purchased the shares in the 1760s. In 1723 a surveyor for the Leathersellers' Company noted that access to some of Colfe's land was "thro' Place House Lane and yard along by the North Hedge of Mr Grimmett's Great Park Field". The six acre Park Field was to remain attached to the surviving half of Place House until its final sale in 1808.

FARMERS
During the eighteenth century the southern half, of which the ownership was disputed in Chancery by various distant heirs of George Edmunds, was occupied by three farming families, the Brookhouses until 1735, the Shepherds until the

6. An Edwardian view of the Elms, Elm Lane. The bay windows were Victorian alterations to the eighteenth century farm house.

late 1770s, and then by the Sabins. Jonathan Sabin acquired the freehold, probably in the 1780s, and pulled down this southern half. It had certainly been demolished by 1791, when J.C. Barrow's drawing was published. Jonathan Sabin had built himself a new house nearby, now known as The Elms, Elm Lane, and his family continued to farm the Place House lands from here until the late 1850s.

Not all of the land formerly attached to Place House was acquired immediately by the Sabins. Some was leased to John Trehearn of Sydenham Road and worked from a building called White House Farm. This probably stood on the east side of Perry Hill on the site now occupied by the shops adjoining the Rutland public house. John Trehearn senior left the remainder of the lease to his nephew John in 1807. The land was acquired by William Sabin of The Elms in 1818.

The northern half of Place House, the property of the Grimett heirs, lasted rather longer. Its land was also occupied by farmers in the first half of the eighteenth century: by William Hyde until 1742, and by William Robinson and his widow until the 1750s, but this half of the house was often shared between the farmers and others. Until 1736 Mrs Christian Castle, a Grimett heiress, lived here.

Richard Brooke, JP, a member of the Stationers' Company, but by trade an East India merchant, bought the freehold in 1763 and 1765, and lived in a part of the house until his death in 1772, while letting the remainder to William Spencer. Brooke "fitted up two of the rooms in Chinese taste, with large screens, decorated with grotesque figures as large as, and some larger than, life, displaying a singular combination of Eastern finery and old English grandeur". At that time the East India Company controlled the Chinese trade. Jane Brooke, the widow of Richard, died in 1784, and the northern half of Place House (possibly by this time the only part surviving) passed to his niece Mary Secker. She let it to Thomas Taylor between 1785 and 1787, to James Taylor until 1802, and then to a Mr Pavott, who remained until 1806. He was the last tenant of any part of Place House in its old form. In March 1808 Mary Secker sold the house and land known as Little Field, Bridge Field, Thoroughfare Field, Park Field, and Gravel Pit Field (about 28 acres in all) to John Forster of Southend. In July 1810 a declaration by Forster and his wife explained that the "Capital Messuage and buildings described in the said indenture" (of 1808) "have been since the execution thereof taken down and removed".

The Barrow engraving (*ill.2*) proves that the southern half of Place House had gone by 1791. This Forster declaration noted above might seem to show equally conclusively that the northern half was demolished between 1808 and 1810, but things are not that clear cut. Maps continued to indicate a large range of buildings on the site until the 1860s, and 'Place House' still figured frequently in parish registers and rate books long after 1810. This may just mean that the name was transferred from the house to the district, but the evidence of Alfred Sykes, whose family had been connected with the Two Brewers since the 1820s, suggests otherwise. In 1914 he wrote that "in my boyhood I frequently played in the ruins of the house, which was then used as a farm building, and I believe some of the brickwork still remains". It seems likely, then, that what survived the Forster dismantlement was converted into outbuildings and accommodation for farm labourers, and remained in this form until the creation of Mary Ann's Place, now Creeland Grove, in the late 1860s.

Perry Hill, Perry Vale and Bell Green

THE POOL VALLEY

Sydenham was almost entirely a farming community until the early eighteenth century, and predominantly so until the middle of the nineteenth. In Lewisham the mills on the Ravensbourne added some industrial variety to the ecomomy, but the Pool River was insufficiently powerful to do the same service for Sydenham. Even so, the Pool did play a vital part in the shaping of the community, because it was the only significant source of drinking water until a piped supply became available in the 1850s. This is one reason why the earliest settlements were in Perry Hill, at Bell Green, and towards the eastern end of Sydenham Road.

The tendency to flooding that helped to make the Pool valley so fertile made Perry Hill the obvious spot for the building of the farmers' houses. The eastern side of the road, in particular, was an ideal location, offering safe, dry sites in immediate touch with the river and the water meadows. We know the names of several of these early Perry Hill farms and smallholdings – Genand Crofte and Cotsumes, Brongers and Nutgrove Hall – but in most cases not their exact locations. The exception is Brongers, which stood between the present Castlands and Datchet Roads.

The name Perry Street, the old form of Perry Hill, is not recorded before the fifteenth century, which may indicate the date at which pear trees began to dominate the landscape. In earlier medieval documents the two local place names are Sydenham (in such variant spellings as Sypenham, Sibbenham, and Cippenham) and Westwode. There are indications that Sydenham usually meant Perry Hill and the Bell Green area, while Westwode was used not only for the great common, but also for most of Sydenham Road.

Fourteenth-century residents included Beatrici Sippenham, Theodichi de Westwode, Egidii Swayn, Robert Brooke, and Walter le Bat. The Batts were the longest surviving of all Lewisham families, found as owners and occupiers of land in Sydenham

7. Perry Hill in 1863.

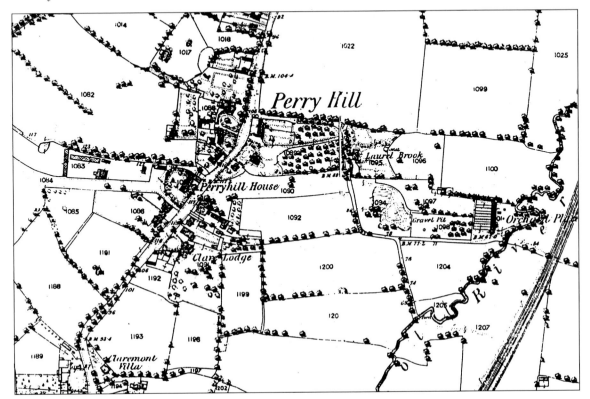

from the thirteenth to the nineteenth century. They gave their name to various local places, no longer identifiable, such as Battislane and Battismede. Another medieval Lewisham family named after Westwood was that of Adam atte Forest, but later usage would suggest that the atte Forests lived at Brockley (the modern Crofton Park) rather than at Sydenham.

LEATHERSELLERS

Our knowledge of the Perry Hill community becomes more detailed after the Leathersellers' Company invested various charitable bequests in the purchase of two farms there in 1627 and 1634. These estates included land on both sides of the road, and various houses on the east or river side. One was Brongers, later White Cottage, and another the forerunner of Clowder's or Perry Hill Farm. At the same time George Edmonds and his sons, the owners of Place House, were selling parts of their Perry Hill land to Abraham Colfe as an endowment for his charities. This shared interest suggested to Colfe the idea of appointing the

wardens of the company as the trustees of his schools and almshouses, and thus brought most of Perry Hill into the control of the Leathersellers' in 1657.

As the direct road from Lewisham to Beckenham, Perry Hill was usually able to support one inn, probably from the late seventeenth century. This was not originally the Two Brewers, but the White Hart, which stood further south, on a site nearly opposite Datchet Road. It was converted into a farmhouse in 1728, and later became the private residence called Radcliffe, which survived until 1911. Its closure as an inn opened the way for the Two Brewers to take its place in 1746. Its first landlord was Thomas Glover, who had previously occupied a public house called the Crooked Billet in Perry Slough, now Perry Vale. The house in which Glover founded the Two Brewers had been built two or three years earlier. Its style was similar to that of numerous houses that once lined the south side of Sydenham Road, though the resemblance was disguised by the large wooden extension built on the forecourt early in the nineteenth century. This original Two Brewers sur-

8. The Two Brewers early in the twentieth century.

9. The Manor House seen from the south-west in the 1830s. Priestfield Road now runs across this part of its garden.

vived until 1926. Another useful addition to the amenities of Perry Hill came in or around 1724 when a smith named Richard Buxton obtained permission to build a cottage on the waste ground fringing the road.

FINE HOUSES FOR COMMUTERS
Since the abandonment of Greenwich Palace by our kings and queens in the middle of the seventeenth century the demand for country houses in north-west Kent had slackened. It revived again in the eighteenth century when the improvements to the local roads achieved by the turnpike trusts made it practical for City men and lawyers to live in what were then the most distant suburbs. In Perry Hill the first house was built for this growing market in 1728.

James Brooke, JP, who possessed the largest estate in Perry Hill outside the grasp of the Leathersellers', did not live on his own land, but at Clowder's Farm, which he leased from the Company. In 1728 he had a handsome mansion built directly opposite the farm, at the highest point of his own estate, and let it to a succession of tenants. James Brooke died in 1750. His son Richard, another active local magistrate who has already been encountered at Place House, continued the same policy, with the result that no member of the Brooke family ever lived in the fine mansion they had created.

The Manor House, as it was later called, survived until 1934, and was home to some of the leading Sydenham families. The Pughs were there from 1785 to 1820, the Rev. Pinkston Arundel French, minister of the Proprietary Chapel in Sydenham Road, from 1820 until his death in 1836, and the

Lawries in the 1850s, after they had sold their own estate to the Crystal Palace Company. The last private residents were the Marriotts, merchants and underwriters, who were at the Manor House from the late 1850s until the Great War.

The second mansion provided for this new market was Clare Lodge, which stood on the site now occupied by Winsford Road and the houses just to the south. It was built between 1754 and 1764 on part of the Leathersellers' estate, then leased to the Brooke family. On the plot assigned to it, which had formerly been an orchard attached to Perry Hill Farm, a formal garden of straight paths and regimented flower beds was laid out. Clare Lodge, which was demolished in 1927, was popular with many successful businessmen, including, between 1840 and 1875, George Halfhide, 'engraver to Her Majesty', Thomas Letts, the creator of the famous diaries (which he printed at New Cross), and William Holland, the Deptford Bridge distiller.

A third example was Perry Hill House, which was built on the Brooke estate, just north of the Manor House, in 1766. Early private residents included Edward King, FSA (1735?-1807), an expert on castles who was briefly President of the Society of Antiquaries, and the Rev. Pinkston Arundel French, who lived here before his move to the Manor House in 1820; but Perry Hill House was mainly notable as a school. The Rev. William Orger, who sometimes assisted French at his Sydenham Road chapel, had a boys' school here in the 1820s and '30s, and Elizabeth Clark turned it into a school for girls in the early 1840s. It was back to boys again under the Rev. Frederick William Miller in the late 1840s and early '50s, but the girls had the last word when the Rev. John Wood Todd

10. Orchard Cottages, Castlands Road, seen from the west bank of the Pool River c.1914.

11. Orchard House in 1833.

and his wife founded here the school that was later to enjoy so much success elsewhere as the Tudor Hall Establishment for Young Ladies (*see pp124-5*).

There were other noteworthy properties in Perry Hill. Orchard House, which stood at the southern corner of Castlands Road, was left to the parish in the middle of the seventeenth century by Walter Hull, an acquaintance of Abraham Colfe. The rent was put to various charitable and administrative uses. There was only one acre attached to the house, but until 1768 it was the nucleus of a farm that included Cast lands and sometimes a great deal more. From 1769 it followed the new trend, and was used as a suburban villa. Orchard House was demolished early in the twentieth century: the terrace now on the site is dated '1910'. In Castlands Road, some three hundred yards east of Orchard

House, stood the early nineteenth century villa known as Laurel Brook. It perhaps had its origin in a small farm, for associated with it were Orchard Cottages, ten dwellings for agricultural labourers that formed a terrace at the bottom of Castlands Road, close to the river. A large house (never given a name) that stood directly opposite Castlands Road was the childhood home of Walter W. Skeat, the great etymologist, and Ivy Wall, the next house to the south, was occupied in the years around 1850 by James Thorne, author of the *Handbook to the Environs of London*.

The market at which such houses were aimed is suggested by this advertisement from 1807. "A very desirable detached villa with land, seven miles from London ... suitable for a small genteel Family, and in a respectable neighbourhood, situate in that cheering and beautiful spot, Perry Hill, Sydenham." The creation of large detached villas in Perry Hill continued until 1856, when Walmer House was built on the east side, in the area now occupied by Datchet Road. The only relic of all this expensive building activity is Swanley, the present no. 145, which was the last farmhouse of Perry Hill Farm. Thomas Tilling, the jobmaster and omnibus proprietor, died there in 1893. He had used the fields as convalescent wards for his sick horses.

Beyond Swanley and the site of Clare Lodge the road begins to fall sharply towards Sydenham. Halfway down the slope there is a bend to the left,

12. *Part of Claremont and its garden c.1880. The figures are thought to be Susannah Todd (wife of William Todd, a warehouseman specialising in woollen goods) and her son Robert.*

and at this point there used to be an open space called Perry Green. A cottage was built here as an encroachment on the waste land late in the eighteenth century, and its garden gradually grew until the whole green had been absorbed. The house, which was rebuilt in 1804 in "brick and rough cast", was known as Claremont. It became a typical Sydenham commuter villa, occupied by such typical local residents as a snuff maker, a Manchester warehouseman, and a fancy goods merchant. Claremont was demolished in 1929, and immediately replaced by a semi-detached pair of houses, one half of which retains the old name. Opposite Claremont stood two pairs of large semi-detached villas known as Meadowcroft. They were built *c.*1830 by a speculator named William Thomas, and leased by the usual range of merchants and barristers. Today the only relic is an outbuilding associated with the most northerly of the four villas, which has been converted into a house. The rest of the Meadowcroft site is occupied by Milverton House and Ardley Close.

PERRY SLOUGH

Perry Rise and Perry Vale were lower than Perry Hill, and of a lower status, for a reason sufficiently obvious from their old name, which was Perry Slough. Even in the 1880s their former 'aguish' reputation was a living memory. There were scarcely any buildings in Perry Rise until the nineteenth century, and only a few cottages in Perry Vale. Indeed, much of the land on either side was the semi-common of Lammas or half-year land (Lord Dartmouth's to the north, Mayow's to the south) and was not legally available for building. The western end of Perry Vale was practically an extension of the common, which it opened out to embrace, and on the south side of the road, on either side of the point where Mayow Road now meets it, there was a wide expanse of waste ground almost as big as Bell Green.

These areas of waste land on the south side of Perry Vale became the key to its development, because from 1774 land-hungry parishioners began to apply to the manor court for permission to enclose small parts of this waste as the sites of cottages. Lord Dartmouth was happy to authorise these encroachments: they were on the Mayow side of the road, not his, and the freehold of the new cottages would revert to him as lord of the manor. Mayow was

13. Bird's Cottages, Perry Vale, c.1930. Valentine Court is now on the site.

furious. In 1788 he wrote to Dartmouth's agent about "an enclosure which he has lately made of a piece of Ground adjoining and bounding part of my estate near Sydenham Common, and thereby cutting me off from an immediate communication with the Lane leading to Perry Slough, which eventually may be of most material injury to the estate, provided I in future should think fit to build on the field so enclosed." He was ignored, and further grants of land were made until the general enclosure of 1810 dealt with all the outstanding pieces of wasteland.

The cottage on one of these plots, first granted in 1787, grew into the mansion known as Dartmouth Lodge. It was demolished to make way for the Ted Christmas houses, nos. 108 to 116 Perry Vale, which were built in 1901. The weather-boarded group known as Bird's Cottages, which stood opposite Westbourne Drive, and thus looked directly onto Sydenham Common, may well have included the "wretched hovel" in which Thomas Dermody died in 1802 (*see p68*). Bird's Cottages were destroyed by a flying bomb in 1944. The first grant of waste land in Perry Vale, made in 1774, provided the site

for Rose Cottage, no. 118, the only surviving example of these squatter dwellings. Over 225 years it has grown by easy stages into the present substantial house.

The most important Perry Rise house was scarcely in Perry Rise at all. The site of Perry Vale Farm, which was built in the early 1790s to take over the land formerly farmed from the Dolphin public

14. Rose Cottage, Perry Vale, in 1991. The central section is the oldest part of this complicated house.

house, is now covered by nos. 15 to 31 Queenswood Road. But until Mayow Road was built the house was approached by a 250-yard carriage drive from Perry Rise. It was on the part of the Mayow estate assigned to William Dacres Adams, who lived here for some years from 1813. In the late 1840s, when the house was occupied by Samuel Laing (1812-97), later MP and Chairman of the Crystal Palace Company, the name was changed to Perrymount House. It was demolished in 1937.

SYDENHAM GREEN

At the bottom of the slope Perry Hill ran into what was called Sydenham Green until the name was changed to Bell Green in the second half of the eighteenth century. Four great upheavals stand between us and any conception of this area as it existed before 1810. First there was the enclosure, which permitted building on the open space. Much of the green was covered with houses in the second and third decades of the nineteenth century. The inexorable growth of the gas works from its foundation in 1853 soon engulfed the only part that had

16. *The farm house and labourers' cottages of Sydenham Farm in Southend Lane, sketched by George Gwilt in 1822.*

15. *Bell Green from the Lewisham Enclosure award map, c.1812.*

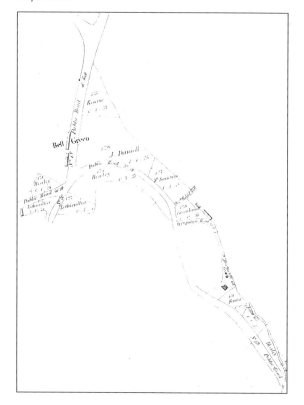

remained free of houses. The situation created by these two events survived until Second World War bomb damage and the wholesale redevelopment of the Bell Green area by Lewisham Council in the 1970s, which involved the demolition of nearly all the early nineteenth century buildings. The last of the four transformations has been the replacement of most of the gasworks complex by a supermarket, with great consequent changes to the road pattern.

In the face of all this it requires a leap of imagination to picture the unenclosed Bell Green as it was before 1810. It amounted to a little over three acres. The greater part of the open space was on the old gasworks site. From a point opposite Perry Rise the boundary stretched away from the road in a south-easterly direction towards Southend Lane and the spot where the Pool River crosses it. The green continued as a tapering fringe for a considerable distance along the north side of Southend Lane. There were smaller sections on either side of Sydenham Road, to the west of its junction with Bell Green Lane, and in the area now occupied by the health centre, and also on the southern side of the curving section of Southend Lane, where the Bell public house is now the most prominent feature. The lane that divided Bell Green from Sydenham Road has had various names. In the seventeenth century it was called Low Lane, and in the nineteenth it oscillated between Bell Green Lane, Kent House Lane, and Verey's Lane. The London County Council had the last word in 1937, when it decided upon the present Bell Green Lane.

The green was fringed by a small number of farmhouses. Those in the entrance to Sydenham Road will be described in the next section. On what was practically an island of old enclosure in the middle of Southend Lane was the headquarters of a 23-acre estate belonging to the parish of St Saviour's, Southwark (now Southwark Cathedral), and known to the parish authorities as Sydenham Farm. The churchwardens tended to let it as an investment to favoured Southwark businessmen, who in turn rented the fields to the more important local farmers. Sydenham Farm was overrun by the expanding gasworks towards the end of the nineteenth century.

THE BELL
Much of the land surrounding the green belonged to the Lethieullier family of Lewisham House. It was divided between several farms. Some twenty acres to the north were probably occupied by

William Stevens until his death in 1694, and certainly by Dorothy Stevens, widow of William, and her son Nicholas. It is not known whether William or Dorothy Stevens were innkeepers, but during the days of Nicholas, who was the tenant from the 1720s or earlier until the 1750s, the farm was known as the Bell Alehouse: it was a common double occupation in the eighteenth century. The last holder of the licence was Richard Perry, who was at the Bell until 1778. The estate was sold by the Lethieulliers in that year, and soon afterwards the house was demolished and the licence extinguished.

The old Bell stood conveniently, as an alehouse should, at the very edge of the green. In modern terms the site would be close to the main drive of the gas depot, north of the big workshop. There is no connection other than the name between the old pub and the present one, which was built in 1843-4 on a different site (formerly in the middle of the green) more than sixty years after the demolition of the original Bell.

Fanciful theories have been put forward to explain how the name Bell Green came to replace Sydenham Green in the second half of the eighteenth century. The prosaic truth is almost certainly that it was called after the Bell alehouse, which was its most prominent building. The name undoubtedly belonged to the pub before it was transferred to the green.

17.   Part of Perry Hill and Bell Green c.1800, showing the area in which the old Bell public house had stood until the 1770s. Its site was probably in Bell Orchard, near to the two ponds.

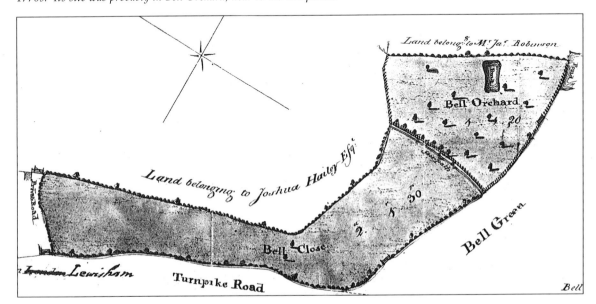

Sydenham Road

NEAR BELL GREEN

Bell Green was the heart of Sydenham from the decline of Place House in the seventeenth century until at least 1810. Fifty years later the junction of Kirkdale and West Hill, where Walter Cobb had just opened his drapery shop, and which is even today known as Cobb's Corner in his memory, had replaced Bell Green as the local centre of gravity. The events that produced this gradual change between 1810 and 1860 were the enclosure of the common, the building of St Bartholomew's Church, the opening of the station, and the arrival of the Crystal Palace on the summit of Sydenham Hill.

Linking these old and new centres is Sydenham Road, which is generally known to local people as the High Street, and was described as such in an 1807 sale notice, though it has never officially borne the name. The earliest map, Ralph Treswell's 1607 survey of the common, shows the western end of Sydenham Road as the 'Waie to Cittnam', and Perry Vale as the 'Waie from Cittnam'. As those two roads lead to Bell Green, Treswell clearly thought of 'Cittnam' as being there. That the emphasis had changed over the following century is indicated by a 1729 plan that shows the eastern end of Sydenham Road, in what is now the region of Home Park, as 'the road from Sidnam to Sidnam Green'. By the middle of the eighteenth century the name 'Sydenham' was certainly being applied most particularly to the area now between Tannsfeld Road and Kent House Road, where there was a nearly continuous range of houses on both sides of the highway, and such focuses of community life as three inns and a non-conformist chapel. But at that period Sydenham Road was still most often referred to as 'the road from Dulwich to Lewisham', even though one 1798 map called it 'Sydenham Street'. In the nineteenth century it was generally known simply as 'the Village' or 'Lower Sydenham'.

18. Sydenham Road in 1799.

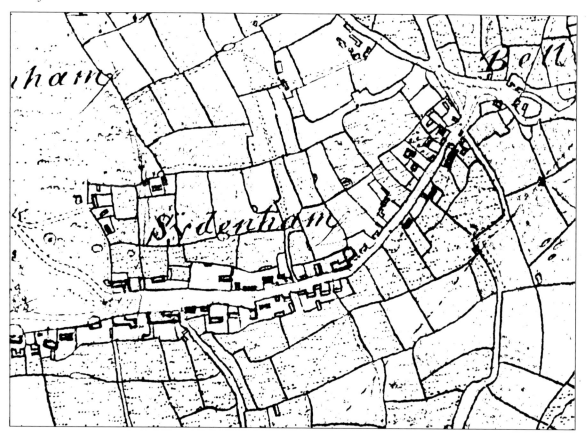

19. The Sydenham Brewery at Bell Green before 1881.

The history of Sydenham Road certainly starts at the eastern end, for when the early settlers from Lewisham had cleared the land on the west bank of the Pool along the line of Catford Hill and Perry Hill, and come to the Bell Green area, they must have found the great North Wood extending down the slope of Sydenham to the left bank of the river. Beyond the green the valley was too flat and marshy to be a tempting site for houses, and soon ran into the spheres of influence of other groups of settlers. The Lewisham people therefore struck westwards into the wood, to some extent via Perry Rise and Perry Vale, but much more seriously and productively along the line of Sydenham Road.

The first old building on the south side of the road was a small farm that belonged to Robert Leigh before 1655, and later to the Lethieulliers. In the eighteenth century the tenants included John Hamborough (in whose barn poor travellers were often found dead) from 1730 to 1742, and Farefax Worrell from 1745 to 1754 or later. In the 1830s Joseph Verey converted it into the tiny Sydenham Brewery. The farmhouse that he adapted to his purpose stood some way back from Sydenham Road because the land in the angle of what is now Bell Green Lane had been part of the green until the enclosure, and the farm had stood on its edge.

When a larger brewery closer to Porthcawe Road replaced it in the 1880s the old building became the Tap, where the Vereys sold their beer direct to the public. In 1881 shops had been built over the ample front garden on Sydenham Road and the address of the beerhouse was changed to Kent House (Bell Green) Lane. It was rebuilt on a smaller scale before being closed at the start of the Great War, and a late 1930s comeback as the Kent House Social Club was ended by its destruction during the Blitz.

This part of Sydenham Road was something of an educational centre. Hope Lodge was the first substantial house west of the brewery. John Batt and his widow ran a small farm of eighteen acres either from this house or from an earlier one on the site for much of the eighteenth century. In the 1840s and '50s Hope Lodge was a girls' school run by Sophia Morris. This and the brewery were part of the old Lethieullier estate, as was Home Park Lodge, but the land and houses between belonged to William Manning in 1678 and afterwards to the lucky Burrells of Beckenham, who rose with remarkable speed from obscurity to a peerage. Gothic Cottage, the nearest house to Home Park Lodge, was probably built in the 1790s, in the gingerbread castle style then in fashion. Between Hope Lodge

20. *Montague Cottage in 1919, after Woodville Cottage, the other half of the semi-detached pair, had been demolished.*

and Gothic Cottage stood an older semi-detached pair, perhaps built *c.*1741. The western half, known as Montague (or Montacute) Cottage, was also a girls' school in the 1860s, conducted by Miss Lucy King. The eastern half, Woodville Cottage, was possibly the earliest of all the known Sydenham schools. One George Earle, schoolmaster, certainly lived in this or one of the immediately adjoining houses during the early 1750s. Woodville Cottage was subsequently the home of the eminent engraver John Cousen (1804-80) during the 1840s. Porthcawe Road and Byron Close stand on the site of all these houses.

HOME PARK

Home Park Lodge developed into one of the major estates of Sydenham, second only to The Lawn in the Bell Green area, but it had its origins in a farm called Rashlands or Rastlands, which belonged in the 1550s to John Clerk, a London clothworker. The earliest known farmers were John Hewes in the middle of the sixteenth century, one of the prolific Batt family *c.*1561, and William Moncleare before 1655. In 1561 the estate was bought by Nicholas Legh or Leigh of Beckenham, and afterwards passed through the hands of Thomas Smith of Woolwich into the possession of the Lethieulliers of Lewisham House. Their tenant for much of the eighteenth century was the energetic Abraham Phillips, who as well as fathering hosts of children by three or more wives was responsible for at least one bastard.

John Greene Lethieullier auctioned most of his Kentish estates at Christie's in 1776. Home Park was lot eight, described as "A compact farm house, out houses, gardens, etc., and about eighteen acres

of land ... now in the occupation of John Guitton, Esq.; the premises are subject to an agreement for a lease to Mr Lepine for forty-two years from Michaelmas 1774, at the annual rent of £18." John Guitton of The Lawn, the great house opposite, had perhaps been using this as his home farm.

It is not clear what happened to the farm as a result of the sale, but by 1794 it belonged to George Prior of The Lawn, and had been rebuilt as a country villa, suitable for occupation by such wealthy men as Henry Tahourdin, who was the tenant from 1796 until 1811, or a little later. In 1833 a lease, probably of 61 years, was taken by a jumped-up Lincoln's Inn solicitor named William Cowburn (1783-1854), who recorded in his 'Scraps of a Family Journal': "We remained a year very prosperously at Eltham, and in May 1833 came to Sydenham, where I had previously bought a nice property ... In April 1834 I began to build a large addition to our House and occupied it in September following. Rapid work for so extensive a building – in fact a House – ten sleeping rooms – Library, a room for Myself, & Offices of all kinds ...With God's blessing this new Habitation etc. will be the means of great comfort to us, I hope for many many years." The front door of Home Park Lodge, as enlarged by Cowburn, stood directly opposite the modern Larkbere Road.

Cowburn had a furious row with the trustees of his wife's marriage settlement before he could extort from them the money to pay for this extension and for the freehold and leasehold estates on either side of Home Park Lodge that he purchased in 1834. These enabled him to indulge in the pleasure of playing the squire, in a style indicated by this circular letter dated 'Sydenham, 7th December 1836':

"I INTEND TO GIVE YOU, and to all my Cottage Tenants, a Jonit [sic] of Meat, a few Potatoes, and some Beer, that you may have a comfortable Dinner with your Wife and Family, *on Christmas Day,* at no cost to yourself.

I take this opportunity of telling you the Rules I shall observe in future as to my Cottage Tenants:-

I will not let a Cottage to any one who will not attend, with his Family, some place of divine worship on every Sabbath.

I will not have a Cottage Tenant who frequents any Beer Shop to spend *improperly* his small earnings, and so neglects his Family and abuses himself.

I will not have a Tenant who is Quarelsome with his neighbours, or in any respect leads a disorderly life.

I will excuse no Cottage Tenant the payment

of his Rent who is in work; but if a Tenant is ill, or out of work, I will allow him time, or find him work, if I can.

In a little less than two years I intend to build more comfortable Cottages, at BELL GREEN, for industrious and deserving Laborers, and I now wish to state that I intend to make my little property there the means of usefulness, and for the bettering the condition of the Poor, and so in every respect an advantage to myself.

Your sincere Friend and well wisher,

W. COWBURN"

Sydenham was ready for Queen Victoria.

It was at the time of Cowburn's death in 1854 that the value of Home Park Lodge began to be undermined by the establishment of the gas works and the decline in the amenities of the Bell Green area that followed. Four more tenants came after Cowburn – Matthew Clement Walker, William Browning, Octavius Horne, and Frederick Ashby. There was some unusual excitement in 1868, when Richard Walker, believing he had been wrongfully deprived of some property, arrived at the house in an excited state and threatened to shoot his uncle Matthew, but in general Sir George Grove's house next door quite eclipsed Home Park as an object of public curiosity.

The estate was offered for sale in 1896, after the expiry of the old Cowburn lease. The auctioneers laid the emphasis heavily upon the opportunities for building streets of small houses over the site of the mansion and grounds to match the properties in Porthcawe Road, Fairlawn Park, etc. that had surrounded Home Park Lodge since 1881. This mortary fate was avoided when the Lewisham Board of Works decided to buy the property as a public recreation ground in 1899. The mansion, though in excellent condition, was demolished in 1901, just as Lewisham Council was seeking a site in the immediate vicinity for a new library. Architects are the natural enemies of old houses, and never recommend conversion if there is the least prospect of a commission for a new building.

West of Home Park stood the old wooden house made famous by the residence there of Sir George Grove between 1860 and 1900. The early history of the estate is difficult to reconstruct with any certainty. There is some reason to believe that in the sixteenth century it was a farm known as Eastridden and Stocketts, and that it was yet another of the Sydenham properties of the Batt family. The building as occupied by Sir George Grove appeared to be in origin a pair of late seventeenth

21. Sir George Grove's house in 1920.

century houses converted into a single dwelling, so it may be significant that in 1697, when the Stocketts estate was bought by Christopher Lowman of Southwark, it was described as two houses now or lately in the occupation of John Scudder, victualler.

If John Scudder kept an inn here, that use did not continue for long, for by 1708 the tenant was Thomas Sheppard, yeoman, who died in 1720. His widow Elizabeth continued to farm the land until the middle of the eighteenth century. Soon afterwards, following the Sydenham trend of the period, it was converted into a gentleman's house. One early occupant was Mrs Maria Hodge, who was a daughter of Sir Edmund Bacon of Norfolk, the premier baronet of England. She moved here from Kenton Cottage (see p43) after her husband, Major Edward Hodge of the 7th Hussars, was killed during the Waterloo campaign.

The great days of the house, when in the hands of Sir George Grove, are described on pages 107-116. After the death of his widow, it was bought in 1919 as a presbytery for the Roman Catholic Church of Our Lady and St Philip Neri, which then stood at the corner of Watlington Grove. The house was demolished in 1929 because one of the priests, Father Dolman, was unhappy about a leaky roof, and the existing presbytery was built on the site. Only the brick extension at the rear, an addition made by Sir George, was retained as part of the new building.

AROUND CHAMPION PARK

Until the middle of the nineteenth century there were no buildings on the south side of the road between Grove's house and the area where Watlington Grove and Kent House Road were built in the 1860s and '70s. (The Prince Alfred, Sir George Grove's favourite pub, was founded at the present 201 Sydenham Road *c*.1860, and moved to the corner of Kent House Road about five years later.) So here it will be convenient to return to Bell Green and examine the most prominent old houses on the north side of Sydenham Road.

The first was Bell Green Cottage, a farm that stood on the edge of the green until the enclosure. It was another part of the Burrell estate, and was occupied by several generations of the Allen family until the death of Henry Allen in 1746, and afterwards by Thomas Pillion. In 1781 it was taken by William Pringle, a seedsman, who turned the estate into one of London's leading suburban nursery gardens. When he died in 1813 he was described in the *Gentleman's Magazine* as "a truly honest man". His son and successor James Pringle was a painter specialising in marine subjects, but he also produced the fine view of Sydenham Common reproduced on pages 74-5. A later tenant of Bell Green Cottage was the actor and dramatist John Baldwin Buckstone (1802-79, *see page 56*), who spent the last few impoverished years of his life here after rebuilding forced him to move from Peak Hill. By that time the area was rapidly losing any pretensions to fashion, and Kirtley Road was being laid out across the former garden of Bell Green Cottage. The house did not survive for much longer.

To the west of Bell Green Cottage stood The Lawn, centre of one of the great estates of Sydenham. In 1718 it was described as a house and lands late belonging to Mr Stiles (probably John Style) and now or late in the possession of Mr Stevens, but by 1727 it belonged to John Anderson, citizen and cooper of London. He remained until at least 1755, in which year he was described as the owner of "an ancient messuage". In the 1770s and '80s the owner was John Guitton, who for a time also leased the Home Park land from the Lethieulliers. Guitton had two interesting tenants after leaving Sydenham in the late 1770s. Joseph Grote, a merchant in Leadenhall Street, who was at The Lawn until 1783, was the eldest son of Andrew Grote of Blackheath, and uncle of George Grote the historian. Jeremiah Sneyd, the tenant from 1784 to 1786, was Chief Clerk successively in the northern and southern departments of the Secretary of State's Office between 1770 and 1791. Senior civil servants at the old foreign office could afford such luxurious suburban retreats because they not only drew a salary but acted as private agents for the affairs of our ambassadors and consuls.

For the following sixty-five years the estate was owned by just two families. George Prior was here from 1787 until his death in 1814, and his widow remained until her death in 1828. She was followed by Thomas Bearda Batard, formerly of The Priory and The Old Cedars (*see pages 43 and 58*), who occupied the house until 1850, except for a brief period, *c*.1832, when he let it to the Rev. S. Sanderson. The Batard family continued to own the estate until it was bought for development in 1861, as described on page 104. The house was rebuilt a few yards to the south in 1862, and re-named Champion Hall. In 1885 it became the second headquarters of the Sydenham Home and Infirmary for Sick Children, and it remained as the central block of the hospital until its closure and demolition in 1991.

The area between the present Champion and Larkbere Roads was occupied by another ancient house, which, like so much property in this part of Sydenham, was once owned by the Batt family. Walter Batt, husbandman, who died in 1607, left the house and four acres to his sons. In 1622, when they sold it to Adrian Evans, a London clothworker, their tenant was Nicholas Neale, weaver. In 1718 the estate was acquired by Edward Hodsdon of the Old House from some remote heirs of Adrian Evans. The house was then occupied by a bricklayer named John Minson or Minchin, who died in 1724. In 1729 Hodsdon leased the property to John Anderson of The Lawn for sixty-one years.

As a result of this lease the house more or less vanishes from the records. Most of the land was used to extend the garden of The Lawn, and the house seems sometimes to have been used by other members of the owning family (by Edmund

22. *The plan of the house given on the 1729 lease from Edward Hodsdon to John Anderson.*

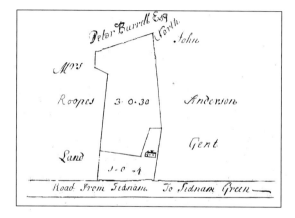

Anderson in the 1750s and '60s) and sometimes to have been divided into several dwellings. In 1779 there were said to be "three brick messuages with convenient offices and gardens" on the estate, yet maps of 1729 and 1843 show only a single building in exactly the same position.

Towards the expiry of the Anderson lease the situation becomes clearer. John Middleton was the tenant in the 1780s and early '90s, and John Fortnom from 1795 to 1798. George Prior of The Lawn had bought the estate by 1800 (probably at the 1786 Hodsdon auction), and it passed to Thomas Bearda Batard in 1828 with the rest of the Prior property. Nineteenth century tenants included Josiah Hardy, who was Highway Surveyor for Lewisham, during the first decade, a Mr Asquith in 1832, Edward Dod Colville junior *c*.1837 to 1851, William Hurt Sitwell in 1855, and the Barber family from 1857 until the 1880s. (Edward Colville, like his father and name-sake who lived at Catford House, was a Registrar in the Court of Chancery.) The old house, which oddly never acquired a name, had been demol-ished by 1894. King Edward's Parade, the worst blot upon Sydenham Road, was subsequently built across the frontage.

On his 1746 map of London John Rocque printed the name 'Whagow House' across this part of Sydenham Road. It is not at all clear to which property he meant it to apply, but the most likely candidate is the large building later known as The Grange, which stood nearly opposite Sir George Grove's house. It was probably built in 1741, when Joseph Constable, who had been farming at Bell Green for many years, established himself here. The old farmhouse was taken over by his son Thomas. As the Constable farm was eclectic, with fields leased from as many as five owners, it did not greatly matter where the farmer lived. The house remained in the hands of the Constable family until 1794, and then passed to James Robinson, another farmer, who died in 1832. The Constables and Robinsons were probably related through the Sheppards of Sir George Grove's house.

The Grange then became a private house, and proved popular with the legal professions. It was occupied by John Atkins, a solicitor, in the 1830s, by William Mello, a broker, in the 1840s, by James Kingsford, another solicitor in the 1850s and '60s, and by Charles Boyle, a barrister, in the 1870s. The house was demolished in 1901/2.

The last house in this group, Hanover Lodge, stood a little to the west of The Grange, in what is now the Sunnydene Street area. It belonged to a Captain Saunders and his widow for much of the eighteenth century, and the family lived here until 1737. The most interesting of their later tenants was Captain Charles Long, who was at Hanover Lodge from 1745 to 1747. He was probably the uncle of Lord Farnborough, the creator of Bromley Hill House. In the middle of the nineteenth century the house belonged to John Addis, the proprietor of Freeman's Wharf, Southwark, who let it to the usual range of merchants and solicitors. A later member of the family, the Rev. William Addis, an Oratarian and a friend of Sir George Grove, re-turned to Sydenham *c*.1880 as the first priest of the new Roman Catholic congregation in the village, and created a scandal in 1888 by leaving the Church to marry. He lived nearby at Clifton Villa, now 221 Sydenham Road. Hanover Lodge was demol-ished in 1901/2. The shops known as Broadway Parade occupy the frontage of The Grange and Hanover Lodge.

Next door (though Sunnydene Street was later squeezed between) stood the little Church of England infant school established by Mary Mayow of the Old House in 1815, with a cottage for the mistress attached. Sarah Raraty kept the school from the 1830s until *c*.1860, followed by a Miss Fiander. The building was taken over by St Michael's parish in the 1860s, and the opening of the present school in 1872 made this old founda-tion redundant. It was converted into two cottages called the School House which were destroyed by a flying bomb in 1944.

THE HEART OF THE VILLAGE

Until the middle of the nineteenth century there were open fields on both sides of Sydenham Road west of the infant school, now occupied by Addington Grove to the north and by Fairlawn Park and Watlington Grove to the south. The Fairlawn Park development is described on page 104. The heart of the village between 1750 and 1850 was located, roughly speaking, between Kent House Road and Mayow Road, neither of which existed during that period. Here were two chapels, three public houses, two forges, and nearly all the shops on which Sydenham depended for its supplies. I will describe the north side first, then return to Kent House Road to deal with the south.

All the properties between 217 Sydenham Road and Berryman's Lane, arose from a 61-year build-ing lease granted in 1732 by Edward Hodsdon of the Old House to a carpenter named Joseph Phillips. The estate consisted of seven acres known as Streetfield and one acre of meadow detached from Six Acre Field. This stray piece was at the eastern end, and is represented today by 215 and 217 Sydenham Road and the land behind. Joseph Phillips commenced his building operations at the western end of the estate, but we will begin here at the modern no. 217, which stands on the site of

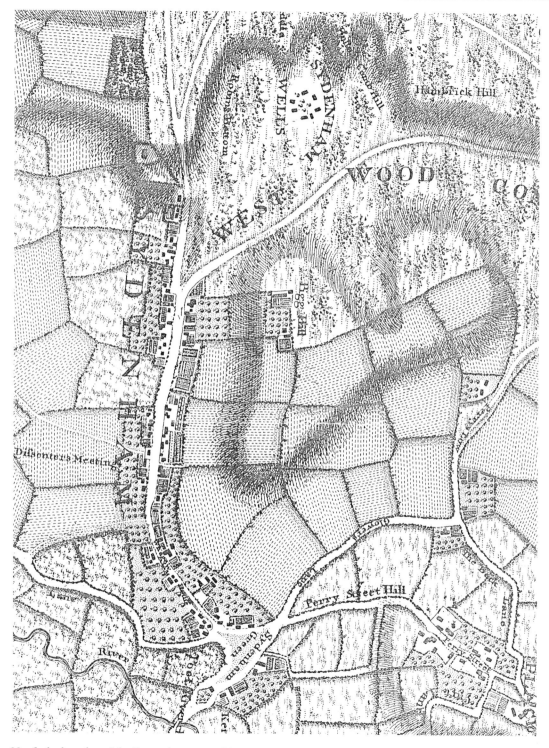

23. *Sydenham from John Rocque's survey of 1741-5.*

24. *The group of houses opposite Kent House Road in 1919. Wilson Place is on the right, the surviving 201 Sydenham Road is in the centre, and on the left are Vine Cottage, Lime Tree Cottage and Mortimer House.*

a large house called Arundel Cottage.

Arundel Cottage was built between 1779 and 1786, in which year it was described as "a timber house, with stable and chaise-house, a garden, and a small meadow, in the occupation of Mr Doughal McPherson and Mr Abraham Kenman." The eight acres leased to Phillips were among the few parts of the old Hodsdon estate that did not pass into the hands of Mayow Wynell Mayow as a result of the 1786 sale. Then or soon afterwards Arundel Cottage was bought by much its most interesting occupant, Hugh French, who lived here for more than twenty years. He was a celebrated physician who served as Master of the Society of Apothocaries and Manager of its Botanic Gardens at Chelsea. He was a Justice of the Peace and for forty years a Deputy Lieutenant for the County of Kent. It was evidently he who gave the house its name, for we have already encountered his son, the Rev. Pinkston Arundel French, in Perry Hill, and will soon meet him again at his chapel in Sydenham Road. From the 1830s until his death in 1856 Arundel Cottage was occupied by James Lance, a civil servant at the Admiralty. In the 1860s it was acquired by Thomas Nothard, who demolished the stables c.1870, and built himself a fine new house on the site. This survives as 215 Sydenham Road, formerly known

as York House. Arundel Cottage was demolished just before the Second World War.

Linden Cottage, sometimes called The Lindens or Linders Cottage, was the first within the seven acres of Streetfield. It stood almost directly opposite Kent House Road, on the site now occupied by the Wesley Hall. It was built at about the same time as Arundel Cottage, and in 1786 was described as "a very neat timber house (in good repair), a yard, and good garden, in the occupation of Mr Sangwin". From 1792 to 1799 it was occupied by Mrs Marryat, formerly of Westwood Hill and afterwards of Peak Hill. She was probably the widow of Thomas Marryat, M.D. (1730-92), and grandmother of Captain Frederick Marryat. Andrew Laurie was here briefly in 1805/6, before establishing himself at Sydenham Hall, and from 1806 to 1810 the tenant was Thomas Hill, whose eccentricities are noticed on pages 71-2, where a description of the house can also be seen. It was bought as a site for the Wesley Hall in 1889, but the Methodists had to wait for the lease to expire in 1892 before they could think seriously about building, and in the meantime they met at 223 Sydenham Road. The present chapel was opened in 1906.

After Linden Cottage there was a terrace of four

two storey brick houses with dormers (perhaps originally designed as only three dwellings), known as Wilson Place. They were built in the 1780s and demolished shortly after the Second World War. They had been badly damaged in 1941. The houses were occupied by gardeners, dressmakers, labourers, etc. The next group will be well known to most Sydenham people, because the first still survives and the rest have only lately been demolished.

The survivor is 201 Sydenham Road, which was probably built *c*.1830. It has been a shop for most of its existence, originally in the tenancy of John Clark, a grocer and cheesemonger. From *c*.1860, though, there was an interesting change of use when this became the first Prince Alfred. John Homewood sold his beer and ale here until the present pub at the corner of Kent House Road was built *c*.1865. Nos. 197 and 199, the former called Vine Cottage, were two tiny brick houses of the 1780s, only recently demolished. Vine Cottage was occupied by William Wright as a glazier's shop in the late eighteenth and early nineteenth century.

Lime Tree Cottage, no. 195, was a much larger brick house of the same date. Its first known occupant was a Frenchman whose name gave the local officials predictable trouble. Between 1789 and 1802 he appears as Monnier, Moineau, Lemonier, Le Monea, and other variants. Later tenants included Robert Westmorland and his widow Sarah between 1803 and 1841, and the wine merchant Mark William Ridgway, former landlord of the Greyhound, from the early 1860s until his death in 1877. Lime Tree Cottage was also demolished in the 1990s.

Mortimer House (193), the last victim of the recent clearance, was a detached brick house standing a little back from the line of nos. 195 to 199. It was built in 1801 for Andrew Simon Willmott, who had briefly owned and occupied the big house to the east (to be described next) and who separated this new house from the main estate before selling it in the same year. In the 1840s and '50s Mortimer House was a boarding school run by the sisters Harriet, Mary, and Elizabeth Litherland, and in the early 1880s it was occupied by a retired schoolmaster named William Knighton. Knighton Park Road was then being laid out nearly opposite.

The large house, one of the largest in Sydenham, that occupied the space between Hazel Grove and Berryman's Lane, is the only one that can certainly be attributed to Joseph Phillips, the original lessee of the Streetfield estate. It was built *c*.1736, and used either immediately or at a very early stage, as a public house. James Donald was the tenant from 1741, and by 1744 he was certainly the holder of a victualler's licence. The sign that he used was probably 'the Bulls', for which William Cooper was

25. A clearer view of Mortimer House in 1980.

licensed in 1753. In that same year the tenant of this house was certainly a Mr Cooper. The building may have ceased to be used as a pub when he moved in 1754, for by the 1760s it was a private house occupied by one Joseph Lancaster. At that time the other houses on the Streetfield estate had not been built, so Lancaster had the entire eight acres for his garden and outbuildings. In 1792 the property was described as:

> "A handsome brick dwelling-house, neatly fitted up, standing in an agreeable part of the town of Sydenham, containing, on the ground floor, a hall, a breakfast parlour, and dining room, with a bow-window; on the first floor, a drawing-room, with bow-windows, and three handsome bed-rooms, with two closets to each, over which are four large good bed chambers, and one smaller. The offices consist of a servants hall, a kitchen, scullery, excellent cellars, a very good laundry, brewhouse, and dairy, all well supplied with good water by leaden pipes; stabling for six horses, lofted over, and double coach-house; a large court-yard, paved, an excellent kitchen-garden, walled and well planted with choice fruit-trees in great perfection; pleasure-ground; fish ponds; a farm-yard, with a cowhouse, piggery, barn, and other buildings..."

Thereafter the house was used by some of the leading citizens of Sydenham, including Charles Bill from 1801 to 1809, and Robert Barber from 1809 to 1819. He was succeeded by Henry Dudin, the Southwark wharfinger and Master of the Old Surrey Foxhounds, who had previously lived at Hill House, Honor Oak Road. The Dudin family were the last owners. In 1853 they sold the estate to a consortium of clergymen, including the Vicar of St Paul's Covent Garden, who had evidently been inspired with optimism by the arrival of the Crystal Palace. They

26. *Hamilton Lodge on the left and Cousin's Cottages on the right, with 157 to 161 Sydenham Road between, as they appeared in 1920.*

demolished the house and sold the ground in building lots under the name of Paxton Park. The three roads called Myrtle, Laurel, and Acacia (now Hazel) Grove, were soon built over the gardens, and five shops took the place of the old house on the narrow Sydenham Road frontage. The corner shop, no. 171, was totally destroyed by a bomb early in the Second World War. The Man of Kent was established on the eastern corner of Hazel Grove in 1861, and rebuilt after bomb damage in 1941.

Berryman's Lane, which marked the limit of the estate leased to Joseph Phillips, is one of the oldest turnings from Sydenham Road, although until the building of Mayow Road it only gave access for carts to the land behind Streetfield before continuing as a mere footpath to Perry Vale. The area between Berryman's Lane and Mayow Road was mainly occupied by cottages, varied by one large house and the Dolphin.

On the western corner of Berryman's Lane stood Cousin's Cottages, a wooden pair fronting the lane, but with the side turned towards the main road given the dignity of a coating of stucco. They were described as "very dilapidated property" in 1940, and were demolished soon after the war. The next group, nos. 157 to 161, were three stucco-faced wooden shops that may originally have been a

single house. If so, it was possibly the home of Joseph Phillips, the carpenter, who lived just to the west of the Streetfield estate that he leased from Edward Hodsdon. In the nineteenth century the three shops were among the most important in the village. John Sinkins the grocer, who was Steward of the Dartmouth Road Wesleyan chapel, had 161, George Cousins the baker was at 159, and 157 was a shoe shop occupied by Henry Waymark in the 1830s and '40s, and afterwards by several generations of the Cusack family. The group survived until the 1950s.

Hamilton Lodge, no. 155, was a double-fronted weatherboarded house, probably of the early nineteenth century. It was demolished in 1931. Next to it was a terrace of five small eighteenth-century cottages that belonged to the Edney family, the village blacksmiths, after whom a street was subsequently named off Wells Park Road. Sadly the street has vanished without trace, and Edney's Cottages were rebuilt in the second half of the nineteenth century, and have long since dropped the name. The forge, later a cycle works and garage, which Thomas Edney had occupied from 1798 or earlier, was at no. 153. In 1807 an optimistic auctioneer calculated that these five cottages were worth forty guineas per annum on account of

27. The rear of Clune House in 1992.

"their centrical situation in the village".

Attached to the western end of the terrace was a larger house called Windemere Cottage, described in 1807 as "a substantial brick-built genteel freehold residence ... particularly suitable for a family, having been recently, at a considerable expence, completely repaired and judiciously fitted up for that purpose, consisting of four sleeping rooms, two parlours, kitchen, wash-house, garden, and fore-court". It was bought by the Trehearns, the Sydenham farmers, and occupied by their widows and unmarried daughters for fifty years. In the 1880s it was replaced by shops, with behind them the Windemere Club, "which old residents speak of with bated breath as though it was a place of ill-repute", as the local paper reported in 1931. When it was sold in 1894 the attractions of the club included a billiard saloon and skittle alley.

Clune House, the next old building, is one of the most unexpected survivals in Sydenham. Few people know of its existence, because the shops numbered 133 to 137 hide it from the sight of passers-by in Sydenham Road, and the view of the back from Mayow Road is nearly obscured by garage buildings and workshops. This was a large and important house, with more than an acre of grounds. It was built in 1805 for Hewitt Cobb of Clement's Inn, a distinguished solicitor who accidentally developed a second career as proprietor of the Theatre Royal at Brighton, of which he acquired the lease by foreclosing a mortgage. He meant to sell it immediately, but the leading lady persuaded him to take over the management. He lost money on the venture, but, like angels throughout the ages, was perhaps compensated in other ways. Hewett Cobb, who was not connected in any way with Walter Cobb of the department store, died in 1822. Another solicitor, George Chilton, followed Cobb, and was here for 25 years, and in

the 1850s and early '60s Clune House was occupied by the cultivated Ogilvy family, who were members of the von Glehn circle (*see p.112*). It sank into commercial use early in the twentieth century, when Sydenham Road was resuming its old position as the main shopping centre of the area.

Between Clune House and the Dolphin there was a terrace of four shops. The one closest to the pub was the village post office in the years around 1840, and this notice of a sale at the Post-office, Sydenham in 1834 may well refer to this same establishment.

> "The stock consists of grocery and spices; glass, china, and earthenware; brown and red ware; ironmongery and tinware; oils and pickles; powder and shot; twines, toys, brushes, and brooms; ready-made clothes; quantity of dairy-fed pork; scales and weights and shop fixtures; capital malt mill with two fly wheels; two chaise carts; 50-gallon iron boiler, copper, beer casks and brewing utensils..."

A comprehensive stock, evoking Tombstone more readily than Sydenham. A few years later the railway began to introduce far more specialised and sophisticated shopping facilities to the village.

THE DOLPHIN

The Dolphin was founded in 1733 by Richard Peake, who either enlarged an old cottage or built an entirely new house on the site. The pub was called The Dolphin in 1733, and was firmly re-established as such by the 1760s, but in between there seems to have been a flirtation with the name 'the Black Horse'. Certainly in 1744 Peake was licensed for a "House known by the Signe of the Blackhor", and the justices are unlikely to have accepted the Black Whore as a name.

Until Perry Vale Farm was built *c.*1790 the public house business was a secondary consideration to the men who leased the Dolphin from the Hodsdons and their successors at the Old House. The pub was also the farm house from which the greater part of the Hodsdon land was cultivated. Richard Peake had 76 acres attached to the pub, and Thomas Boxall, the carpenter who took a 21-year lease in 1768, increased this to 108 acres. It was probably Boxall who began a division between the farming and innkeeping aspects of the estate by building a new farm house behind James Edgelar's shop (*see p.49*), more or less on the line now taken by Mayow Road. Boxall did not live in Sydenham at all, but sub-let the various parts of his property. In 1775 a Mr Flynn was the farmer, and John Dowse the publican. When the bulk of the land was transferred to Perry Vale Farm on the expiry of the

28. *The old Dolphin in the 1920s.*

Boxall lease in 1789, the house on the Mayow Road line became the home farm of the Mayow family, the new owners of the Old House.

After 1789 the Dolphin settled down to the regular routine of a small village public house. The head leases were held by capitalists and brewers who sub-let to a long succession of publicans, none of whom stayed very long or made any great mark. The old pub was demolished in 1935, and replaced by the existing building, which is now happily known as the Dolphin again, after a mercifully brief deviation. Modern licensors will apparently sanction any name.

There were several cottages adjoining the west side of the Dolphin in the eighteenth century, but they were replaced in 1807 by a terrace of three known as Mayow Cottages, to which a fourth (nearest to the pub) was added soon afterwards. This last house was the first to go, for it was added to the site of the Dolphin when rebuilt in 1935. The others survived until displaced for the garage at the corner of Mayow Road in the 1950s. No. 115 was John Pendrid's forge in the 1830s and '40s, and 113 was the Mayow gardeners' cottage. It was after Mayow Cottages that the long frontage of the Old House completely changed the character of Sydenham Road, so here we will return to Kent House Road and examine the south side.

WEST OF KENT HOUSE ROAD

Nos.160 to 176 Sydenham Road, the shops curving round the western corner of Kent House Road, stand on the site of a farmhouse built in 1800 by John Daniel of Mincing Lane, and occupied by him for a few years before he leased it to John Trehearn, whose farmhouse was then one hundred yards to the west (*see p.35*). The land attached to the Daniel farm had once belonged to the Hodsdons of the Old House, and in 1713, when purchased by Edward Hodsdon, was known as Wakers Croft. It was leased to Thomas and Samuel Scudder, the leading Sydenham butchers, until 1763, and then to William Waghorn, a bricklayer. His death in 1771 may have frustrated a building scheme.

The land was frequently sold and resold after the break-up of the Hodsdon estate, before being bought by Daniel in 1800, but for most of the time it was occupied by the Trehearns, who made this the centre of their operations after 1817. They had been butchers, but now concentrated on dairy farming, and their house eventually came to be known as the Sydenham Dairy. In 1849 John Griffith, architect, of 16 Finsbury Place, produced a plan for creating Kent House Road across the fields, but nothing happened for some years, and it was not until the early 1860s that houses were

29. *The corner of Sydenham Road and Mayow Road in 1920. On the right are the cottages between the Dolphin and Mayow Road, now replaced by a garage.*

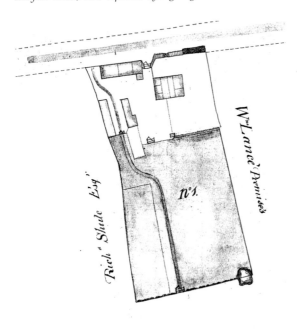

30. *John Trehearn's farmhouse and yard in 1807. The buildings hard up against the road were Covell's Cottages.*

built on the new road. The Trehearns carried on until 1853, and other dairymen succeeded them, making use of the land that remained.

There was a cottage next to the farmhouse, on the site now covered by 170 to 176 Sydenham Road. It was usually occupied by one of the Trehearns, but in the 1840s was let to Ann Selley, whose name appears in some records as Mrs Silly. She was perhaps related to the Samuel Scilly who was a Trehearn tenant on the north side of the road in 1799, and the various shoemaking Selleys who lived in Sydenham during the nineteenth century.

The next old house stood on the site now occupied by 142 and 144 Sydenham Road. It belonged to the Morphew or Morfee family, and in 1700 was left to Jeffrey Morphew by his father William. It was then occupied by George Wood. In 1729, after the death of Jeffrey Morphew, it was described as a "tenement with orchard or backside and garden, containing half an acre, at Sippenham or Sittingham, formerly in the occupation of Robert Batt ... and now of Elizabeth Morphew".

From the early 1770s until his death in 1818 the tenant was William Lance, the principal baker in the village. When Thomas Dermody was in hiding at Perry Vale in 1802 he asked his friends to "direct to me at Mr Lance's, baker, Sydenham, Kent". He could walk from his cottage to the shop along the Berryman's Lane footpath. William Lance's widow and daughter continued the business until 1828,

31. The view from what is now Hazel Grove presumably painted, in 1920, from an 1897 photograph. On the left are Covell's Cottages, and on the right is the surviving no. 128 Sydenham Road.

when it was taken over by William Frederick Ion (or I'on), who remained until the 1870s. His shop and Oxford House, which had been built against its eastern wall in the 1840s, were demolished c.1894 to make way for the existing shops.

On the line of Knighton Park Road, for the sake of which it was demolished in the early 1880s, stood the old Trehearn headquarters, from which the family moved in 1817. It was a butcher's shop as well as a farmhouse for at least eighty years, occupied by Thomas Scudder from 1727 or earlier until his death in 1746, by Samuel Scudder until 1780, and then by the two John Trehearns, uncle and nephew. The elder Trehearn was a belligerent semi-literate character who once wrote an angry letter to Lord Dartmouth protesting about his policy of creeping enclosure. By 1832 the old farmhouse had become a doctor's surgery, occupied by Alexander Scott until the 1840s, and by Francis Corbould until he moved to 2 Westwood Hill in 1853. In the 1850s it was the private residence of Mark William Ridgway, former landlord of the Greyhound, before he moved across the road to Lime Tree Cottage. In its last years the old house became known as Paxton Lodge, or Cottage. On part of its garden a house called Springfield was built in 1857. This survives converted into shops as 138 and 138a Sydenham Road.

On the western corner of Knighton Park Road stood the ancient wooden terrace known as Covell's Cottages, 132 to 136 Sydenham Road. The Covell

family were butchers at 136 from the 1820s or '30s until 1868 (when they retired to Paxton Lodge), and also at one time tenants of Kent House Farm. The cottages were probably built originally for labourers on the Scudder/Trehearn farm. They were demolished in the 1960s, and a garage took their place.

We now come to a surviving group of old houses, all probably built in the 1790s. No. 128, although greatly altered, is still essentially the house occupied by Hunt and Winton, builders, carpenters and undertakers, from 1817 or earlier. They were heavily engaged in the development of Sydenham Common after the enclosure. In 1840 the business was taken over by the Barrett family, who remained for many years. No. 126, sometimes called Cromer House, was for a time the private residence of William Henry Barrett, one of the partners in the firm.

The terrace next to the chapel was known as The Firs. It has been divided into three houses since the 1830s, but before that 122 and 124 were occupied as a single house of some distinction. By 1798 the tenant was John Sutton, who was apparently a job master and livery stable keeper. In 1808 Thomas Campbell playfully planned an elopement with Fanny Mayow, until he discovered that she was a Tory, and declared that he "should have hired a post-chaise from John Sutton (maugre the expense)". In 1817 the Rev. John Keen Cookesley moved here from The Priory (*see p.43*). He was

32. The Firs, 120 (on the right) to 124 Sydenham Road, in 1992.

chaplain of Pinkston Arundel French's proprietary chapel almost next door, and was running a school here at The Firs in 1826. French himself may possibly have occupied the double house in the early 1830s, but after that the division was made that has remained ever since.

The first tenant of 124, after this division, was the versatile Edmund Brown, estate agent, insurance man, registrar of births and deaths for the Sydenham district, and occasional school master. He also took in lodgers. He and his widow occupied the house for fifty years. The most interesting tenant of 122 was Thomas Clifford, former landlord of the Greyhound, who was here in the 1860s. The third house in The Firs, no.120, was the Manse of Samuel Marsh, minister of the chapel next door, during the late 1860s and early '70s. Marsh took pupils here and sometimes described the establishment optimistically as the Grammar School. The house was sadly spoiled by conversion into a car showroom, but the upper floors are externally unaltered.

THE CHAPEL

The Sydenham Road Chapel is one of the oldest and most curious buildings in the district. Its origin is a mystery. In 1706 and 1707 one Mrs Quicke, the widow of a Nonconformist minister, gave "an eminent instance of her charity" by "setting up and carrying on, for the last two summers successively, the ministry of the gospel, at her own charge, in

33. The Sydenham Road Chapel c.1930, when it was the All Saints' church hall.

a poor ignorant village, Sydenham, in Kent, not many miles from this city, and unto which many wealthy citizens with their families, in the summer, ordinarilly resort". Ignorance is to be understood here in its theological sense of freedom from exposure to the teachings of Jean Calvin.

This summer mission has generally been considered the origin of the chapel, but there is no direct proof of this. All we can say for certain is that John Rocque's map of 1746 shows a 'Dissenters Meeting' on the site, but that he attaches the name to a building that presents its long side to the road. Rocque's evidence is not the strongest, but it does agree here with the architectural assessment of the existing chapel, which suggests that it may date from the middle of the eighteenth century. Before that the congregation probably met in a private house. Rocque also shows a footpath leading directly from the chapel to Penge, initially on the line of the modern Trewsbury Road. It is possible that this footpath was established by worshippers from that hamlet constantly crossing the fields, for Kent House Lane already gave adequate access from Penge to Sydenham Green.

A Victorian account claims a Mr Barron as minister from 1760 to 1767, but if so he must have lived at a distance and visited Sydenham only on Sundays, for there is no record of him as a resident. From 1767 until 1794 Dr John Williams (1727-98) brought some intellectual distinction to the chapel and the village. He was a well-known Greek scholar and acted for many years as Librarian at his namesake Dr Daniel Williams's Library. His only recorded local address was at Sydenham Place (*see pp.48-9*) in the 1770s. After 1777 his duties at Dr Williams's Library probably obliged him to live in town.

In 1794 the lease of the chapel expired. The owner of the site, and of much other land on the south side of Sydenham Road, was the Rev. Henry Pratt, Vicar of Orpington. He granted a new lease to Dr Hugh French of Arundel Cottage (*see p.28*), who turned the building into an Anglican chapel for his son, the Rev. Pinkston Arundel French, who had graduated from Oxford in 1786. The many wealthy new residents in the village certainly needed a local chapel to save them from the long journey to St Mary's at Lewisham, or to St George's Beckenham, which some of them preferred to patronise. It seems that French, who when he was in Sydenham usually lived at various houses in Perry Hill, kept the pew rents, but employed curates or chaplains to do the bulk of the work at the chapel, especially after his college presented him to a Somerset rectory in 1803.

These assistants generally supplemented their incomes in the traditional manner by opening schools. The first of them known to us, John Keen

Cookesley, certainly did. He officiated from 1814 until 1826 or later. It was presumably he that Thomas Campbell encountered at "our village chapel" in 1815. "I have been doomed to hear a proser – with an east wind tormentung my rheumatic jaw, and nipping my toes – preach for two hours on the shortness of time; while I need hardly say that his sermon proved anything but his text!" In the late 1820s and 1830s William Orger combined work at the chapel with running his school at Perry Hill House, which he leased from the French family.

Thomas Palmer Hutton took over after the death of Pinkston French in 1836. He probably accepted pupils at his house in Sydenham before setting up a successful school at Summerfield in Honor Oak Road in the 1840s. The chapel was "repaired in 1845, and a handsome spire in the Gothic style added, at a cost of £1,000, defrayed by subscription". In 1847 Foster Rogers was the minister. He was succeeded, from 1850 until his death at the end of 1861, by William Burgess Hayne, who lived at 13 Jew's Walk. He was followed at both the chapel and the house by Charles Stevens, who remained until he was appointed the first incumbent of Holy Trinity in 1866.

The chapel was then leased by Samuel Marsh, whom we have met as the master of the 'Grammar School' at 120 Sydenham Road. It was in his time that the chapel became known as Christ Church. He conducted Anglican services, but was technically a Non-conformist minister until he was ordained in 1873. In that year Christ Church returned to the official Anglican fold as a chapel of ease to St Michael and All Angels. When All Saints' was opened in Trewsbury Road in 1903 the old chapel became its church hall.

THE STEVENS ESTATE

Two of the three houses between the chapel and the Golden Lion were demolished to make way for Trewsbury Road in the early 1880s. The one nearest the chapel was the home of Thomas Dyteman, the leading bricklayer in the village until his death in 1837. It was then the first Sydenham home of Robert von Glehn, whose family played such a great part in Sydenham life in the 1860s (*see pp.112-116*). The third house, which survives as no.118, was the home of the Belbin family for several generations. The younger Charles Belbin, who flourished in the 1850s and '60s, as well as being a plumber, painter, gas fitter, and house decorator, was a keen cricketer and marksman, and successful enough to have his portrait painted in oils to adorn the ancestral shop.

The Golden Lion was probably founded in the

34. *Sydenham Road c.1860, by C. Adams. The Ouzman house and the Congregational Chapel and British School are on the right. In the distance are the Golden Lion and the Sydenham Road Chapel, with its spire intact. The sign of the Dolphin can be seen on the left.*

35. *No. 118 Sydenham Road and the Golden Lion in 1992.*

1740s. The first landlord of whom we can be sure is John Robinson, who was here from 1743 until his death in 1746. Other notable licensees were Daniel Ross from 1809 to 1836, and the jovial Susannah Hardy (later Trehearn) from the 1840s to the 1860s. She married and buried two landlords before taking charge again in her golden after-noon, when she was still described as the "fair mistress" of the inn. The Lion was the best equipped of the Sydenham public houses, and it became a focus of popular social life. In the 1850s, when the pub may have been entirely rebuilt, there was added a "splendid new Music Hall 60 feet long, to be let for dinner parties, concerts, balls, etc.". Later in the century the pub was known as the Golden Lion and Palace of Varieties. There was a fine bowling green, quoit and skittle grounds, and facilities for shooting matches. The cricket ground behind the pub was the headquarters of Sydenham Albion, the best of the local clubs in the middle of the nineteenth century.

Between the Golden Lion and the modern Girton Road were squeezed some eighteen shops and cottages, few of them of any great age or individual interest. Most of this area was still an open field until the second half of the eighteenth century. In addition to the shops on the main road there was a group of four cottages behind numbers 98 to 102. Although they were built long before he arrived in Sydenham they came to be called Dawson's Cottages after William Henry Dawson, who lived at The Cedars (*see p.41*) from the 1850s to the '70s. They survived until 1957. Next to the Golden Lion was the shop to which William Andrews moved the village post office in 1842 from its original position nearly opposite. The oldest surviving shop in this group is no. 104, which was built for his own use in 1847 by William Bridgland junior. The only large detached house stood directly

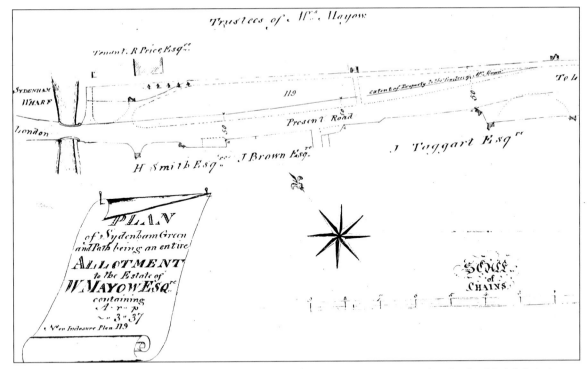

36. *The Sydenham Road greens in 1834. Features on the north side of the road are Doo's Wharf and Ralph Price's house. The names to the south are Haskett Smith of Newlands, John Dudin Brown of Malvern House, and James Taggart, the owner of the Stevens estate.*

opposite Mayow Road. In the 1840s and '50s it was the home of Thomas Hunt, formerly one of the building firm of Hunt and Winton at no.128. He was one of the main developers of Sydenham Park.

Immediately to the west of this house Sydenham Congregational Chapel was built in 1819. Since their loss of the old chapel in 1794 the Independents had worshipped on the common near Peak Hill (where "the preacher was sometimes interrupted by the foolish people ringing a large bell"), in a tent, and in a cottage at Lower Sydenham. For more than twenty years after the building of the chapel there was no resident minister, but in 1842 the Rev. Alfred S.Ray took charge. The congregation was frequently split by the schisms characteristic of this denomination, and after 1850 the chapel chiefly served as the British (that is, Nonconformist) School until it moved to Kirkdale in 1861. Next door to the chapel stood a handsome double fronted brick house that was occupied for seventy years or more by the Ouzman family, who were the principal tailors in Sydenham until competition grew with the arrival of the Crystal Palace. All the old houses between no. 98 and the line of Girton Road were demolished in the early 1890s to make way for the existing shops.

At this point the character of Sydenham Road changed quite markedly. The bustling village of shops, pubs and chapels gave place to a quiet street of large houses in heavily wooded grounds. This alteration in the atmosphere was emphasised by the beginning of the Sydenham Road greens, a series of enclosures bordered by posts and rails, and studded with trees, first on the south and then on the north side of the road, that screened the big houses from the passing traffic. In modern terms, these greens extended all the way from Mayow Road to beyond Silverdale, the creation of which in the early 1870s made the first breach in them. The rest lasted until the fatal 1880s, when so much of old Sydenham was destroyed. The surviving greens in Lewisham High Street and Rushey Green will give some idea of what Sydenham Road lost with them.

It will be most convenient to begin the description of this new phase of Sydenham Road on the south side, where the first large houses formed part of the same estate as the shops and cottages last described. In fact everything on the south side from Trewsbury Road to Newlands Park (an old footpath and lane) belonged to the same succession of owners from the seventeenth century until 1851.

In 1658 John Stevens the elder of Bromley settled the estate on his son John on the occasion of his marriage with Marie Ellys of Chichester. It then consisted of five farms or smallholdings "all in a certain street or place commonly called Sydenham".

1. messuage and 2 barns, orchard, garden, and land, 10 acres, in occupation of Thomas Glover

2. messuage and one barn, stable, garden, orchard, and land, 4 acres, in occupation of Thomas Moseley

3. messuage, barn, stable, orchard, garden, and land, 4 acres, in occupation of Thomas Hanford

4. messuage, barn, and orchard, in occupation of Adam Allingham

5. messuage, barn, stable, garden, orchard, and land, 10 acres, in occupation of John Bridgell.

It is not possible to identify these five holdings with any certainty, but one might guess that the two ten acre farms were the ancestors of the houses known as Elm Grove and The Priory, described below, and that the Golden Lion originated from one of the others. The estate remained in the Stevens family until the death of John Stevens of Chislehurst *c.*1790. It was then bought or inherited by James Taggart, also of Chislehurst, and from him passed in 1834 to his wife's family, the Bascombes. Disputes among the Bascombe heirs ended in a Chancery suit, and the auctioning of the property in small lots in 1851.

The first house after Ouzman's was Cedar Cottage or The Cedars, which stood in grounds of four acres on what is now the western corner of Girton Road. The site of the house was later occupied by the Granada Cinema and has since been taken by the Safeway supermarket. Much of Girton Road covers the garden. Cedar Cottage cannot have been one of the 1658 farmhouses, for it was built, apparently on a fresh site, in 1807/8, for George Reveley of 42 Lamb's Conduit Street. Later tenants had interesting literary connections. From the 1820s until his death Cedar Cottage was occupied by John Rivington (1779-1841), head of the publishing firm. His son, John the younger (1812-86) remained for a few years before moving to Sydenham Park. The Rivingtons were succeeded by George Beadnell (1773-1862), a friend of Charles Dickens. George's daughter Maria was Dickens's first love and the model for Dora in *David Copperfield*.

When auctioned in 1892 Cedar Cottage was

37. *John Rivington (1812-86).*

described as commanding "an extensive view in the direction of the Surrey Hills and Knockholt Beeches" and contained "nine bedrooms, two dressing rooms, bath room, large billiard room, drawing room, dining room, and morning room, butler's pantry, servants' hall, kitchen, and usual offices". Like most estates in Sydenham at that time it was sold more with a view to development than occupation. The house was demolished in 1894 or shortly afterwards.

Next to Cedar Cottage, and behind the first of the greens, stood a pair of wooden houses known as Hawkhurst Lodge and Kenton Cottage. They were probably of a similar style and date to the surviving pair near the corner of Newlands Park and others that used to exist in Sydenham Road. Most began as genuine cottages for gardeners and small-holders, but were gentrified as the area became more fashionable. Hawkhurst Lodge was certainly respectable enough by 1798 for the marriage of its tenant, Samuel Parsons, to be reported in the *Gentleman's Magazine*. A later occupant was the solicitor Henry Charles Chilton, son of George Chilton of Clune House opposite, who moved here in 1836, after his marriage with Fanny

38. *The main front of Elm Grove c.1840. In the foreground is one of the Sydenham Road greens.*

39. *The garden front of Elm Grove in 1874, painted from Penge Lane (now Newlands Park) by Helen Thornycroft.*

Malin of The Bridge (*see p.48*). Hawkhurst Lodge achieved some undesired publicity in 1867 when the recent tenant, William Hurst, a stockbroker's clerk, was prosecuted for the theft of thousands of pounds from his employers. Kenton Cottage was long the home of the Hodge family, who were friends of Thomas Campbell. The death of Major Edward Hodge during the Waterloo campaign was introduced into his *Ode to Burns*. Both houses were involved in the ruin of Cedar Cottage and Elm Grove and demolished in the 1890s. The shops numbered 66 to 72 Sydenham Road are now on the site.

Elm Grove, the next house, was the largest on the old Stevens estate. In 1868 it was described as "the most pleasant and delightful residence in the village of Sydenham", and for once an estate agent scarcely needed to exaggerate. The original building on the site was probably one of the farms in the 1658 list. It was rebuilt *c.*1785 for Dr Samuel Farar (formerly of Norman Cottage, *see p.47*), but is chiefly associated with Richard Shute, another friend of Campbell, who was here from the 1790s until his death in 1819. He was an 'eminent silkman' with business premises at 27 Ivy Lane, near St Paul's Cathedral. A later tenant, Richard Preston Beall, who lived here in the 1850s and '60s, was also in the silk trade. In 1867 he moved to Longton Hall, where he provoked the Taylor's Lane riots (*see pp.127-8*). The eight acres of land attached to Elm Grove were too valuable to give it any chance of survival. The house was demolished in 1894, and Tannsfeld Road was laid out across the grounds ten years later.

Between Elm Grove and Newlands Park there was another large house, which was probably also a descendent of one of the 1658 Stevens farms. By 1771 it was occupied by Baron D'Aguilar. It fell empty late in the century and was pulled down so that Richard Shute of Elm Grove could build a fashionable villa on the site in the Strawberry Hill Gothic style. The architect he employed was George Tappen, the Surveyor to Dulwich College, who probably lived at the time in Honor Oak Road (*see p.64*). The Priory, as the new house was called, was completed in 1804. Shute had taken a 61-year building lease of the property from James Taggart. He did not intend The Priory for his own occupation, but as an investment, and in 1804 he let it to Thomas Bearda Batard, later of the Old Cedars and The Lawn (*see pp.58 and 25*).

A most interesting tenant of The Priory, though a very brief one, was Miss Lucy Jordan, one of the daughters of the Duke of Clarence (later William IV) and Mrs Jordan, the actress. The house was apparently taken for her as a suitably smart address from which to marry Col. Hawker of the 14th Dragoons, which she did on the 30th of April 1810. Her sister Mrs Allsop may also have lived here when she settled in the village in 1813. Later occupants included the Rev. John Cookesley, afterwards of The Firs (*see pp.35-6*) and John Towgood Kemble, who subsequently moved to Kirkdale.

A 21 year lease of the house was taken by Charlotte Dence in 1874, but she died in the same year and it passed to her nephew John Dence, who began to plan the development of the estate. Rosedale, the surviving house next door to The Priory (now no. 40) was built by him in the late 1870s on the site of the old stables. Dence did not live to see his schemes realised, but the thirty houses in Newlands Park known as Priory Villas (later nos. 104 to 46) were built in the early 1880s, shortly after his death. The Priory survived the loss of its grounds and remained a picturesque feature of Sydenham Road for another ninety years, first as a more modest private house, then as the Priory Preparatory School, which closed in 1923, and finally as the Priory Garage. It was demolished *c.*1969, and the post office and the attached

40. The last fragment of The Priory as part of the Priory Garage in 1969.

42. Sydenham Road, just east of Newlands Park, in 1919. On the left is Wood Minna Cottage (or Priory Villa), which has now lost the section in front of the chimney stack. In the centre are the surviving Grove Cottage and Priory Cottage, and on the right the similar pair that used to stand at the corner of Newlands Park.

41. Grove Cottage and Priory Cottage, 34 and 32 Sydenham Road, in 1960.

shops to the west now cover the site. The Naborhood Centre has taken the place of the Queen's Hall or Naborhood cinema, which had been built in 1910 on a corner of the old Elm Grove garden.

Beyond Rosedale, mentioned above, and the small wooden building with shops in front, which is a surviving fragment of the coachman's cottage on the Priory estate, lie the two oldest buildings in Sydenham. Grove Cottage and Priory Cottage, now nos. 34 and 32, probably date from the beginning of the eighteenth century. The pair may originally have formed a single house, and the building must certainly then have had all its walls constructed of wood. The distinctive brick and stucco front elevation would have been added as a fashionable embellishment in the second half of the eighteenth century, when there was a growing market in the village for genteel cottages.

The story of the houses cannot be traced with any confidence before the early 1760s, when Grove Cottage was occupied by a Mr Halford or Alford, and Priory Cottage by William Staples, whose widow was to remain until 1795. John Lemaistre and his widow were the tenants of Grove Cottage from 1765 until 1794, and during the middle decades of the nineteenth century two sisters named Mary Ann and Hannah Parks earned a living here as linen drapers. The successor to Mrs Staples at Priory Cottage (though only for a year or two) was the Rev. Pinkston Arundel French, who had just taken possession of the Sydenham Road chapel (see

pp.36-7). Its only other notable occupant was Olga von Glehn, one of the talented daughters of Robert von Glehn, who found a refuge here as a teacher of languages when the reduced circumstances of the family forced the sale of Peak Hill Lodge in 1886.

Because of the gradual widening of Newlands Park there is now only room for a narrow shop between Priory Cottage and the corner, but there was formerly a pair of houses here of a similar style to the original Grove and Priory Cottages. This pair was never gentrified, probably because the acute angle of Newlands Park gave no room even for a small garden, and by the 1840s the two cottages had been combined as a shop. This was first used by the butcher Thomas Covell, but in the 1860s it became a drapery under the name of the Manchester House. The old wooden building behind the shop, and the ramshackle extensions in Newlands Park (originally the butcher's stable and slaughterhouse), survived until seriously damaged by bombing in 1943.

THE FENNER ESTATE

Newlands Park, known as Penge Lane until the 1880s, is not marked on John Rocque's map of 1746, although well-established by the end of the eighteenth century. The omission may be one of Rocque's mistakes, but in any case illustrates the point that this was not an important route until the rise of Penge in the 1850s. Indeed Penge Lane remained a private toll road until John Harding, the proprietor for fifty years, was bought out by the developers of Newlands Park in 1878, when the gate was demolished. It stood at the boundary line of

43. *The rear of the pair of houses at the corner of Newlands Park in 1920. The roof of Grove Cottage and Priory Cottage can be seen above the wooden stables and slaughter house in Newlands Park.*

Beckenham and Lewisham, where Newlands Park still narrows. The lane marked the end of the Stevens estate and the beginning of one of almost equal value belonging to the Fenner family. It extended west more or less to the line of the railway, and amounted to nearly sixty acres, much of it over the parish boundary in Beckenham.

The first of the seven Fenner houses stood on the western corner of Newlands Park. In the second half of the nineteenth century, after rebuilding, it was known as Ellesmere House. The first known tenant was Thomas House, who was here for upwards of thirty years until his death in 1794. After that William Fenner, the owner of the estate, who was Master of the Stationers' Company in 1786, occupied the house (or sometimes Malvern House next door) until 1807, when he was succeeded by Dr William Langford, the disgraced Canon of Windsor (*see p.68*), who died here in 1814.

In the nineteenth century it was most often a girls' school. Miss Harriet Girling first used it as such in the 1830s, before moving to Percy Cottage, Charles Street, now 8 Charlecote Grove. Ellesmere House was rebuilt in 1841 for Charles Toller, a proctor (attorney in the ecclesiastical courts) who remained until 1857. It was then a school again, either boarding or day, until it was demolished and replaced by the present 28 and 28a in 1899. The most successful teachers were the Misses

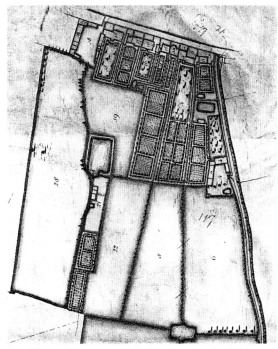

44. *The northern part of the Fenner estate in 1795. Sydenham Road is at the top and Penge Lane (Newlands Park) on the right.*

45. *Ellesmere House c.1899. On the right is the almost entirely demolished Malvern House.*

46. *Sydenham Road seen from the railway bridge in the 1860s. On the left is the largest of the greens. The shop in the centre is the Manchester House, at the corner of Newlands Park, and on the right are Ellesmere House, Malvern House (with the gazebo), Norman Cottage, Arden Cottage, Ivy House, and Mayow Lodge. The opening on the right is not Venner Road, but the entrance to the Newlands stable-yard. The chapel spire is visible in the distance.*

47. Norman Cottage and Arden Cottage in 1979.

Sanders, who remained from the 1850s to the 1880s. Later ventures, including that of the improbably named Mdlle. Marie Grogan, were more short-lived.

Malvern House, next door, was the second largest on the Fenner estate. Its grounds of nearly five acres extended down Newlands Park nearly to Tredown Road. It was occupied by Peter Ogier in the 1760s, and then briefly by Baron D'Aguilar before he moved to the forerunner of The Priory (*see p.43*). The most notable tenant was Joseph Marryat, MP (the father of the novelist Captain Marryat) who was here from 1801 to 1815. Later tenants included John Dudin Brown, who was a partner in the wharfage business of Henry Dudin (*see p.29*), and John Wheeley Bevington of the Neckinger leather mills at Bermondsey. His daughter Mary, Lady Quilter, was the mother of Roger Quilter, the composer. Malvern House was auctioned in 1898 as being "ripe for building purposes, and cottages, small villas, and business premises are in very great demand". The house was demolished soon afterwards, and nos. 24a to 26a were built on the site.

Next to Malvern House stood two large semi-detached houses that survive, very much altered, as nos. 24 and 22a Sydenham Road. They were called Norman Cottage and Arden Cottage. The first known tenants were Abraham Henman and a Mr Paget in the 1760s and '70s. The building seems then to have been converted into a single house occupied by Samuel Farar until Elm Grove was rebuilt for him, and then by John Coates until he moved to Sydenham Place c.1797. The most notable tenant of Norman Cottage after the building was divided into two dwellings again was William Roberts, who was the leading surgeon in Sydenham from the 1820s until his death in 1849. His widow and daughter remained until the house was converted into a builder's works and yard in

the 1880s. A shop has been built over the front garden, but the upper part of the eighteenth century house remains little altered.

Arden Cottage was long the home of Miss Betty Wynell Mayow, a cousin of Mary and Fanny Mayow of the Old House. It was saved from destruction in the 1880s by its usefulness as a laundry, and in the twentieth century the laundry buildings extended hugely over the back garden and beyond. But the front has remained free from any shop, and the two-storey bay survives from Arden Cottage's long-lost days as a private house.

A similar pair, Ivy House and Mayow Lodge, filled the space between Arden Cottage and Venner Road until they were demolished in the 1880s. The earliest known tenant of Ivy House was a Mrs Godden in the 1760s. For the first third of the nineteenth century the Lekeux family lived here and caused serious spelling problems for the parish officers. They were followed by Mayow Wynell Adams, who was at Ivy House for more than thirty years before he inherited the Old House on the death of his aunt, Frances Mayow, in 1874. Mayow Lodge was occupied by Robert Fuller in the 1760s and '70s, and by Betty Mayow in the late 1840s, before she moved to Arden Cottage, but from early in the nineteenth century it was generally used by one of the Smith family from Newlands, next door.

Newlands was the biggest Fenner house, with twelve acres of ground in Lewisham parish, and more beyond in Beckenham. A Mr Godden lived here in the early 1760s, and was followed by William Wilson, the owner of a hardware warehouse in Cannon Street, until 1788. For the next two years 'Mr Aislibie' lived here. This was probably Benjamin Aislabie, the twenty-stone wine merchant who was later at Lee Place. Despite his weight he was a determined fox hunter and a keen if unskilful cricketer. He served as the first Secretary of the MCC, and his portrait may be seen at Lords.

In 1790 the lease of Newlands was acquired by Haskett Smith of 9 America Square, who subsequently bought the freehold. The Smith family were to remain until they sold the estate for redevelopment in 1877. They were very wealthy, and Newlands was only one of several houses that they owned. Haskett Smith died in Bedford Square, at the age of ninety, in February 1840. His son William inspired great confidence with three addresses, Newlands, 20 Hyde Park Terrace, and Great Peathing Lodge, Leicestershire. In 1870, when aged 79, William Smith was foolish enough to marry a Spaniard, Victoria Caballero, of little more than half his age. She moved to Newlands with all her relations and installed a priest, Ralph Cooper, as domestic chaplain and virtual head of the household. As the historian of Roman Catholicism in the village has explained it:

"In 1870 Mrs Victoria Smith, a Spanish lady, came to live in Sydenham. With her she brought her own private Chaplain, who would say Mass in an out-building attached to the house. Local Catholics were admitted ... On average, about forty or fifty Catholics attended every Sunday. This was the beginning of Mass for the people within the boundaries of Sydenham ... When, in 1872, Mrs Smith retired to a Convent in Roehampton, her Chaplain left the district."

If this date of 1872 is correct the Smiths must have parted, for he did not die until 1876. Writing two years later, Mayow Adams recorded the event with regret both personal and social:

> "Mr Smith, one of the oldest of our neighbours, died on the 5th August 1876, and in consequence thereof his property, one of the old places of the village, near the bridge and running down south by the side of the railway to the Chatham and Dover line, is now sold, and is to be cut up, making another sad alteration in the appearance of the neighbourhood."

The heirs sold the estate to the British Land Company in November 1877, and Venner Road was soon run through the site of the old house.

SYDENHAM PLACE

The bridge here makes a sharp break in the road, and this has been emphasised by the buildings on the west side being numbered as part of Kirkdale. But in its various forms the bridge has only existed for two hundred years, a short time in the history of Sydenham, and it is logical to continue this survey of Sydenham Road to the foot of Westwood Hill. The Fenner estate ended with Newlands, and beyond it the buildings on the south side belonged to Lord Dartmouth, the lord of the manor of Lewisham. It was usual for roads to debouch onto commons, to assist the herding of animals, and it was equally common for these wide openings to be gradually narrowed by encroachments. Lord Dartmouth was happy to sanction them because any houses the squatters built became his freehold property. The shops from Venner Road to (but not including) the Old Cedars stand on ground taken from the common in this way during the eighteenth century.

The first old house on these enclosures was known as The Bridge in its last years. It occupied most of the space between Venner Road and the railway cutting. John Cooper was the occupant from 1754 until 1766, during part of which period

48. Dr John Williams. (Permission to reproduce this portrait is granted by the Trustees of Dr Williams's Trust and the National Portrait Gallery.)

George Cooper was landlord of the Greyhound nearly opposite. It may have been a school early in the nineteenth century, when a Mr Redman was the tenant, for Thomas Campbell's sons learnt the rudiments from the Misses Redman, "called Redman, for they teach men to read", according to the boys. The Bridge was involved in the ruin of Newlands in the 1870s, and Station Parade was built on the site.

Several small cottages were removed when the canal was cut across the road in the first decade of the nineteenth century. The first house to the west of it was on the site now occupied by the shop numbered 276 Kirkdale. It was built on waste ground *c.*1742 for a barber named William Russell. In 1805, when occupied by Richard Bargrove, it was described as "a brick messuage, stable, and coach house opposite the Greyhound". The house acquired the name 'Caledonian Cottage' in the 1840s when occupied by a retired Scottish jeweller named Andrew Beaton. His niece Margaret Stronach, who inherited in the 1860s, was the last occupant. Caledonian Cottage was demolished in the early 1870s.

Next door, on the site of 262 to 274 Kirkdale, stood Sydenham Place. This began as a pair of large semi-detached houses, probably built in the 1750s. In 1805 they were described as "two great houses, stable, and chaise house". The first known

49. The centre of Sydenham in the 1850s, seen from the entrance to Kirkdale. The Greyhound, in its old alignment towards Kirkdale (and formerly the common) is on the left, the original booking hall of Sydenham station (demolished 1979) is in the centre, and Sydenham Place is on the right. (This illustration is also reproduced on the jacket of this book.)

tenants were Edward Walker and a Mr Bond in 1763. The most distinguished was Dr John Williams, the minister of the Non-conformist chapel, who lived here in the 1770s. He probably occupied the western house, which had a smaller garden. John Hartshorne, a cheesemonger from Great Tower Street in the City, acquired the lease of both houses *c.*1813, when he left Perry Vale Farm, and occupied the eastern half himself until the 1830s.

Sydenham Place was rebuilt as a terrace of four houses *c.*1840. For twenty years people of wealth and respectability continued to live here, but then three of the houses fell into the hands of George Ware, a booking clerk at the station, and were converted into lodgings. Sydenham Place was demolished *c.*1870, and the site remained vacant until Caledonian Cottage could also be removed, and allow the comprehensive redevelopment of this valuable site in what was by then known as Central Sydenham. The six shops that were built in 1875, now 262 to 276 Kirkdale, incorporate the cruciform motif that was found on the old Sydenham Place.

THE OLD HOUSE

The last section of Sydenham Road to be described is the north side from Mayow Road to the Greyhound. This was the Old House estate, and the great growth of its garden and grounds under the Hodsdon and Mayow families prevented any intensive development here until late in the nineteenth century. The small number of houses in this part of the road may even have declined after 1700, as the Hodsdons sought greater privacy and grandeur – in a way that was common during the eighteenth century – by clearing away the houses and cottages of their neighbours. As late as 1815 the Mayow family demolished one that stood exactly on the line later taken by Mayow Road, and used the space for their new kitchen garden. This house had been occupied by James Edgelar, a shopkeeper, since the 1780s.

The Old House, the centre of Sydenham's largest estate, was formerly known as Brookehouse Farm, because it had been owned or leased in the sixteenth century by Richard Brookhouse, a member of the prominent local family that has already been

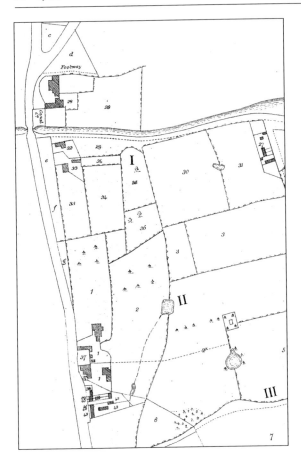

50. Part of the Mayow estate in 1815. No. 1 is the Old House and its home farm, 43 the Dolphin, 33 Ralph Price's house, 32 The Cottage, 28 The Greyhound, and 27 the Dog Kennel houses.

51. Mayow Wynell Mayow by Sir Thomas Lawrence c.1806.

encountered at Place House. The farm belonged to Edmund Style in 1621, and in 1658 was sold by John Style, for £2,404, to Sir William Wylde, an eminent judge who lived in Lewisham High Street. He had built up a large estate in the parish, but the interests of his sons lay elsewhere, and in 1713 they sold Brookehouse Farm to Edward Hodsdon, a Southwark wine merchant, for £2,000. It then extended to about 110 acres.

Edward Hodsdon was buying land in the Sydenham area with great eagerness in the years between 1713 and 1719. In addition to Brookehouse Farm he acquired from various owners some fifty acres, mostly in the form of woodland, immediately adjoining. This gave him control of nearly all the land between Sydenham Road, Perry Vale, and the common. Other, detached, pockets of land that he bought during this spending spree included the forty-acre Coleson's Coppice, which was later to be the origin of Forest Hill (see p.61).

Brookehouse Farm was probably occupied by Alexander Lindsay, a butcher, in 1713. He died early in 1715, which may have been when Hodsdon moved to Sydenham. There is no direct evidence to show when he rebuilt the house, but the style of its main section would be consistent with his having done so immediately. Finance would clearly have been no obstacle. The Old House remained basically the same until its demolition in 1902, although the bow-window at the rear was a later addition (perhaps of the 1780s, as the house had been "lately improved at a considerable expence" in 1786), and there was a Victorian canted bay-window on the western side. Mayow Adams had the house thoroughly restored by the architect Charles Frederick Reeks in 1876, shortly after he inherited the estate from his aged aunt. The site of the Old House is now occupied roughly by nos. 85 to 95 Sydenham Road, or perhaps rather by the back yards of these shops and the service road behind, for the house stood some way from the road.

By the time of his death in 1737 Edward Hodsdon had established himself as the great landowner of Sydenham, and secured his credit with the other local magnates by becoming a pillar of the bench of magistrates. It was clearly his intention to pursue the traditional ambition of successful eighteenth

52. The garden front of the Old House c.1900, shortly before demolition.

century tradesmen by founding a line of country gentlemen. But the Hodsdons were unlucky. Edward's only son, another Edward, died unmarried in 1739. The great inheritance passed from him to his cousin, Thomas Hodsdon of Bushey, who moved to Sydenham and lived at the Old House. He was married, but left no legitimate offspring at his death in 1766. In his will he gave a life interest in half of the estate to his widow. The other half became the absolute property of Sarah Bowles,

"daughter of Jane Bowles of Sydenham, widow". No relationship or other connection is given in the will to explain this generous bequest, but it seems possible that Sarah was Thomas Hodsdon's daughter.

The Old House inheritance rarely brought good fortune with it. Susannah Hodsdon, the widow, died in 1773, and Sarah Bowles, by then Sarah Bunce, in 1774. The estate, in smaller and smaller shares, was divided among numerous Hodsdon great nephews and nieces, and various relations of Sarah Bunce and her husband. Inevitably this led to confusions and arguments that quickly developed into a tangle of Chancery suits. Meanwhile, the Old House itself had been available for letting since Susannah Hodsdon moved to Lewisham High Street in 1769. Edward Russell was the tenant who took a 21-year lease of the house and garden, paying his rent nominally to a host of infant landlords, but in reality to various attorneys and Masters in Chancery.

One obvious function of Chancery was to enable lawyers to buy property cheaply, for few laymen would dare to meddle with the complicated titles disposed of by order of the court. Thus Mayow Wynell Mayow, who was Solicitor to the Excise Office, snapped up most of the old Susannah Hodsdon half of the estate at a Chancery auction

53. The west side of the Old House, probably in the 1890s.

in 1786. He had already secured the remainder of Edward Russell's lease, and was able to live at the Old House while negotiating with the man who had bought the old Sarah Bunce half at an earlier auction. In 1787 they reached agreement and the central block of the Hodsdon estate was re-united for the first time since 1766 in Mayow's hands.

This success was not repeated in the lottery of parenthood. The Mayows produced five daughters, but no son, and the estate seemed about to be broken up again. This was prevented by a tacit family agreement to fix the ultimate inheritance upon a grandson, Mayow Wynell Adams, who was born in the Old House in 1808, the year after the death of Mr Mayow. This understanding was partially broken when the youngest of the five daughters married unexpectedly and demanded her fifth share; but the most easily detached portion (the Greyhound and the Silverdale area) was chosen, and the rest eventually passed to Mayow Adams. He had to wait until 1874 for his full inheritance, as his aunt Fanny Wynell Mayow lived to be 91. The full part played by the Mayow family in the social life of Sydenham is described elsewhere (*see pp.68-71*).

The difficulty of finding an heir to the Old House persisted to the last. Mayow Adams had only one child, a daughter who died before her father. She married and had two sons, one of whom was groomed to take over at Sydenham, and paraded at Old House festivities as the young master. But as soon as Mayow Adams died in 1898 Herbert Mayow Fisher Rowe decided that such an estate was an anachronism in the changing circumstances of the area, and promptly sold it. The property was auctioned in 1900, and the Old House was demolished two years later. In the interval it had probably served as headquarters for Edmondson and Sons, who were rapidly building the Thorpe Estate across the old garden.

THE SILVERDALE AREA

Until 1870 the remainder of the northern side of Sydenham Road held only two houses. The garden of the Old House ended nearly opposite Newlands Park. From there almost to the bridge ran Barefield, which formed the garden of a large wooden house. It may have been built *c.*1750, for the earliest known occupant was a Mr Willson, who was living here in 1753. When the house was leased to James Morris in 1757 it was described as "a timber messuage, coachhouse, stables, and out buildings, with about nine acres of meadow land, adjoining to Mr Hodsdon's garden".

The most notable and long-lasting of the later

54. *Sydenham Bridge over the Croydon Canal, seen from the north in 1836. The house on the left is The Cottage, and beyond it, on the far side of Sydenham Road, is part of the house known as The Bridge. Doo's Wharf is on the right.*

tenants was Ralph Price, who was here from *c*.1815 until his death in 1860. He was the son of Sir Charles Price, bart. (1748-1818), who was Lord Mayor of London, MP for the City, and a great oracle on all commercial questions. Ralph Price looked after the family bank while his father was absorbed in politics. In 1816 he "determined to give up his house in Chatham Place and to reside wholly at Sydenham, by which he should save much expense, and it would be better for the Health of his Family. The inconvenience attending it, said He, will be confined wholly to myself, and that I shall submit to and go there and back agreeably to an arrangement I shall make." This part of the Mayow estate had been acquired by the Rev. Henry James Wharton, Vicar of Mitcham, by his marriage with the youngest of the Mayow daughters. He demolished the Price house in the late 1860s, and soon laid out Silverdale directly across the site.

A smaller house known as The Cottage was built in the first year or two of the nineteenth century beside the towing path of the canal then being dug. It was built for James Hogg, who had taken a lease of what was later the Price house in 1791. It is not clear in which of the two he lived after The Cottage was ready in 1803. In the 1830s the lease of The Cottage was acquired by Ralph Price, who used the house to lodge various members of his family. His son-in-law Robert Still, a solicitor, was living there in 1841. The Cottage was demolished *c*.1870, and Railway Approach is now on the site.

THE GREYHOUND

Sydenham Road officially ends at the railway bridge, but historically it continues to include everything up to the Greyhound. The Railway Tavern, the first building on the west side of the

bridge, is the modern successor to a public house established by George Ware, the former railway clerk and lodging-house keeper (*see p.49*) in 1868. The two shops next door, 321 and 323 Kirkdale, are older than they look. They were built *c*.1845 for Henry Doo, the coal merchant whose wharf on the canal had been removed during the construction of the railway. Doo was the first occupant of no. 323.

The last building to be described is the Greyhound, Sydenham's leading public house. We can be fairly certain that the pub did not exist in 1713/14, as it was not listed when this part of the Old House estate was bought by Edward Hodsdon. By 1727 it is mentioned by name (the only pub so distinguished) in the earliest surviving Lewisham rate book. This naming may indicate that the building was both new and prominent. It is likely enough that Edward Hodsdon, the wine merchant, would be quick to establish an inn on his new estate. The first known landlord was Joseph Hyde, who was described as a vintner when he was buried at St Mary's church in 1729, and the second was Thomas Pulkinghorn, who married Joseph Hyde's widow.

The old Greyhound was a wooden building set well back, and facing not south onto the road, but west onto the common. The present side entrance is in the position of the original front door, and parts of the old wooden Greyhound still survive at the rear of the pub. The huge extension towards the south that changed the alignment of the building and doubled its size, was built in 1873, by Abraham Steer of South Norwood Park. Whether facing south or west the Greyhound bore its true name, denoting its origin as a hunting inn, for about 275 years until a fatuous brewer changed it to something unintelligible in 1996.

55. Nos. 321 and 323 Kirkdale and the Railway Tavern in 1989.

56. The older, partly timber-built section at the rear of the Greyhound, as it appeared in 1989.

The Fringe of the Common

PEAK HILL

Peak Hill is the oldest inhabited part of Upper Sydenham. Its height, which would have been far more striking before the building of so many houses disguised it, made this a natural advanced bastion of enclosure from the manorial waste. The approach to Peak Hill from the side entrance of the Greyhound, along a road now called Spring Hill, dips at first into a small valley. This was formerly the course of a stream that rose on the common and eventually found its way into the Pool River near Bell Green. The true field called Peak or Pig Hill

began on the northern slope of this valley, and it is only with this area that the present section is concerned.

The name seems at first sight to follow a classically sanitising path from Swine Hill via Pig Hill and Peak Hill to the modern Spring Hill; but the story may not be quite that simple. Early in the fourteenth century one Egidii Swayn held land "at Swaynesfeld adjoining Westwode". It is most likely that Swayn was named after the pig field in which he lived or worked, but there is always the possibility that the place was called after the man. Another complication is that there was an almost equally old name for the area. Ralph Treswell calls it Highe feilde on his 1607 map of the common (*ill.78*), and shows two houses there, at the north-eastern and north-western corners.

These two houses are the key to an old misunderstanding about Peak Hill. They became the basis of a lasting division of the field into two

57. *The old 1 and 2 Peak Hill c.1870. Thomas Campbell lived at no. 2 on the left.*

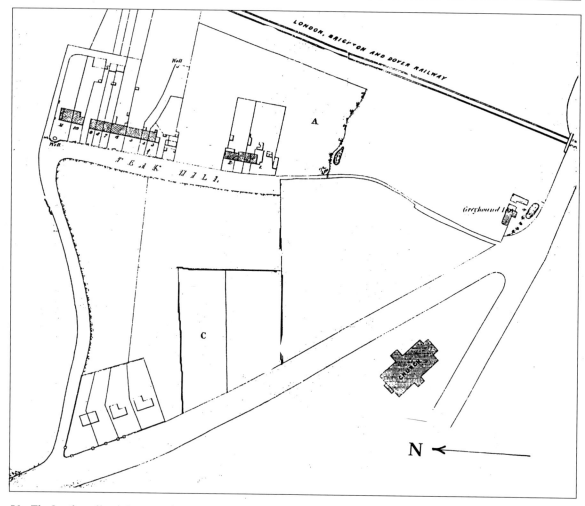

58. *The Leathersellers' Company houses on Peak Hill in 1844. Campbell's house was no. 2, and Buckstone's no. 3, formerly the Fox and Hounds.*

estates, one of which became the property of the Leathersellers' Company, the other of the Hodsdons and Mayows of the Old House. There was no road called Peak Hill until the nineteenth century. The Leathersellers' houses faced directly onto the common westwards, the Hodsdon/Mayow houses northwards. Two important events of the early nineteenth century changed this situation radically. When the Croydon Canal was cut through Sydenham it ran more or less down the dividing line of the two estates, with the result that the eastern half was cut off from any direct communication with the western, first by the canal and later by the railway. A few years later the enclosure of the common deprived the Mayow houses of their northern outlet, and left them isolated, approachable only via footpaths across the Old

House estate. Very soon it was forgotten that this eastern half had ever been a part of Peak Hill.

When Abraham Colfe was defending the common from enclosure at the beginning of the seventeenth century he unearthed some evidence of its antiquity that clearly bears on the history of this eastern portion of Peak Hill. The documents were "two ancient deeds, the one in the fift [1417/18], the other in the ninth [1421/2] yeare of King Henry the fift [showing] that the land of one Batt of Lewisham, called Highfield, doth bound on the North, super Comuniam de Westwood, upon the comon of Westwood".

In 1714 Edward Hodsdon bought Highfield House and about five and a half acres of land from John Style of Merton. The property was described as having Westwood Common and Bay Riddons to the north, just as Ralph Treswell shows it on his map of a century earlier. In 1712 Highfield House was occupied by a farmer named Henry Billiter, who died in 1721. After the Greyhound was established and hunting became an important local sport Highfield House served as the kennels of the local pack. Its isolated position in a corner of the common made it ideal for the purpose. By the time Thomas Hodsdon died in 1766 the old farm had degenerated into "three cottages standing in one of the fields let to Armitage [of the Greyhound], called the Dogkennel Houses ... and occupied by the labourers of Sydenham". The number of cottages rose to four, then five, but the poverty of the tenants never altered. In the first half of the nineteenth century many recipients of the parish charities lived at the Dog Kennel Houses. They were finally demolished in the 1830s, and Silverdale now runs across their site.

When Edward Hodsdon bought Highfield House in 1714 it was described as being bordered on the west by "lands heretofore Andrews". 'Heretofore' was in this case nearly a century earlier, for it was in 1627 that George Andrews and others sold to the Leathersellers' Company a large farm mostly in Perry Hill, but also including "High Field alias Pig's-hill". This must have been the house at the north-western corner of Peak Hill shown on Treswell's map of 1607.

Until 1784 the Leathersellers' used to let their whole Sydenham estate to a single tenant, who may have sub-let the Peak Hill house. Before the 1720s none of the Leathersellers' tenants made any move to add more houses to the one shown here in 1607. It probably continued to be the headquarters of a small farm. There is even a possibility that in time it became an inn called the Green Man, for James Brooke of Perry Hill (*see p.15*), who took a 61-year lease from the Leathersellers' in 1723, is listed in the 1728 rate book as "Mr Brooks or tenant at pig hil at ye Green man". The entry is unfortunately interlined in a tantalisingly ambiguous way.

It was James Brooke who began the development of Peak Hill as a terrace of quality houses suitable as summer residences for City people, or as pleasant retreats for retired merchants. There was only one house here in 1727. Three more were added in 1728, another in 1733, and two in 1736. Whether the original house was incorporated into the terrace or demolished and replaced in not known. It would certainly not have been a regular composition. Grote's Buildings at Blackheath is an existing common-side terrace that may give some idea of its appearance. The seven houses established by 1737 were not always quite consistent in number because a tenant would sometimes occupy

59. *John Baldwin Buckstone by Daniel Maclise, c.1837.*

two adjacent houses, and knock them together, and occasionally a house would be sub-divided, but basically they remained unaltered until the Brooke lease expired in 1784.

The Leathersellers' had a pair of semi-detached houses built at each end of Peak Hill in the 1790s, and the road was eventually numbered 1 to 11. James Brooke's central terrace became nos. 3 to 9 under this arrangement. No. 3 served for a time as the Fox and Hounds, Peak Hill's second public house. The Green Man is not heard of again after 1728, but the Fox and Hounds had a longer history, at least from the 1760s to the '90s. Its name is a further indication of the importance of this corner of the common as a hunting rendezvous. The building had ceased to be a pub by 1803. Later, when it was known as Pevril House, it acquired a further convivial celebrity as the home of John Baldwin Buckstone (1802-79), the comedian and actor-manager (*see p.25*).

Another notable Peak Hill institution was the Sydenham House Academy, which began at no.5 and expanded into no.6. It was founded in 1804 by George Charles Kerval, the man who discovered Roman medallions on the common in 1806, and gave them to the British Museum. One of Thomas Campbell's sons was a pupil, and the poet liked to see him at "all hours of the day on the playground of the Common before Kerval's school". This was to prove the schoolmaster's undoing, for when this land was awarded to the Leathersellers' Company at the enclosure he rented it at an extravagant price, and was soon bankrupt. Other teachers followed at nos.5 and 6: William Davis in the 1820s and Mary Evans in the '30s.

The Leathersellers' Company let Peak Hill on 52-year building leases from 1793. The new houses that resulted had several points of interest. The southern pair was built for William Holness, who lived at no.1 for more than fifty years. His tenants at no.2 included Sarah Marryat, probably the grandmother of the novelist, and Thomas Campbell, who took a 21-year lease in 1804, and remained until 1820. His life in Sydenham is described on pages 70-71. The northern pair, nos.10 and 11, may originally have been a single house called Elm Cottage. In the 1840s and '50s no.11 played an important part in the life of the village because an engineer named Joseph Carter deepened and improved a well in the front garden, and sold the water that he pumped from it to his grateful neighbours. (*See pp. 131-3*)

The beauty of Peak Hill was spoiled by the enclosure and the gradual loss of the open access and uninterrupted views the houses had enjoyed. Writing in 1866 Joseph Edwards sadly contrasted the old and the new:

"Before Sydenham became so much built over this was a very lovely spot, Sydenham-hill in front, Wells-road winding to the left, the fine old trees in the "Jews walk", the old windmill in the distance, and but few houses around, made the prospect a pleasant one in front, while at the back not a house could be seen from the windows. In Campbell's time there was no railway at the back nor any carriage thoroughfare past the house in front... In those days no gas lamps lit the place at night, nor any drainage made the little stream offensive. It will perhaps now scarcely be believed that within fifteen years since this little brooklet was so swollen by a summer storm that a boy was carried away by it and drowned in this lane. Now there are gas lamps and a sewer. The orchard on one side is built over and the meadows on the other are the Greyhound pleasure grounds."

The Leathersellers' saw the intensity of building with which other Sydenham landlords were crowding their estates, and decided that eleven houses were not enough. In 1874 John Baldwin Buckstone wrote to a friend that he had lived in Peak Hill for fourteen years, but that now the Leathersellers

had decided to demolish all the old houses, "and build fashionable villas". When the materials of "the houses now being pulled down at Peak Hill" were sold in 1875 the salvage included "2 antique carved wooden chimney pieces taken out of the house formerly the residence of the Poet Campbell".

Peak Hill Lodge, which was built *c*.1836 for the Rev. Thomas Bowdler, the first minister of St Bartholomew's, and just failed to last a hundred years, was not part of the original Peak Hill. Its site was on the common until the enclosure. The house is especially associated with the von Glehn family, for which see pages 112-16.

COOPER'S WOOD
The old coppice known as Cooper's Wood might be defined in modern terms as extending nearly to Westwood Hill on the north, to the railway line on the east, and to the borough boundary on the south. On its western side the wood gave place to open common between the Shenewood Estate and Lawrie Park Gardens. Westwood Hill follows the line of the old track from Sydenham to Dulwich, which ran across the common rather than along its edge, leaving a strip of waste ground to the south. As a result the houses built on the edge of the common, in Cooper's Wood, lay up to one hundred yards south of the track. During the enclosure process, when the track was adopted as the road now known as Westwood Hill, the owners of the Cooper's Wood houses acquired the waste land between their estates and the road, which gave them magnificent front gardens. One of these still survives at the Old Cedars. It was enclosed and allotted to the owner of the house in 1812.

Cooper's Wood was a part of the common until the sixteenth century. It is not known precisely when it became detached, but it is quite likely to have been in the 1540s, when Henry VIII sold the similar Coleson's Coppice on the north side of the common. Whenever it happened, it was an illegal act, and one that continued to be disputed for centuries. One of the original motives for these sales may have been to preserve the timber, which elsewhere on the common had suffered severely from the depredations of men and beasts by the time the King acquired the manor of Lewisham in 1531. But if the enclosure of Cooper's Wood was originally partial and conditional the restriction was soon forgotten. Development probably began here in the middle of the seventeenth century, under the stimulus of the discovery and popularity of Sydenham Wells, and there were certainly four houses in Cooper's Wood by the 1720s. Five more were added by 1753. But the enclosure had never

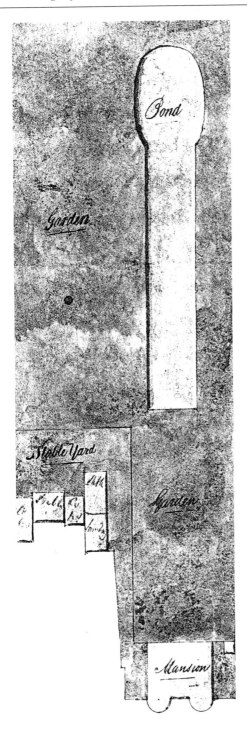

60. *Westwood House in 1810. The blank space
beside the mansion contained the pair of wooden
houses built by the Puplett family.*

been accepted as a *fait accompli* by the people of
Sydenham, and as late as 1754 George Thornton,
the landlord of the Greyhound and tenant of the
western part of Cooper's Wood, had difficulties
when his fences "were thrown down and pros-
trated by persons claiming right of common" and
he "ceased to receive any benefit from the estate".

The only pre-enclosure house to survive in
Cooper's Wood is the Old Cedars, at the bottom
of Westwood Hill, which belonged in the eighteenth century to the Batt and Fenner families of
Beckenham. It originated before 1727, but was
rebuilt on a larger scale, probably in the early
1770s. The eighteenth century portion is now hard
to spot at the front because it is wedged between
large extensions of 1872 and 1992, but can be readily
seen at the back. The first occupant who can be
located here with any confidence is John Holden,
or Holding, who died in 1728. In the 1760s and
'70s, when Cooper's Wood seems to have been the
Jewish quarter of Lewisham, Moses Pabia (or De
Paiba) was the tenant. The Old Cedars is a modern
name, in use only in the twentieth century. In the
1890s the house was known as Wunderbau, but
before that it was quite anonymous.

The next house was Sydenham Hall, the position
of which is indicated by Hall Drive. It began as
a farmhouse, probably in the seventeenth century.
Oliver Baukham, the tenant until 1732, was certainly living in Sydenham by 1699. In 1733 the
estate was bought by the celebrated builder Edward
Strong the Younger of Greenwich (1676-1741), who
executed many of the major works of Wren,
Vanbrugh, and Hawksmoor. He lived here until
1739, and may well have rebuilt or extended the
house. Strong left Sydenham Hall to his son-in-
law Sir Thomas Parker, the judge (1695?-1784),
noted for his strict views on boxing:

"Parker, Chief Baron, held that bruising,
   Deemed so delightful and amusing,
   Is an illegal dang'rous science,
   And practis'd in the law's defiance."

In the late 1750s and early '60s Parker let the
house to the Irish portrait painter Nathaniel Hone
(1718-84), a foundation-member of the Royal
Academy. His exhibition of 1775 included 'A View
from one of the Huts on Sydenham Common, some
years ago'. Sydenham Hall must have been rebuilt
*c.*1805, for it was described as "newly erected"
when bought by Andrew Lawrie in 1806. Thereafter it was the principal Sydenham home of the
Lawrie family until they sold the estate to the
Crystal Palace Company in 1852. The house survived, latterly as a school, until 1939.

61. *The garden front of the Old Cedars in 1886. The original eighteenth-century house is on the left, the 1872 extension on the right.*

West of Sydenham Hall, more or less on the line now taken by Lawrie Park Avenue, was Abbey's or Abbott's Farm, an old house occupied during much of the eighteenth century by the Garrard family, and afterwards the Lawrie home farm. The name may indicate some antiquity, as the land in Beckenham on this edge of the common belonged to the Abbey of Bermondsey before the Dissolution, but the farmhouse in Cooper's Wood is unlikely to have existed before the seventeenth century. Part of the land was in Beckenham, and the farmhouse may have been there before Cooper's Wood was enclosed.

In what is now the area between Lawrie Park Avenue and Shenewood stood five eighteenth-century houses, none of which long survived the enclosure. Three were built in 1737 on land then belonging to Edward Strong of Sydenham Hall, and it is quite likely that he designed them. From their valuation, and the standing of their tenants, the houses must have been substantial, yet they stood on a plot only fifty feet wide. They must have been a terrace of tall houses in an essentially urban style that would only have looked appropriate in this edge of common context if extended into a much longer row. Nos.13 to 21 Clapham Common North Side, built between 1714 and 1720, would have offered a recent precedent. If Strong did have any plan for a more extensive development here it was cut short by his death in 1741. From 1802 until 1810 (when he died) the largest and most westerly of these three houses was the

country retreat of Josiah Dornford, JP, who also had a large house in New Cross Road. He was a correspondent of William Cowper, and a pamphleteer on various subjects, notably prison reform, in which field he was a disciple of John Howard. The last two of the five houses between Abbey's Farm and Westwood House were a large wooden semi-detached pair built by the Puplett family *c.*1750, immediately adjacent to Westwood House.

All these lesser Westwood Hill houses were demolished by the Lawrie family between 1800 and 1840, as they decided that privacy was more important than revenue. The odd result was that in 1735 there were four houses in Cooper's Wood, in 1775 the number had grown to nine or more, but by 1840 only the original group – the Old Cedars, Sydenham Hall, Abbey's Farm, and Westwood House – survived.

The last of these, Westwood House, was perhaps the most interesting of all. The first building on the site was an inn, with a bowling green attached. In the 1720s and '30s it was owned by Peter Hambly of Streatham, and the landlord was Thomas Venables. The name of the inn is not known for certain, but it may have been the Three Compasses, or the then appropriate World's End. Its establishment in such a remote spot was perhaps connected with the discovery of the Sydenham Wells in the 1640s. It was not possible to establish a large inn on the common itself, and the Westwood House site was the nearest available on its borders, a mere six hundred yards from the wells. In the eight-

62. *Sydenham Hall c.1905, when it was James Crosland Mallam's preparatory school.*

eenth century the inn would also have been well placed to benefit from the Sydenham Fair (*see pp.83-4*), which regularly brought crowds of thirsty revellers to the common, and it is perhaps significant that it was demolished in 1766, the year in which the fair was suppressed.

In its place was immediately built a large mansion with huge bays flanking the front door, and a strange test-tube shaped lake or pond in the back garden. In 1767 it was purchased by David Ximenes, a Sephardi Jewish merchant with a City office in Mark Lane. He was to make a lasting impression on Sydenham's topography. One of his first moves was to obtain the manor court's permission to enclose a small portion of the common in front of Westwood House, to give it a more impressive carriage drive. It was almost certainly also Ximenes who had the idea of planting an avenue of elm trees across a corner of the common, so as to transform this drive into a magnificent vista. This was the origin of the street with the much discussed name 'Jew's Walk', which in its earliest recorded use, in 1819, was written as 'the Jew's Walk'. The elms were damaged in the 1850s by the vandalism of the

workers building the Crystal Palace, and after unavailing efforts by Sir Joseph Paxton to save them, they were replaced by chestnuts.

The most notable of the later occupants of Westwood House was Lady Charlotte Campbell, who was here from 1812 until 1818 or a little later, and formed part of the Thomas Campbell circle (*see p.72*). In 1818 the mansion was bought by Andrew Lawrie, and when he died in 1824 it became the dower house of his widow Margaret. Unlike Sydenham Hall, it was not required by the Crystal Palace Company in 1852, but the Lawries only retained the house for another three or four years before being tempted to sell by the explosion of land prices in Sydenham. The purchaser was George Wythes, who was already busy developing the surplus Sydenham Hall acres as the Lawrie Park estate. Westwood House survived until 1881, when it was enlarged and substantially altered for Henry Littleton (*see p.116*). After serving for forty years as the Passmore Edwards orphanage for the children of teachers the new Westwood House was demolished in 1952, and replaced by the estate known as Shenewood.

OLD FOREST HILL

'Forest Hill' is a modern and artificial name, not in use until the 1790s. Then it referred only to Honor Oak Road north of Westwood Park. The fifteen or so houses on this half mile of road, with their gardens stretching back to the old Lewisham boundary on the west, and almost to the Devonshire Road line on the east, maintained the exclusive use of the name until the 1840s, when the new houses built at the southern end of the road, formerly part of the common, also began to be considered part of Forest Hill. In 1847 one of them, South Bank, was described as "near Forest-hill, Sydenham". From there the name spread to London Road and Dartmouth Road, and in time came to embrace the whole wide suburb.

The site of the original Forest Hill houses was a forty-acre wood on the northern edge of Sydenham Common variously known as 'Coulton's Wood', 'Westwood or Calton's Coppice', 'Cawlton's Coppice' and finally and most usually as 'Coleson's Coppice'. This does not exhaust the list. In modern terms it might be very roughly described as being bounded by Dunoon Road, Devonshire Road, a line from Devonshire Road to Westwood Park (running somewhat south of Ewelme Road), Westwood Park, and the first stretch of Horniman Drive extended north to meet Honor Oak Road opposite Dunoon Road.

It formed part of Westwood Common until Henry VIII obtained possession of the manor of Lewisham in 1531. In 1545 the king sold the wood to John Pope for £1551 13s 8d. This was an astonishing sum when compared with later sales, especially as the extent was then estimated at only twenty-eight acres. It was undoubtedly an illegal act, as this was common land, but where was the man brave enough to explain that to Henry VIII? The sale saved this part of the common from the fate of most of the other Westwood coppices, which were rapidly laid waste by their royal owners. The wood was described as Coulton's in 1607, and as Calton's in 1630. One 'Coulton' is recorded as the owner at some point after 1545, having acquired it from Pope. He was almost certainly the Thomas Calton who was granted the manor of Dulwich at the Dissolution. His widow Margaret Calton or Coulton sold the manors of Dulwich and Camberwell, with 120 acres of wood in Lewisham, to Lord Giles Pawlet and William Chevall in 1569/70. Coleson's Coppice was owned by Sir Thomas Gardiner in 1614, and by Sir Francis Galton of Stepney in 1630, when he sold it to Robert Matthew of East Greenwich. Matthew resold in 1645 to Abraham Deskene, a London weaver, for £119. The property was then described as:

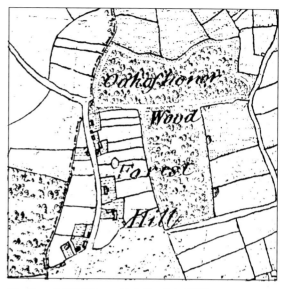

63. *Forest Hill (Honor Oak Road) in 1799.*

"All that land and wood commonly called...Westwood otherwise Calton's Coppice...containing by estimation forty acres...now or late in the tenure or occupation of John Hudson his assignee or assigns...situate and being in the parish of Lewisham...between the lands and woods now or late of Bryan Annesley Esq. belonging to Brooke House on the East part, the Woods called by the name of Westwood there on the South part, certain Lands or Coppices of Wood now or late of Francis Muscamp Esq. on the West part, and the lands and Woods there called Kallywell Spring in the parish of Camberwell in the County of Surrey on the North part."

The wood formerly owned by Bryan Annesley (of Lee, died 1604) was Honor Oak Wood, later part of the Earl of St German's estate; "the woods called Westwood" were Sydenham Common; Muscamp's land and Kallywell Spring were across the parish and county boundary in Camberwell. Kallywell was clearly a corruption, for the manor of Dulwich and much other property in Camberwell had belonged to the Prioress of Haliwell in Middlesex before the Reformation.

In 1707 James Deskene, grandson of Abraham, who had retired from weaving and wrote himself a gentleman, sold the wood for £80 to Thomas Vickers, citizen and Merchant Taylor of London. In 1719 he sold it in his turn to Edward Hodsdon of the Old House, Sydenham Road for £470. The description of the estate in these two conveyances is identical. The striking difference in the price may be partly explained by a note made by Dean

Stanhope, Vicar of Lewisham, in his account book. (Mr Archer was his curate.)

> "Sept. 30, 1720. Memorand. That I have besides made my Demand of Tithes for Colstons Coppice felld this year by Edwd. Hoddesdon Esq. but that claim is not yet adjusted between us. Mr Archer delivered my letter of Demand and received a Civil answer."

Evidently the wood was mature and ready for thinning in 1719, but not in 1707.

Up to this date the wood had been bought and sold as an investment by landlords who may never have seen it. It was let to various tenants, perhaps timber merchants: to John Hudson before 1645, and to Francis Ligoe of Deptford before 1707. Hodsdon was the first recorded owner who lived nearby. Since this wealthy wine merchant had acquired the Old House estate in 1713 he had been eagerly purchasing more land all over Sydenham. His other woods in the immediate vicinity of the Old House he grubbed up and converted into farmland, but he retained Coleson's Coppice unaltered in his own hands.

The first tentative step towards development was made by Edward Hodsdon junior, shortly after his father's death in 1737. Among the lands acquired by Edward Hodsdon senior had been seventeen acres called Smiths Hills that adjoined the western edge of Coleson's Coppice on the Camberwell side of the boundary. In March 1738 the younger Hodsdon leased these seventeen acres to John Edgson, a brickmaker, for 45 years. At the same time he leased to Edgson for 61 years a cottage and one acre in Lewisham parish, detached from Coleson's Coppice, at the small rent of one pound per annum. This was in consideration of Edgson's agreeing to build a barn on the southern part of the one acre, and perhaps also in acknowledgement (though this is not stated) of his having already built the cottage. It was certainly not mentioned when the elder Hodsdon bought the wood, and so can safely be assumed to have appeared between 1719 and 1738. Possibly it was built in 1720 to facilitate the harvesting of the coppice.

It is difficult to establish the exact location of this cottage as it did not survive far into the nineteenth century, and had no successor, but the evidence points to its having been at the south-western corner of the wood, near the present junction of Westwood Park and Horniman Drive.

On the Camberwell portion of his leasehold estate John Edgson built a brick and tile kiln, from which it is probable that the material for many Sydenham houses was supplied over the next sixty or more years. Certainly there were no brickworks in Sydenham Village itself at this time, which no doubt explains the prevalence there of timber or part timber houses. In giving Edgson a lease on such easy terms Hodsdon may have been preparing plans for building brick houses on some part of his estate. If so they were swiftly cut short by his death in 1739.

The cottage in Coleson's Coppice was occupied on and off by John Edgson and his heirs until c.1815, when it was apparently demolished, but they occasionally let it. From 1741 to 1743 a Mrs Woodhouse was the occupant, and in the 1760s and early 1770s John Capps or Cupp was the tenant of the kiln and the cottage. Like any source of free heat in any age the "Brick kilns at Sydenham Common" proved a popular resort for tramps, and several who died there were buried at St Mary's church in Lewisham during the 1760s and '70s.

Despite its long history of sale and resale, which might have been expected to give the Hodsdons an unimpeachable title to the wood, in 1755 Thomas Hodsdon, the cousin and heir of Edward junior, was sued in the Exchequer Court by a Lewisham freeholder who claimed that Hodsdon had prevented him from exercising his common rights in "Coulton's or Coulson's coppice, parcel of Sydenham Common". The plaintive, who had been so cruelly prevented from gathering his few poor bundles of firewood, was the wealthy London cooper, John Anderson. He lived close to Hodsdon in Sydenham Road, in a house that was rebuilt as Champion Hall in 1861 (on a slightly different site), and was subsequently the Sydenham Children's Hospital.

This was probably a test case, in which Anderson was merely the representative of the body of Sydenham residents. There was a local agitation at this time to reverse the universal tendency of commons to shrink. In 1754 it had expressed itself violently on the other side of Sydenham Common, when the fences around Cooper's Wood, in the Westwood Hill area, were repeatedly destroyed by people claiming the same rights that John Anderson put forward a year later in respect of Coleson's Coppice. Historically the agitators were right. Coleson's and Cooper's Coppices had been common land two hundred and fifty years earlier, and had still been partially accessible to the Lewisham freeholders in 1614. By the 1750s it was too late to establish such a claim, and both woods continued to be confidently bought and sold as viable freehold land, even though there was still a bloody battle to be fought in the hopeless cause.

Coleson's Coppice descended with the rest of the Hodsdon property, and was eventually bought in 1786/7 (at the sales at which Mayow Wynell Mayow bought the Old House) by Samuel Atkinson, a cheesemonger from Tooley Street, Southwark. Atkinson was to be the unlikely father, and perhaps god-father, of Forest Hill.

AN AFFRAY AT SYDENHAM

At this date there was not even a road through Coleson's Coppice, although Ralph Treswell's 1607 map of Sydenham Common (*ill. 78*) shows a 'Waie to Peckham' on the eastern edge of the wood, near the present line of Devonshire Road. John Rocque's map of 1746 indicates only what is now Wood Vale in this vicinity. It was between 1787 and 1789 that Atkinson, as a first step to opening up the estate for building, created the present Honor Oak Road, which in 1789 was described as "a new road or carriage way from Peckham Rye to Sydenham Common". Until *c.*1816, when the enclosure commissioners extended it southwards, the road stopped short at the present junction with Westwood Park. Beyond that point there was only a track across the common that did not follow the direction of Honor Oak Road, but ran further west, going on to take the line of Sydenham Rise to Sydenham Hill.

It was probably in 1788 that Atkinson had a house, The Hermitage, built for himself on his new estate, and as early as January 1789 he was selling building plots fronting the new road. His actions were not accepted tamely by those who believed that the wood was still common land. In October 1792 *The Times* reported the death of one Michael Bradley (who had a cottage near the Bell Green end of Sydenham Road) in an 'Affray at Sydenham':

> "It appears that this Bradley and others belonging to Sydenham Parish, went a few days since on a piece of land called Colson's Wood, to ascertain their rights of commonage, which have been held upwards of 200 years. A Mr Atkinson met the deceased and his associates, and asked them their business; - they replied, there was a footway across, which right their fore-fathers had enjoyed and so would they. Atkinson said they should go no further - and the first man who did, he would shoot. - Bradley was shot, and died.
>
> The Wednesday following, Atkinson purchased the right of this wood and pasturage, consisting of 52 acres, out of Chancery for £350 - and has since enclosed it.
>
> The Coroner's Inquest sat on the body of Bradley on Friday and Saturday, the 19th and 20th of October, at Sydenham, and brought in their verdict, Manslaughter against one Atkinson of the said parish. The man was shot in the leg by a pistol, which fractured the bone, and a mortifi-

cation ensued. The deceased has left a family and four children, and Atkinson has absconded."

There are numerous obvious inaccuracies in this account. One was corrected in the next issue, which included a note that "we are desired by the friends of Mr Atkinson to state, that he has not absconded in consequence of the unfortunate accident which occurred in the affray at Sydenham". Whether he was able to persuade the world, or the courts, that it was all an accident is uncertain. Atkinson continued to own the estate, and apparently to superintend its development, but he probably decided it was no longer prudent to live in the parish. By 1793 The Hermitage was occupied by a tenant.

SYDENHAM NEW TOWN

The Bradley affair did not interfere with the sale of building plots. By 1794 five houses had been built, by 1798 a dozen. In 1789 the property was described as being on Sydenham Hill, but by 1797 the name Forest Hill had come into use. Was it invented by Atkinson in the spirit in which a modern developer might call his estate Sunny Bank or Riverside Gardens? The choice may have been influenced by Forest Place, the old name for Brockley Green Farm, then the nearest substantial building to Coleson's Coppice. There is evidence that a wood in the Devonshire Road area, which belonged to the farm, was called 'Forest Hill' in 1834. Was the wood named after the road, or the road after the wood?

With a brick and tile kiln next door, and a wood being felled to make way for the houses, building conditions were certainly favourable. Perhaps progress was comparatively slow in the period 1789 to 1793, as against 1794 to 1798, because the builders were waiting for the timber on the site to be seasoned. Of the fifteen houses that appeared on the estate between 1788 and 1817 five survive either in their original form, or as early rebuildings. Three of these are grouped together at the junction of Honor Oak Road and Westwood Park, a spot that was the edge of the common until the enclosure.

Hill House, 64 Honor Oak Road, was probably built *c.*1796, and extended over the next decade or two. Imaginative estate agents are fond of describing houses of this type as hunting lodges. It is a safe rule to disregard such stories, but Hill House may be the exception to prove the rule. It was owned for many years by the Southwark warehouseman and corn factor Henry Dudin (*see p.29*), and he seems to have occupied it for several years from 1807. Dudin was the Master of the Old Surrey

64. *The rear of the White House in the late 1940s.*

Hunt, which met frequently at Sydenham and Forest Hill at that period. There are even indications that the north wing was originally a stable block, and an unexpectedly large one for a house of this size.

Ashberry Cottage, 62 Honor Oak Road, the most attractive of the surviving houses, is named rather inaccurately after Joseph Ashbarry of Holme Lacey, the owner in the 1830s and '40s, and perhaps before. There was a real cottage on the site from the end of the eighteenth century, but the present substantial house was not built until the 1820s. The unofficial blue plaque on the building stating that the Duke of Clarence and his mistress Mrs Jordan

lived here is obviously incorrect. Quite apart from the lack of any evidence linking the couple with Forest Hill, it must be remembered that they parted in 1811 and Mrs Jordan died in 1816, at a time when the building on this site was tiny; yet Mrs Jordan had fourteen children (ten by the duke) and a proportionate staff of servants.

The third survivor in this group is the White House, 2 Westwood Park, which began as a small cottage *c*.1798, and was rebuilt in its present form between 1809 and 1817. Its coach house has been converted into a separate dwelling. This small group also included three houses that have now been demolished. The Hermitage, which has already been mentioned as Samuel Atkinson's house, was occupied for the last few years of his life by the surgeon and journalist Frederick Knight Hunt (1814-54). He was the editor of Dickens's *Daily News* and author of *The Fourth Estate*, a classic account of the newspaper business. The house, which stood at the end of the lane called The Hermitage, was demolished in the 1850s, and replaced by a large semi-detached pair that survived for just over a century.

Next to Ashberry Cottage stood a 1790s pair known as Carlton House and Havelock House. The first occupant of Havelock House was a Mr Tappen, almost certainly the architect George Tappen (*c*.1771-1830), who was Surveyor to Dulwich College and designer of The Priory in Sydenham Road. Was he also responsible for this pair, and perhaps other houses in Honor Oak Road?

65. *Hill House, 64 Honor Oak Road, at the beginning of the twentieth century.*

66. The main front of Fairlawn early in the twentieth century.

The present, Edwardian, Havelock House stands some way north of the original.

The other old houses on the west side of Honor Oak Road have all been demolished, though the early Victorian coach house to Manor Lodge has been converted into the present no.18. Manor Lodge itself, which stood just north of Canonbie Road, was built in the mid-1790s for Robert Wissett, JP, an East India Company official who died in 1820. It was replaced by the present house called The Manor, in Canonbie Road, in the 1930s. The remaining two houses on this side have been replaced by Fairlawn School. The Limes, the older and smaller (only eight bedrooms), stood opposite the Christian Fellowship Centre. It was built in the 1790s. Fairlawn, a fine house built between 1808 and 1816, served as a military hospital in the First World War, and was badly damaged by a flying bomb in 1944. Directly opposite Dunoon Road a small public house called the Royal Oak did business until the 1880s, when it migrated to Forest Hill Road. It's old site was in Camberwell until the boundary was altered in 1900.

There were two early 1790s houses named Oakfield and Fonthill Lodge, both demolished, on

67. The Manor House, 53 Honor Oak Road, in 1983. The central section is the original building of c.1815. The extension to the right incorporates the old service wing and stables.

the east side, just south of Dunoon Road. In the 1860s the tenant of Oakfield was Robert Adams, a well-known revolver maker. The central block of the Christian Fellowship Centre (no.39) is, although greatly altered during years of institutional use, another of the survivors of old Forest Hill. There has been a house on the site since the 1790s, perhaps even from the late 1780s. In the 1870s it was known as Bay House. The large extension to the south was added soon after 1886, when it became the Forest Hill House School. The central section of no.53 is the last of the survivors, the Manor House. It was built *c.*1815, and cobbled into the present block of flats in 1931/2.

Midway between Tyson and Benson Roads stood a large and graceful pair of houses built *c.*1793, and called Brookville and Cedar Lodge. Mrs Ann Tyson was the first owner and occupant of Brookville, the northern house. Tyson Road was built across part of its garden (and the large fish pond) in the 1870s. Among the tenants was Sir John Cowan, bart. (1774-1842), who was Lord Mayor of London in 1837/8. His young widow Sophia, "a very handsome woman" according to that excellent judge, Benjamin Disraeli, lived on here for a few years after his death. Cedar Lodge was occupied from the 1840s to the '60s by William Oakley, the father of the architect of St Augustine's Church. Brookville and Cedar Lodge were demolished in 1961, and the site is now occupied by the Tyson Estate. At the bottom of the Brookville grounds, about 250 yards east of Honor Oak Road, there was a cottage and nursery garden occupied by Thomas Trinder in the 1830s and '40s, and later by James Rutherford and others. Tyson Gardens in Devonshire Road is now on the site.

The last house on the east side was the largest in Honor Oak Road. The Grange, which was replaced by Benson and Ewelme Roads, and had occupied a site between them, had twelve bedrooms, and at its peak some fifteen acres of garden "beautifully laid out in lawns, gravel walks, flower beds, rockeries, ornamental water, etc." The drawing room was "decorated at a cost of over £200" by Owen Jones, who designed some of the courts at the Crystal Palace. The house was built in the early 1790s for Edward Howis, an oil and colourman

68. Bay House as the Forest Hill House School, c.1905. Bateman was one of the pupils. The 1880s assembly hall on the right has now been raised to two storeys, with a flat roof.

69. Cedar Lodge in 1952.

with a shop at 216 Piccadilly. The firm were later oil men to Queen Victoria. In the 1840s The Grange was let for a time to Alexander Rowland junior, the son and successor to the Macasser Oil King of Rosenthal, Rushey Green. The last owner and occupier, here from 1854, was John Crossley Fielding, a stockbroker. It was presumably he who employed Owen Jones. The Grange was demolished in 1882.

Before the present name became established in the 1880s Honor Oak Road was described in a bewildering variety of ways. 'Forest Hill' was widely current from the 1790s to the 1850s. Other versions were 'New Town' in 1819, 'the road from Sydenham to Peckham Rise' (i.e. Rye) in 1824, 'Old Forest Hill' in 1862, 'Forest Hill Road' in 1867, and 'Peckham Road' in the 1860s and '70s. In the early days, before the enclosure of the common opened up road communications to the south, the new settlement was more often thought of as part of Peckham than Sydenham, and even in the 1820s the address was given as 'Forest Hill, near Peckham'.

Sydenham Society 1800 to 1850

70. *Thomas Dermody.*

OBSCURITY

Sydenham had few intellectual stars before 1800. The eminent jurist William Aubrey was the tenant of Place House in the 1590s. Edward Strong, the builder, Nathaniel Hone, the portrait painter, and John Williams, the Greek scholar, lived briefly on the edge of Westwood Common in the eighteenth century, and Williams had a more extended connection with the village as minister of the Independent Chapel for nearly thirty years. With these slight exceptions the only known residents with interests more extended than the fields they farmed were the City merchants who settled here in increasing numbers after Edward Hodsdon established the trend in 1713.

At the beginning of the nineteenth century Sydenham was obscure enough to seem an ideal hiding place for those wishing to escape the unwanted attention of the world and its bailiffs. Thomas Dermody (1775-1802), the libertine Irish poet, after a brief career in which he tried bookselling, teaching, scene-painting, soldiering (both as a private and an officer), and journalism, fled to Sydenham in 1802, to escape his creditors, and died of consumption in 'a wretched hovel' in Perry Slough.

Another who found refuge here was the antiquary and art connoisseur, the Rev. William Langford. In 1806 Joseph Farington recorded in his diary that "Dr Gretton gave me a sad account of Dr Langford late one of the Masters of Eaton, who absconded on account of debts amounting, it is said, to £26,000.– His income from Boarders and from preferment was so large, the Doctor said, He ought to have been worth £100,000. – It is now reported that He is in Nottinghamshire & passes under the assumed name of Doctor Loyd." By 1808 the news was better. "Dr Langford, Canon of Windsor, now resides & does the Church duty at Lewisham in Kent. His creditors do not molest Him, but an arrangement has been made & His debts are gradually liquidating." The fugitive owed this haven to Edward Legge, the Vicar of Lewisham, who had been appointed Dean of Windsor in 1805, and was naturally anxious to regularise the outlaw existence of one of his canons. Dr Langford had in fact not settled at Lewisham, but at Ellesmere House in Sydenham Road (*see p.45*),

where he died. His coffin plate listed the preferments that should have kept him solvent: "William Langford, D.D., Chaplain of His Majesty, Canon of Windsor, Fellow of Eton, Rector of Newdigate, and Vicar of Isleworth, died January 21st 1814, aged 71".

THE MAYOW CIRCLE

By that time the mists of obscurity had begun to rise from the village. The change had been prepared in the 1780s by the settlement of Mayow Wynell Mayow at the Old House, principally as a summer residence. This had no great immediate impact on the social and cultural life of Sydenham. Mayow, though "one of the worthiest of human beings", was merely a wealthy solicitor, but he did have five clever and attractive daughters. As they grew to womanhood, and it became clear that there would be no son to rob them of their inheritance, distinguished young men clustered around the Old House.

One was William Dacres Adams (1775-1862), then Private Secretary to the Prime Minister, William Pitt. He held the same position under the Duke of Portland, and in 1810 received the lucrative appoinment of a Commissioner of Woods and Forests, which he held for twenty-four years. Adams married Elizabeth Mayow in 1804. Another member of the Old House circle was Thomas Peregrine Courtenay (1782-1841), one of the two MPs. for Totnes, the other being the father of his close friend William Dacres Adams. Courtenay, who lived at Clay Hill between Beckenham and Shortlands, married Anne Mayow in 1805. He had a moderately successful political career, rising to be Vice-President of the Board of Trade, and later wrote what is still the standard life of Sir William Temple. Peregrine Courtenay, as he was generally known, was the son of the noted pluralist Henry Courtenay (who among many other good things was Rector of Lee and Bishop of Exeter), and brother of the eleventh earl of Devon. But for all his high connections Courtenay was a poor man for a Regency MP, and stood greatly in need of a wealthy wife.

The most distinguished young man to frequent the Old House was also perennially short of money, despite the high prices paid for his portraits. Thomas Lawrence (1769-1830), not yet Sir Thomas, was probably also drawn in by his friendship with William Dacres Adams, who was his chief source

72. *The young Thomas Lawrence, drawn by George Dance in 1794.*

71. William Dacres Adams by Sir Thomas Lawrence, c.1810.

of political news and advice. He sometimes hurried down to Sydenham in a post-chaise to obtain it. Lawrence painted portraits in oils or pencil of several members of the family: Mr Mayow, his daughters Mary, Fanny, and Caroline, and Dacres Adams and his sister. The Mayows became major collectors of his work, and in time the Old House gallery also included portraits of the Duchess of Gloucester, Thomas Campbell, Sydney Smith, Lady Lawley, Mrs Inchbald, and Mrs Woolf, plus two Lawrence self-portraits. The Rev. Sydney Smith was included because he was another regular guest of the Mayow family.

Lawrence had almost as great a genius for flirtation as for painting. Throughout his career he was constantly carrying his relationships beyond what might have been thought the point of no return, before emerging unscathed from the Reichenbach Falls of marriage. In this he greatly resembled that other celebrated Sydenham lothario, Sir Arthur Sullivan. But even Lawrence could not always escape without suffering a social penalty, and once or twice he was even forced to pay compensation for breach of promise. There is some ground for suspecting that it was an entanglement with one of the Mayow sisters, most likely Fanny, that abruptly ended Lawrence's friendship with the family. In December 1815, when Lawrence was asked by a friend to use his influnce with Adams, he replied that "unfortunately He and Mr Adams had lately ceased to be acquainted in consequence of some matter of a nature to cause a discontinuance of their friendship". A few weeks later the same friend recorded that "Sir Thomas Lawrence called this morning, & we had conversation respecting a settlement with a Lady and Her Brother". Even after his quarrel with Adams Lawrence continued to visit Sydenham as the guest of Ralph Price, who lived in Sydenham Road, only three hundred yards from the Old House.

THOMAS CAMPBELL

That Lawrence was romantically involved with one of the Mayow sisters is only a matter of speculation, but there can be no doubt about the case of Thomas Campbell, another man represented in the Old House portrait gallery. Campbell moved to Peak Hill from Pimlico in 1804, at a time when his reputation as a poet was growing steadily. *The Pleasures of Hope*, which he published in 1799, had already passed through seven editions, and become the rallying point of poetical conservatives. But fame had not yet brought fortune, or anything like it, and the expense of furnishing his new house left him deeply in debt. In these depressing circumstances the enthusiastic welcome he received in the village was doubly gratifying.

"Life became tolerable to me", he wrote later, "and, at Sydenham, even agreeable. I had always my town friends to come and partake of my humble fare on a Sunday; and among my neighbours, I had an elegant society, among whom I counted sincere friends. It so happened that the dearest friends I had there, were thorough *Tories*; and my *Whiggism* was as steadfast as it still continues to be; but this acquaintance ripening into friendship, called forth a new liberalism in my mind, and possibly also in theirs." These Tory friends were the Mayows, who made Campbell free of the Old House circle, and introduced him to such Sydenham Road families as the Hodges of Kenton Cottage and the Shutes of Elm Grove. Campbell was soon also on friendly terms with the Marryats of Malvern House. Frederick Marryat, their famous son, then a boy of twelve, was later closely associated with Campbell's journalistic career in London.

Campbell quickly became intimate with the Mayows, and was constantly in and out of the Old House, but his wife was seen there far less often. He had married his cousin Matilda Sinclair in 1803, and their two sons were born at Sydenham in 1804 and 1805. With two babies on her hands, and a house to manage on a precarious income, she had

73. *Thomas Campbell, as caricatured by Daniel Maclise in 1830.*

much to keep her at home; and as the family was entirely dependent upon Campbell's literary earnings it was equally natural that he should frequently seek a refuge from "the double-drumming" of his sons' legs and the tantrums of his demented cook. The Mayows placed their summer-house at his disposal as a quiet place for writing, "where Thomas Hughes the gardener's wheelbarrow, or scythe, is the only sound I hear". Soon he was finding more companionship, certainly more intellectual companionship, with the unmarried Mayow sisters (the Three Graces, as he called them) than he had ever enjoyed with his wife. She had a more Scottish outlook on life and literature than he, as one of his biographers recalled.

"I wish you would make my husband write novels like Sir Walter Scott", said Mrs Campbell to myself.

"Why Mrs Campbell? I do not think he would make a good hand at that kind of writing."

"Because you know that Lady Scott says to her husband when she wants a new dress - 'Watty, my dear, you must write a new novel, for I want another dress!'"

At first the three sisters seemed to attract Campbell equally, but before long he began to discriminate. Caroline, "an angel without wings", was the first to fade from the picture. By 1807 a distinct role had been found for Fanny, who, he wrote, "is indeed, and I will call her, my sister". That left Mary Mayow. She and Campbell were certainly in love, and would probably have married had he been free. When Matilda died in 1828, after Campbell had been forced to move to London by his editorial duties, their friends assumed that they would. "It was the opinion of all, mutually acquainted with the parties, that Campbell was taking a most prudent and well-considered step. The lady was a woman of good family and fortune, and endowed with those virtues, which give sanctity and security to the domestic hearth." But a combination of his flightiness and her ill-health imposed delays, and the moment passed. To the end of his life Mary Mayow was Campbell's most intimate correspondent, and on his death-bed "the only question he had strength to ask was respecting the health of a much valued friend at Sydenham".

The contemporary fame of Campbell, hard for the modern reader of his poems to understand, made Sydenham a place of pilgrimage between 1804 and 1820. Famous visitors to the little house on Peak Hill included Mrs Siddons, Lord Byron (who knocked at the door, but found that Campbell was not at home), Thomas Moore, Samuel Rogers, and George Crabbe. Two eminent American guests were Washington Irving and George Ticknor, who thought Sydenham beautiful, and "more like an American village than any I have seen in England".

THE POETICAL DRYSALTER

For a few years between 1805 and 1810 there was a third house in the village that attracted a remarkable stream of distinguished visitors. Linden Cottage in Sydenham Road was then the country retreat of Thomas Hill (1760-1840), who was "a drysalter in Queenhithe, a man of narrow education, of no literary attainment, while his manners were by no means those of a gentleman. He managed, however, to draw the wits about him, giving *recherché* dinners at Sydenham, never costly. He was in reality their 'butt'; some liked but none respected him. One of his friends pictures him as 'a little, fat, florid man - an elderly Cupid'. Another says 'he had a face like a peony'. He had a rare collection of books [the finest private library of poetry in the country, according to Southey], of which he knew only the titles and their marketable value." Hill became the inspiration for a great many comic characters in the plays and novels of

74. *Thomas Hill, a portrait sketch by Daniel Maclise c.1834.*

the period, for as he said one day to Coleridge "If I am not witty myself, I am the cause of Wit in others".

The many entertaining accounts of these meetings show that if the wits came to laugh at their good-natured host, they remained to enjoy themselves, and took away pleasant and vivid memories. James and Horace Smith, the authors of *Rejected Addresses*, were familiar guests at Linden Cottage, and Horace left this account of Hill's Sundays.

"His large literary parties were always given at his Sydenham Tusculum, which, though close to the roadside, and making no pretensions to be a 'cottage of gentility', was roomy and comfortable enough within, spite of its low-pitched, thick-beamed ceilings, and the varities of level with which the builder had pleasantly diversified his floors. The garden at the back, much more useful than ornamental, afforded an agreeable ambulatory for his guests, when they did not fall into the pond in their anxiety to gather currants - an accident not always escaped. Pleasant and never-to-be-forgotten were the many days that I passed beneath that hospitable roof...

On those summer afternoons, we mounted the little grassy ascent that overlooked the road, and joyfully hailed each new guest as he arrived, well aware that he brought with him an accession of merriment for the jovial dinner, and fresh face-tiousness for the wit-winged night! Let it not be thought that I exaggerate the quality of the boon companions whom our Amphitryon delighted to assemble. If we had no philosophers who could make the world wiser, we had many a wit and wag who well knew how to make it merrier. Among those most frequently encountered at the jollifications were Campbell, the poet, then occu-pying a cottage in the village, and by no means the least hilarious of the party; Matthews, and sometimes his friend and his brother comedian, Liston; Theodore Hook; Edward Dubois, at that time editor and main support of the *Monthly Mirror;* Leigh Hunt and his brother John; John Taylor, the editor of the *Sun* newspaper; Horace Twiss; Barron Field; John Barnes, who subse-quently became editor for many years of the *Times* newspaper; and some few others." [The only woman admitted was Mrs Matthews, the wife of the actor,] "who seems to have been voted a bachelor for the occasion".

HIGH SOCIETY

These loud and wine-drenched parties in the heart of the village were far removed, in space and tone, from the typical society of Westwood Hill, which was where the other Sydenham literary celebrity of the period lived. Lady Charlotte Campbell (1775-1861), the youngest daughter of the fifth Duke of Argyll, had married her cousin, Col. John Campbell, in 1796. He died ten years later, leaving her with nine children and very little money. Her first expedient for supporting her family was to accept the position of lady-in-waiting to the Prin-cess of Wales, then living separated from the Prince at Montagu House, Blackheath. The second was to try her hand at writing. In 1812 she published her novel *Self-Indulgence,* the first of many, and moved to Westwood House, where she could be near, but not too near, the vulgar and indiscreet princess.

Her arrival at Sydenham was warmly welcomed by Thomas Campbell, who claimed her as a distant cousin and "my chieftain's lovely daughter".

75. *Lady Charlotte Campbell, from the portrait by John Hoppner.*

Westwood House was close to Peak Hill. It was one of the prominent features of the view from Campbell's front windows, and he described Lady Charlotte, with only slight exaggeration, as his "next door neighbour on the Common". He was soon writing that she "is a great accession to me. I spend evenings very often with her and her sensible Swiss governess." Acquaintance with the lady-in-waiting naturally led to an introduction to the Princess of Wales. Campbell was alarmed by her expressed intention of descending on his little house in Peak Hill, but Lady Charlotte managed to divert this onerous honour, and the meeting took place at Blackheath instead. Campbell dis-tinguished himself, by his own report, in dancing a Highland reel with the Princess.

Lady Charlotte went abroad in 1814, and was much on the Continent during the next four years, but she retained the lease of Westwood House, and returned to it in 1818 with a new name. At Florence she had that year married a young clergyman, Edward Bury, who was no richer than the late Col. Campbell. As Lady Charlotte Bury she was now obliged to resume her literary career, and soon moved her family to London, where the material for her silver fork novels could be gathered more easily.

SYDENHAM.

FOR ONE NIGHT ONLY.

EXTRAORDINARY COMBINATION OF NATIVE TALENT!

ON THURSDAY EVENING, 17TH DECEMBER 1840,

MRS. PRICHARD'S HUMBLE SERVANTS WILL HAVE THE HONOR
TO PERFORM THE COMEDY OF

THE RIVALS,

WITH NO SCENERY OR DECORATIONS.

Mrs. Malaprop	Miss Marianne Colville.
Lydia Languish	Mrs. Edward Colville.
Julia	Mrs. Thomas Hardy.
Lucy	Miss Colville.
Sir Anthony Absolute	Mr. Peter Hardy.
Captain Absolute	Mr. Edward Colville.
Sir Lucius O'Trigger	Mr. Henry Humphreys.
Faulkland	Mr. William Hardy.
Acres	Mr. H. Smith.
Fag	Mr. Thomas Willis.
David	Mr. John St. Barbe.
Coachman	Mr. Francis Lysons Price.
Boy	Mr George Chilton, *minimus.*

STAGE MANAGER AND PROMPTER—T. D. HARDY, ESQ.

PERFORMANCE TO COMMENCE AT EIGHT O'CLOCK PRECISELY.

PAX ET AMOR.

VIVE L'HÔTESSE!

76. *A silk playbill for a performance at the Old Cedars (Mrs Selina Prichard's house) in 1840. The cast was largely recruited from the big houses of Sydenham Road.*

At this period nearly all the families composing the high society of Sydenham lived along the half mile of road between Westwood House and the Old House. The Mayows and Prices, the Lauries of Sydenham Hall, the Prichards of the Old Cedars, the Smiths of Newlands, came to be regarded, or to regard themselves, as the old families of the village, even though the most firmly rooted of them had been there only sixty or seventy years when everything began to change in the 1850s.

Common and Enclosure

"'Tis bad enough in man or woman
To steal a goose from off the common;
But surely he's without excuse
Who steals the common from the goose."

WESTWOOD COMMON

At the time of its enclosure in 1810, even after centuries of wholesale and piecemeal encroachment, Sydenham Common covered nearly five hundred acres – almost twice the size of Blackheath. By itself it accounted for more than a tenth of the whole extent of the parish of Lewisham. Today some 16,000 people live on its site, which comprises nearly half of Sydenham and Forest Hill.

Sydenham Common was anciently called Westwood, because it was at the western edge of the parish of Lewisham, and it was originally a part of the Great North Wood – north of Croydon – from which Norwood takes its name.   Like Norwood, Dulwich, and the other parts of the Great North Wood, Sydenham provided a good income for the lord of the manor through the systematic farming of its timber. Under the rule of the Abbots of Ghent (until 1414) and the Priors of Shene (until 1531) Westwood had been divided into coppices, one of which was felled each year in rotation, though a proportion of the better trees were allowed to grow to maturity in each. If the example of the Archbishop of Canterbury's Norwood was followed, the coppices did not cover the whole extent of Westwood, but were interspersed with tracts of open common where the villagers could graze their cattle and gather fuel.

That the coppice system was collapsing early in the sixteenth century is strongly indicated by the survey carried out for Henry VIII after he extorted Lewisham from Shene Priory in 1531. It was no doubt in the interests of the king to paint a picture of hopeless decay, for it was not his plan to reinvigorate the coppice system. His new dockyard at Deptford was in constant need of timber, and here was a free source conveniently close at hand. But coppices were of limited use. For masts and planks mature trees were needed. Some of these would have been available at Westwood, but it seems likely that Henry's instruction to his steward was to thin the coppices and allow all the promising trees to grow. Certainly it was not until the reigns of his children Edward and Elizabeth

77. *Sydenham Common painted by James Pringle, the Bell Green nurseryman, in 1812, just before the enclosure. His point of view was the telegraph station at the bend of Sydenham Hill, opposite the top of Kirkdale. The dog, the woman, and the coach are all proceeding down Kirkdale. The canal reservoir is the main feature on the left. Beyond it, and reflected in it, are the Peak Hill houses. The Jew's Walk trees are conspicuous on the right, leading to Westwood House. Further down Westwood Hill Sydenham Hall, the Old Cedars, and Sydenham Place stand out from the trees.*

that the wholesale felling of Westwood was carried out. The route by which the Sydenham trees were carted to the dockyard can still be traced along the line of Stanstead Road, Brockley Rise, Brockley Road, Upper Brockley Road, Tanner's Hill, Deptford High Street, and New King Street – an ancient and nearly straight road of almost three miles. Part of it (perhaps at one time all) was known as Butt Lane.

By the beginning of the seventeenth century most of the common had been stripped of mature trees for the benefit of the navy. The two areas that remained well-wooded were Coleson's Coppice and Cooper's Wood at the northern and southern fringes (*see pp.57-63*), which had only been protected by means of a partial enclosure, which soon inevitably shaded into a complete one. Except for these semi-private woods, the common had been largely stripped of timber. In 1605 this made it a tempting object to "Henry Newport of Lewi-

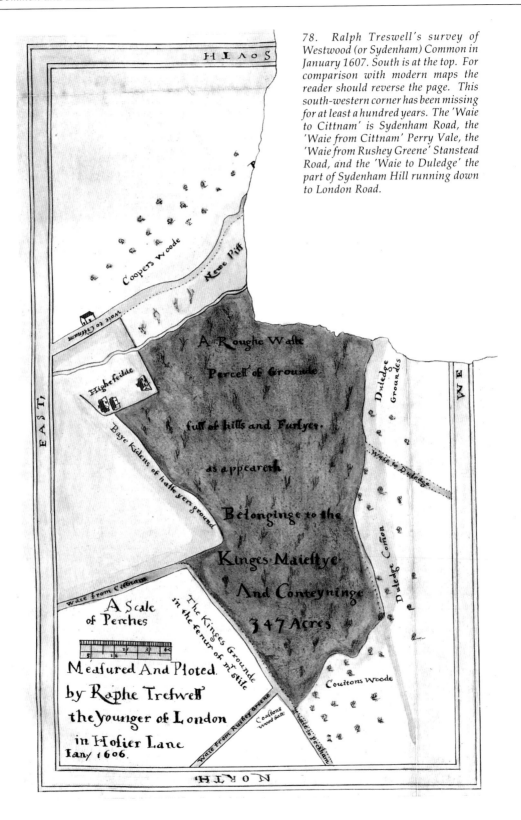

78. *Ralph Treswell's survey of Westwood (or Sydenham) Common in January 1607. South is at the top. For comparison with modern maps the reader should reverse the page. This south-western corner has been missing for at least a hundred years. The 'Waie to Cittnam' is Sydenham Road, the 'Waie from Cittnam' Perry Vale, the 'Waie from Rushey Greene' Stanstead Road, and the 'Waie to Duledge' the part of Sydenham Hill running down to London Road.*

79. The most celebrated of the cottages at Sydenham Wells (see p. 78) was the Green Dragon, 'the dwelling of Alexander Roberts', which was sketched by Thomas Bonner (or Bonnor) c.1770.

sham, gentleman, and yeoman of ye boiling-house to King James" who, searching hungrily for a scrap to beg from his master's table, lighted on Westwood Common. Newport persuaded the King to regard this morsel of five or six hundred acres as part of the demesne land of the manor, and in that belief James leased Westwood to him.

Most of the inhabitants of Lewisham were still small farmers and husbandmen who relied heavily on the free pasture available at Sydenham. In many parishes where the commons were small a rationing system was enforced, whereby freeholders were entitled to graze only a specified number of cows and sheep and pigs in proportion to the size of their estates, but Westwood was so big that no restrictions were applied. This had encouraged large numbers of squatters to build cottages at Sydenham, where they supported themselves almost entirely by grazing animals. In one of the petitions that "the inhabitants of the Parrishe of Lewsham" now fired off in all directions, they pointed out (probably with considerable exaggeration) that there were "above 500 poore housholders with wives and manye children greatly relieved by the sayde Common and would be utterly undone yf yt should be unjustly taken from them". If that had happened their support would have become the responsibility of the parish, which no doubt helps to explain why the opposition to Newport was so generously supported by the richest landowners in Lewisham.

Three years of legal manoeuvring ended inconclusively in 1608. In 1614 Newport acquired two allies in Robert Raynes, sergeant of the buckhounds, and Innocent Lanier of Greenwich, one of the eminent family of court musicians, and jointly with them took out a new sixty-year lease from the King of 347 acres of Westwood at a rent of forty marks a year. "Presently the Patentees began to make ditches about the common and inclosed it and drave out and killed sundry of the cattell of the inhabitants". There were violent scenes at Sydenham when the more hot-headed parishioners levelled the ditches and broke down the new gates, and Lanier's servant responded by driving off the animals pastured on the common, killing some in the process, and by burning the furze that the poor people used for fuel.

In 1614 Abraham Colfe, the Vicar of Lewisham, who organised the resistance to the enclosure, adopted a more peaceful approach by leading a deputation of "neer 100 people young and old .. through ye city of London and a little on this side of Topnam high-crosse petitioned King James who very graciously heard ye petition and ordered the Lords of his Privy Counsell should take a course that he might be no more troubled about it". There were still several legal setbacks to overcome, but with the King anxious to avoid trouble on the politically sensitive question of enclosures the final verdict was given in favour of the inhabitants of Lewisham at the end of 1615.

80. *One of the other old cottages at the Wells developed into the settlement called Rose Retreat, near the top of Wells Park Road, seen here c.1930.*

SYDENHAM WELLS

The other seventeenth century event of importance to the common was the discovery there in the 1640s of a number of medicinal springs, which quickly became celebrated as Sydenham, or Lewisham – or Dulwich Wells, from the nearest place widely known to Londoners. By 1651 the flood of summer visitors to Sydenham was so great that the government issued a proclamation ordering them to behave with decorum. When this did no good cavalry was sent to maintain order.

Evelyn visited the wells in 1675 and noted that they were "much frequented in Summer time". When Daniel Defoe passed this way early in the eighteenth century he also "saw Dullige or Sydenham Wells, where great Crouds of People throng every Summer from London to drink the Waters, as at Epsome and Tunbridge; only with this difference, that as at Epsome and Tunbridge, they go for the Diversion of the Season, for the Mirth and the Company; for Gaming, or Intrieguing, and the like, here they go for meer Physick, and this causes another difference; Namely, that as the Nobility and Gentry go to Tunbridge, the Mer-

chants and Rich Citizens to Epsome; so the Common People go chiefly to Dullwich and Stretham; and the rather also, because it lyes so near London, that they can walk to it in the Morning, and return at Night; which abundance do; that is to say, especially of a Sunday, or on Holidays, which makes the better sort also decline the Place; the Croud on those Days being both unruly and unmannerly."

An early attempt was made "by the instigation of a forward and active person" to enclose and monopolise the waters, and a handsome well was dug, but "no sooner was the well finished, though supplied with water very plentifully, but it lost its taste, its odour, and effects; which was so manifestly observable that thereupon there was immediately a final end put to that specious project". After this fiasco the profits arising from entertaining the visitors at the wells and at the houses on the edge of the common were widely diffused among the residents. At the height of the spa's popularity there may have been as many as a dozen wells clustered near the junction of the present Taylor's Lane and Wells Park Road. Small enclosures were permitted around each, with a cottage to house the proprietor and shelter the water drinkers. The influx of invalids and pleasure seekers undoubtedly stimulated building activity around the common. Although most visitors came on day trips from London, some of the wealthier ones took lodgings. Inns like the Greyhound and the Three Compasses were probably built, in part at least, for the accommodation of the water drinkers.

The Sydenham Wells had their greatest triumph late in the eighteenth century, when George III spent a day tasting the waters, while his privacy was protected by a picket of soldiers around the cottage. That king's patronage, though, was perhaps a dubious advertisement. At any event the popularity of the wells did not survive the enclosure. Probably their vogue had always depended more on the beauty of the common than on the quality of the waters (which one witness flatly described as "very nasty"), and after 1812 Wells Road developed into an area of slum housing. The wells were not used after the 1830s. The last of the associated cottages to survive was the Green Dragon (*ill. 79*), which stood in Wells Road (now Wells Park Road), opposite Taylor's Lane. It was destroyed by a flying bomb in 1944.

ACTIVITIES ON THE COMMON

By 1810 Sydenham was already to a large extent a suburban community, with public coaches and private carriages taking a significant proportion of its leading citizens to work in the City and Westminster. But at this early stage of suburban development few of London's satellite villages had produced the social organisations and facilities that we now take for granted. This meant that Sydenham Common played an even more prominent role in the life of the surrounding community than an open space like Blackheath does today.

The oldest activities on the common were naturally fuel gathering and the grazing of animals. The importance of the former must have been reduced by the opening of the Croydon Canal, which brought cheap coal to Sydenham. As for grazing, there were always plenty of sheep, which were kept from wandering off into Dulwich by a gate across the road at the top of Westwood Hill, a spot once known as Low Cross, later as Rockhills. Mayow Adams, who was born in Sydenham in 1807, recalled that "my Aunt used to tell me of a Shepherdess by the name of Neville, dressed after the manner of a Shepherdess in a Pantomime, crook and all." But an earlier account, probably by that same aunt, Miss Mary Mayow, gives a less idyllic portrait:

81. The Greyhound drawn by G. Shepheard in 1839, when the landlord was William Ridgway.

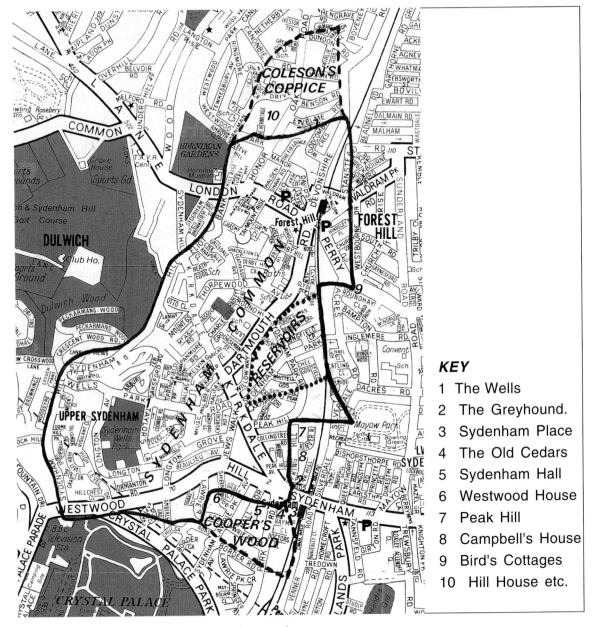

82. The extent of Sydenham Common indicated on a modern map.

KEY

1 The Wells
2 The Greyhound.
3 Sydenham Place
4 The Old Cedars
5 Sydenham Hall
6 Westwood House
7 Peak Hill
8 Campbell's House
9 Bird's Cottages
10 Hill House etc.

Neville, the shepherdess, who brought her flock so regularly to the common from her hovel at the lower village, that the sight of her rope-girdled coat, red petticoat, and high-crowned beaver, were signals as much to be depended on as the clock.... Poor Neville! she was the last of the shepherdesses. There was nothing Arcadian about her; indeed, if report were true, her character was as far from straight as the iron crook she carried. She

had what the neighbours called 'an awkward trick' of substituting their live lambs for her dead ones; and it was well for her that her large flock could tell no tales ... Poor Neville! she died in 1814, in Lewisham workhouse – a sad end for the relic of the golden age!

When Thomas Campbell first moved to Sydenham in 1804, he was standing at his door admiring the

83. The Croydon Canal and the south side of Sydenham Bridge as painted by William Hodges c.1830. On the right is part of the house known as The Bridge.

fine view, and growing poetical, when "my wife cut short my reverie by asking if we had a right to keep pigs on the common!" This too, he complained, from a woman with the romantic name of Matilda. Later, Campbell's young sons enjoyed chasing sheep on the common.

The livestock must have had an exciting time, because another favourite activity at Sydenham was hunting. Several old names in the area are reminders of this. The Dog Kennel Houses (*see p.56*) stood until the 1830s in the remote corner of the common now occupied by Recreation Road and Silverdale. The old Fox and Hounds inn was a feature of Peak Hill in the eighteenth century, and the Greyhound (under its foolish temporary disguise) still dominates the western end of Sydenham Road, where the common began. It was founded *c.*1720. 'The Greyhound' was a favourite name for hunting inns, and especially for those associated with the famous Old Surrey Hunt of Mr Jorrocks. In his heyday, the 1820s, the Old Surrey met at the Greyhounds at Dulwich or Croydon, and hunted all over this area. In 'The Swell and the Surrey', one of the stories in *Jorrocks's Jaunts and Jollities*, the swell from the Melton Mowbray Hunt leaps across the Croydon Canal, but Jorrocks is able to

keep up with him by bribing a bargee to ferry him over.

There is little doubt that before 1812 the Greyhound at Sydenham was one of the Old Surrey's meets. The Master in the years around 1800 was the warehouse owner Henry Dudin, who lived at Hill House, Honor Oak Road, on the northern edge of the common, and later moved to Sydenham Road (*see pp.63-4 and 29*). Even after the enclosure hunting continued for a time, and the new Fox and Hounds in Kirkdale, which was opened in 1830, became a haunt of the West Kent Hounds and others. In 1868 it was recalled that in its early days the pub was "visited by huntsmen from miles around, as it was a place of meeting , and stag and foxhounds of celebrated packs were kept in the adjoining yard".

Wealthy sporting grocers of the Mr Jorrocks type were very much of the same class as many Sydenham residents, some of whom subscribed to the Old Surrey; but there were other forms of hunting that did not meet with local approval. In 1786 Lord Dartmouth's agent reported:

> I saw Mr Pownall yesterday, who tells me that there is a very great nuisance in this Parish, goes

The GRAND REVIEW on SYDENH

The Prince and his party were drove to the summit of a hill where they made a stand for nearly an hour & a half but where at len fawoured their flight & left the several battalions masters of the field his Majesty followed the enemy on foot at the head of

84. *The mock battle of 1792 provided the inspiration for one of Isaac Cruikshank's political allegories. In his 'The Grand Review on Sydenham Common', George III, Pitt and Burke are seen putting the Prince of Wales, Fox, and their opposition friends to flight. Sheridan is the fallen Whig.*

ION

at to the bottom setting fire to the furze & hedges the Smoke of which
to the foot of the hill when he remounted & returned back to the lines.

under the sanction of your Lordship, by making use of your name; he says there is a Pack of Hounds kept by a man at Sydenham, who is nothing more than a day labourer, and is frequently out, and a parcel of Idle fellows attending the Hunt, who he says ought to be imploying themselves in the maintainance of their familys; as your Lordship is at no expense in keeping the hounds, they that are must in course reimburse themselves out of the Game they kill. Mr Pownall says if they are not Protected by your Lordship he will order the Dogs to be shot.

Nothing more is heard of this hunt, which may have been the one with its headquarters at the Dog Kennel Houses.

The common provided an excellent venue for military displays, especially the sham battles for which its broken terrain was so suitable. George III attended several of these during the 1790s. One he observed with the royal family from carriages drawn up on Peak Hill. A later account gives some details.

Many still live who remember those days; ... they will relate how soldiers took the place of sheep, and how bullets whizzed where nightingales had sung. Yes, I saw Dulwich Wood in possession of the French, and marked them retreat before the brave English troops of Sydenham Common. I noted the valour of the Oxford Blues, and the shots of the City Rifles, the courtly grace of the Prince of Wales, and the noble bearing of the royal dukes [and heard] the Duke of York's March as it played from the tents on Peak Hill. [For years afterwards the local boys] fought over again the sham-fight upon that very spot ... the common was the Aldershot of our children, and there was not a furze-bush or hawthorn-tree that had not been taken by the French, only to be retaken by the English.

The wealthier residents of Sydenham were pleased to see large numbers gathered to watch the manoeuvres and cheer the King, but they were far less happy about other events that attracted crowds of common people onto the common. In the middle of the eighteenth century it became the venue of a popular fair, which by 1766 had so alarmed the "principal inhabitants of Lewisham and Sydenham ... and the villages adjacent" that they mounted an impressive and successful petition to the Quarter Sessions at Maidstone to have it suppressed. The petitioners described the fair as:

...an unlawful Assembly of diverse loose idle and disorderly Persons held on the Common or Waste called Sydenham Common ... particularly

85. George Scharf captioned this 1828 view 'Canal near Norwood', but there can be no doubt that his painting shows the lock at what is now Honor Oak Park. The house to the right of centre was built between 1815 and 1828, became the property of the London and Croydon Railway company in 1836, and was demolished between 1843 and 1863. Ashdale, the present 103 Honor Oak Park, was built on or near the site c.1865.

on Sundays in the Months of May June and July to the great Annoyance and Disturbance of the ...Inhabitants... That such meetings or Assemblys consist of several Hundreds of the most dissolute and profligate Persons of both Sexes from all Parts of London and its Environs where they by Violence hold a Fair or Mart for buying young Birds and Birds' Nests, which are brought thither for Sale by Farmers' Servants and other labouring Men for several Miles round and where spirituous Liquors are retailed in Huts without Licence to the great Encouragement of Drunkenness, Gaming and all other Debaucheries to the ruin of many Apprentices and other young Persons who are induced to attend these Meetings to the great Neglect of their Masters and Familys and the Encouragement of Vice and Immorality ... That these Assemblies begin very early on Sunday Mornings and continue during the whole or greatest Part of the Day drinking and idling about in the Fields and Hedges, and in their Way there commit many Outrages by breaking the Windows Gates ... Hedges and Fences and hunting and killing Sheep, milking of Cows, stealing Poultry and other Effects of the Inhabitants."

made to expel them; but in the end it was the builders, not the magistrates, who drove them away. There certainly was a great deal of crime on or about the common. A later account records that "carriages were stopped in broad daylight; our own squire was robbed of his watch before seven in the evening, and never afterwards travelled without a robbing-watch, made up expressly for the occasion; and it was necessary to appoint a patrol, armed with a blunderbuss, to meet the coach daily at the bottom of our hill". In November 1800 *The Times* reported that "On Sunday afternoon a young man, well mounted, stopped Mr Bulcock, banker in the Boro', on the Dulwich Road, and robbed him of his money, and within a few hours five or six other robberies were committed on the same road." James Bulcock lived at the Old Cedars on Westwood Hill.

In 1805 Thomas Campbell was walking with his wife on "a solitary part of the common" nearly within sight of his own house on Peak Hill.

> An ill-looking man, mounted on a beautiful horse, passed us. He went to both sides of the hill, came back and returned, and came back again, after looking on the road to see if it was clear. On coming close to us he demanded our names. I spoke to him strongly at first, and threatened to call for assistance. He half dismounted; but hearing me holla to some workmen in the neighbourhood, he took his seat again, and after some incoherent expostulations with me - rode off. I got Mrs Campbell, with difficulty, home in strong fits.

This possible highwayman was caught and taken before the local magistrate, who much to Campbell's disgust fined him a small sum and released him.

A great addition to the amenities offered by the common was made after 1801 with the construction of the Croydon Canal, which opened in 1809. The venture proved a commercial disaster, but there were compensations for the non-shareholding residents. The canal had a reservoir at Sydenham and another, which still exists, at Norwood. The range of activities still offered at Norwood Lake – fishing, sailing, swimming – were all once available at Sydenham, plus others that are no longer allowed there, officially at least: duck shooting, for example. Mayow Adams recalled that the canal "was much used by the young men of the neighbourhood, myself among the number, for bathing in summer and skating in winter". He also mentions that Henry Doo the coal merchant, who had a wharf at Sydenham Bridge, hired boats as a sideline.

The sport, or trade, of netting birds on the common continued long afterwards. This fair was duly banned, but the love of unruly pleasure could not be kept down for long, and a fair held on Trinity Monday and the two following days in the Kent House fields of Lower Sydenham became a feature of village life for much of the nineteenth century – despite the Rev. Thomas Bowdler's attempt to suppress it in 1836.

The banning of the fair on the common in 1766 did not end the worries of the local householders. The Great North Wood was a favourite haunt of the Gipsies, who for centuries had been famous here for their fortune telling. They tended to be blamed for any unsolved crimes in the surrounding villages, and from 1797 vigorous efforts were

Sometimes on a Sunday afternoon, when we could get the fellows together, we had the four-oared boat and pulled up to Croydon". [Or sometimes they would row] "the other way to the first lock, about half-way between Forest Hill and Brockley. Occasionally we had, in the summer evenings, a pic-nic in Penge Wood, boiling our kettle, gipsy-fashion, while listening to the nightingales.

Where there is boating and swimming there is also, of course, drowning, and that was another popular activity on the common. The Royal Humane Society provided rescue equipment at the Dartmouth Arms, but it frequently arrived too late. In 1822 William Bear was drowned in the reservoir while chasing a duck he had shot. A more dramatic incident occurred in 1807 when a young gentleman fell into the reservoir and was ultimately drowned after Timothy Stollard, the landlord of the Greyhound, allegedly refused to lend his boat for a rescue attempt. As a result Stollard lost his licence, but got round the problem by putting up a man of straw until the magistrates forgave him. The reservoir was a source of anxiety to Thomas Campbell when visitors left his house after dark. Cyrus Redding records an occasion when "there was no conveyance back to town. Campbell wished me to remain the night, but I declined his invitation, set off late, and walked on towards the reservoir nearly in front of his house. Supposing I did not see it, he called out to me to take care of my footsteps."

THE ENCLOSURE

The great enclosure movement of the second half of the eighteenth century and the early part of the nineteenth was obviously motivated predominantly by greed, but during the Napoleonic Wars food shortages and a sharp rise in the cost of living provided it with a convenient cloak of patriotism. The government was very anxious to bring more land into cultivation and went out of its way to ease the passage of enclosure bills.

The projectors of the Lewisham enclosure had one striking point in common: none of them lived at Sydenham, and the only one who owned land there was the lord of the manor, Lord Dartmouth, who owned land everywhere. He and John Forster of Southend, the two who stood to gain most, were the principal sponsors of the scheme. The earl was a veteran politician, and an old hand at enclosures, having taken a leading part in one at Basingstoke. Forster was thus described by Sir Francis Baring, himself no novice in business matters: "I know Forster well, and that he is formidable, but how

you could attempt to manage a man who manages the rest of the World is what I do not understand. I expect no favor from him." The details of the plan, as disclosed at a public meeting, were given to Baring by his agent in November 1809.

I rather think Lord Dartmouth is the original promotor of the Inclosure ... Sydenham Common and all the wastes, excepting Blackheath, have been measured - it appears that Sydenham Common consists of 480 acres - and the rest of the wastes excepting Blackheath to not more than 20 acres ... - that part of Blackheath which is in the Parish of Lewisham was guessed to be about 150 or 200 - the reason why it has not been ascertained is that Lord Dartmouth has made up his mind to consent to no inclosure which shall comprize that land, which he is determined to keep in its present state as a kind of natural ornament ...

The discussion turned principally by an objection by Mr Marryat, and other Sydenham people to the inclosure of part and not the whole of the Parish - their objection in point of pecuniary Value was correct - they said if you inclose only Sydenham Common, the freeholders near Blackheath to whom it is [neither] useful or pleasureable will come and participate with us in the allotment – whilst we shall derive neither pleasure or profit from Blackheath remaining in a state of Common – whereas if Blackheath is inclosed the freeholders thereabouts will be satisfied by an allotment from it in respect of their rights on Sydenham Common, whilst we shall be put into the enjoyment of our rights on Blackheath, by a larger allotment of Sydenham Common. ... The discussion ended in resolving itself into two questions – first whether the parties present were inclined to promote inclosure of the whole parish – this was carried in the affirmative by all who gave any opinion ... Kent is to state this resolution to Lord Dartmouth, to see if he will alter his mind as to Blackheath - without his consent as Lord of Blackheath and Sydenham Common no inclosure can take place.

The next question proposed was whether, if Lord D. would not consent to inclose the whole, the parties would consent to a partial inclosure – the general opinion was in the negative ... I reserved this for you, stating it to be a question between pecuniary profit, and ornament, and that [as] it was in a great measure a matter of taste I could not anticipate what you would wish, hinting at the same time that in a rich Country ornamental pleasure ground of a publick nature was a desirable object, but that it might be paid for too dearly. – you are therefore quite open to support Lord Dartmouth or the Sydenhamites, or to be mediator between them.

The earl held firm, and when Sir Francis Baring and Lord Eliot decided to support him his agent wrote confidently, and revealingly, that he was "extremely glad to find Sir Francis Baring is so steadily inclined to co-inside with Lords Dartmouth and Eliot in the Inclosure of Sydenham Common and the half year Lands, and of keeping Blackheath open. I have no doubt but by perseverance we shall carry our object, for though there are many Persons against the measure their property is inconsiderable."

The Mr Marryat mentioned by Sir Francis Baring's agent as the leader of the Sydenhamites was Joseph Marryat MP (*see p.47*). He was clearly angered by the enclosure scheme – passionate tempers were a family characteristic – but he was not necessarilly moved by concern for the interests of his poor neighbours. Marryat did not own the large Sydenham estate, Malvern House, that he occupied, and as a parliamentarian he must have known that leaseholders stood to gain little or nothing from enclosure acts.

Whatever his motives Marryat became an influential element of opposition to the plan. Another was the Adams family. William Dacres Adams, the son of an MP, and himself the Private Secretary to two recent Prime Ministers, had married the heiress Elizabeth Mayow in 1804. Their son, Mayow Adams, later recalled what happened:

"The Act was passed after much opposition from some of the inhabitants...; the second reading in the House of Commons being carried by a majority of only one, it so happened that my grandfather, William Adams, Esq., then M.P. for Totnes, and another Member were shut out of the division, or the result would have been different."

THE EARLY DEVELOPMENT OF THE COMMON

The commissioners appointed under the enclosure act divided the land between the qualifying Lewisham freeholders, and their decisions determined the broad outline of development on the common. The larger plots, destined for the wealthier landowners, were on the higher ground to the south, the west, and the north. The smaller ones tended to be in the east, and were concentrated near the main roads across the common. The sudden glut of building land created by the enclosure must have depressed the price of houses in Sydenham, and those wealthy enough to do so waited for a better opportunity before building on their allotments. Most of the poorer beneficiaries were obliged to act quickly. As a result the early development was predominantly in the form of cottages, many of them wooden, and all built in or around Kirkdale

86. The view down Kirkdale in 1836. The building just to the left of St Bartholomew's is the Fox and Hounds (before rebuilding), and the open space behind its sign is the undeveloped Church Meadow.

87. Willow Walk c.1930. These cottages were no. 12 (the bungalow) and 14 to 20.

88. Nos. 89 and 91 Kirkdale in 1991.

and Wells Park Road, two old tracks adopted by the enclosure commissioners, and in Dartmouth Road, their most important creation. More than two hundred cottages were built here between 1812 and 1843.

The greatest concentration was in the area later known as the High Street: Kirkdale from Wells Park Road to Dartmouth Road, and Dartmouth Road from Kirkdale to Willow Walk. With these were associated the cottages in Cheseman Street (formerly known as Skeet's Lane and Russell Street), in Willow Walk, and in Charlecote Grove, formerly Charles Street. Many of the original buildings survive in Kirkdale and Dartmouth Road, hidden behind shop fronts. The least spoilt examples are in Kirkdale: the stuccoed nos. 124 and 126, and the wooden 89 and 91, just north of the Dartmouth Road junction. A few old cottages survive in Charlecote Grove, and one (no. 7) in Cheseman Street, but Willow Walk has been completely rebuilt.

The other substantial groups of cottages were in Wells Park Road and its offshoots – Mill Gardens, Springfield, and Taylor's Lane – and at the northern end of Dartmouth Road, in the tapering sliver of common between the road and the canal. Here

89. *Mill Gardens c.1930. The buildings were, from left to right, Hill (or Hilton) Cottage, Wood Cottage and Stanley Cottage, a semi-detached pair, Rose Cottage, and Home Cottage, which survives greatly altered.*

90. *Some of the old Dartmouth Place cottages in the 1890s, by which time they had long been converted into shops numbered 79 to 63 Dartmouth Road.*

91. The back-to-back pair of Ashtree Cottage (on the left) and Rouselle Cottage, Mount Gardens in 1973.

92. The Orchard, Mount Gardens, with part of The Chalet in the background, in 1991. The gabled dining room of The Orchard was added to the original three-bay house in 1858.

the twenty-five or more houses built south of the Dartmouth Arms public house were known as Dartmouth Place. All have now been rebuilt as shops. The development of Wells Park Road (formerly Wells Lane) spread out from the cottages attached to the various wells near the Taylor's Lane junction – the only buildings on the common before the enclosure. From there the ribbon of building stretched mainly eastwards to link up with the 'High Street' area of Kirkdale. The only surviving examples of this earliest post-enclosure development in the Wells Park Road area are the rather remote wooden pair in Taylor's Lane and Home Cottage in Mill Gardens, all three greatly altered in recent decades.

The best preserved group of early cottages on the common is something of an anomaly. The land towards the top of Kirkdale on which Mount Gardens was built was one of the large allotments on high ground which usually remained undeveloped for at least thirty years after the enclosure, and on which large houses were nearly always ultimately built. Mount Gardens proved the exception to both rules, for the land was sold in small plots even before the commissioners' award had been ratified, and the cottages that appeared here were among the earliest on the common. The back-to-back wooden pair known as Ashtree Cottage and Rouselle Cottage, built *c.*1815, has remained unaltered because the restricted site allowed no room for expansion. But as Sydenham Hill and upper Kirkdale developed into an area of fine houses and wealthy residents the other cottages tended to grow. The Orchard and The Chalet, the two substantial houses at the end of Mount Gardens, had much more modest origins.

In the first three decades after the enclosure the building of larger houses on the common was restricted not only by the glut of land, but by the

lack of any effective water supply. The digging of a deep well had to be included in the cost of any projected development on the higher ground, and this additional expense must have persuaded many landowners to bide their time. But in spite of these difficulties twenty or more large houses were built during this early period.

One group was established at the lower end of Honor Oak Road, on its eastern side, and in the adjacent part of London Road. Summerfield, no. 74 Honor Oak Road, is the surviving example. Round Hill House, in the rising ground between Dartmouth Road and Kirkdale, was built in the early 1820s. There were six large houses in the upper part of Kirkdale. The older three, on the west side, dated from the early 1820s. Of these the one still standing is Milverton Lodge, no. 24, which was part of the Mount Gardens development. The more substantial houses on the eastern side were the work of a builder named James Hunt, who had his office in Idol Lane near the Tower of London. That was in the parish of St Dunstan-in-the-East, which received an allotment on the common because of its charity estates – the site of St Dunstan's College and others – elsewhere in Lewisham. The parish authorities leased the allotment to Hunt, who built himself the mansion called Woodthorpe between 1830 and 1833. The house has given its name, curiously inverted, to Thorpewood Avenue. Hunt then bought or leased adjoining plots, and built various houses and cottages on them between 1833 and his death in 1869. The earliest and most prominent were Tudor Lodge and Seymour Lodge, built in the mid-1830s between Woodthorpe and Charlecote Grove.

Six houses appeared on the east side of Sydenham Hill before 1843. Bellevue was built in the 1820s

93. *Seymour Lodge, Kirkdale, probably in the 1880s.*

by William Little, a cloth worker with premises in Catherine Street, Covent Garden, and replaced by The Cedars, the present no. 34, in 1898. The two acre allotment at the southern corner of Wells Park Road was awarded to the parish at the enclosure, to be used as a gravel pit, and for fifteen years loaded carts carrying away this vital road making ingredient must have been a regular sight in Sydenham Hill. But by 1828 the gravel was exhausted. The parish officers thought of obtaining a private act of parliament authorising them to sell the land, but abandoned the idea when they found it would cost £250. After a long delay the local magistrates gave permission for the sale and in 1837 the two acres were bought for £310 by a stockbroker, Frederick Augustus William Murthwaite Helps, who built Rock House (no. 24) on the site in 1841. It survived until the early 1960s.

Trinity Hospital, Greenwich, was another charity that received an allotment on the common. In the 1820s John Forster of Southend obtained a lease of the land and in partnership with a local builder, John Verge, erected two houses, the substantial Old Grange, no.20, which was close to the road, and The Cottage, no.22, a smaller property that was largely hidden towards the rear of the seven and a half acre plot. Both were badly damaged during the war, and 20 to 24 were replaced by St Clement's Heights in the 1960s.

The remaining two pre-1843 houses on the east side of Sydenham Hill, and the only ones that still survive, were also built for the Forster family. The Elms, no. 18, which was extended southwards in 1894-5, but is otherwise unaltered, may date from the 1830s. The Wood, no. 16, was built as two

houses in 1841, but almost immediately converted into one. This happened because the widowed owner, Rebecca Wells, married a Rushey Green builder named Charles Atkins in 1842, and the couple decided to settle here. The Wood continued to grow throughout the nineteenth century, and especially between 1855, when Lady Hunloke became the tenant, and 1858, when the sixth duke of Devonshire died. Lady Hunloke was the duke's old mistress. It is certain that the Cavendish fortune financed the lavish improvements to the house that raised its rateable value from £115 in 1849 to £201 in 1857, and very probable that the extensions were designed by Sir Joseph Paxton. The duke was a frequent guest at Paxton's nearby house, Rockhills, and the two men maintained a constant intercourse with 'the fat ladies', as they called Lady Hunloke and her daughter.

Until the 1840s the only large new house that appeared on the former common land in Westwood Hill was another Forster creation. Westwood Cottage, which was built in the 1820s, was replaced by Horner Grange in the early 1880s, and what remains of Horner Grange after the recent fire is now the main block of the Sydenham High School. Although the Forsters built Westwood Cottage and a few early houses on Sydenham Hill, such development was not their priority before the 1850s. John Forster obtained about 22 acres on the common from the enclosure commissioners. By various exchanges, purchases, and (if all else failed) leases, he soon built this up into a formidable landholding that enabled him to dominate the area between Westwood Hill, Sydenham Hill, and Wells Park Road. His son Edward lived at Westwood

96. The Wood, 16 Sydenham Hill, in 1991

94. The Elms, 18 Sydenham Hill, in 1991. The nearest bay was added in 1894-5.

95. (Below) The area of the Forsters' Sydenham Common farm at its peak in the 1830s, indicated on the enclosure award map of c.1812, at which time John Forster's holdings were far less extensive.

Cottage, the farmhouse from which all this carefully acquired land was managed. At its peak, in the 1830s, this Forster farm on Sydenham Common extended to some 115 acres. In fact, despite all the early developments described above, at least three quarters of Sydenham Common remained as agricultural land until forty years after the passage of the enclosure act.

The Double Boom

SYDENHAM PARK

In 1835 Sydenham was a charming Kentish village – perhaps more reminiscent of New England if George Ticknor is to be believed – and Forest Hill barely existed. They were linked to London by expensive coach services that made them a suitable residence only for the wealthy commuter. Thomas Campbell found that his occasional trips to and from town cost him 5s 6d, and when his editorial duties required a daily attendance at the office after 1820 he could no longer afford to live in the village. By 1865 Sydenham and Forest Hill were large and ever expanding suburbs, fully integrated with London by rapid and regular train services. This thirty year transformation was the result of two great waves of building development, of which the second and larger caught and overwhelmed the first.

The railway boom began with the purchase of the Croydon Canal in 1836 by the London and Croydon Railway Company, which laid its tracks along the general route of the canal and at some points in its bed. The two stations at Sydenham and the Dartmouth Arms (later Forest Hill) were opened in 1839. The Sydenham reservoir acquired by the company in 1836, as part of the canal property, was of no direct use to the railway. But the projectors of the line were shrewd enough to see

98. Robert Harrild (1780-1853).

97. The London and Croydon Railway in 1839. The view is south towards the Dartmouth Arms (Forest Hill) station, and the distant tower of St Bartholomew's church.

99. *The plan from George Allen's Park End sale of 1842. 'Frederic Place' was a very short-lived name for this part of Sydenham Park.*

that the two stations would create a demand for building land and good houses in their vicinity, and that this site between the two was ideally placed to exploit it. It was a fine site, certainly, but it was not immediately land. Even after the feeder streams had been diverted and the reservoir drained the muddy wilderness was scarcely calculated to appeal to developers or potential home owners. The malodorous wasteland must have been strewn with the dumped rubbish of thirty years, the remains of abandoned boats, and the bodies of drowned men and beasts. Before the reclaimed land could be offered for sale it was necessary to make the two basic roads, so that all the intended plots could have a useful frontage, and to provide "pleasingly scattered groups of flourishing ornamental plantation, studded with several thousands of fruit and forest trees, flowering shrubs, etc., of great beauty and variety", as the auctioneers were to describe the finished job.

The two original arteries were Park Road, now Sydenham Park Road, and the topically named Albert Road, now Sydenham Park.

The land, thus beautified "at considerable cost" was brought under the hammer in twenty-eight lots on the 9 July 1841. The principal purchasers, and developers of the estate, were Robert Harrild, Thomas Hunt, William Henry Whittle, and George Allen. Harrild (1780-1853), the printer and printing machinery manufacturer, who had lived at Round Hill House since the early 1820s, bought most of the plots at the northern end of the reservoir, directly opposite Round Hill. This may have been as much a decorative and defensive measure as an investment, to prevent developments of a kind liable to depress the value of his own house. For a time he kept deer at Redberry Grove. When he built on these plots, between 1845 and his death, it was mainly in the form of detached houses. One of them, Alpine Cottage, no. 4

100. *Nos. 5 and 6 Albion Villas (built for Robert Harrild c.1847) when they were being used as the Sydenham Home and Infirmary for Sick Children in the late 1870s.*

101. *Another of Robert Harrild's creations was Park Road Cottage, which stood next to Holy Trinity church, at the corner of Sydenham Park and Sydenham Park Road. It was demolished in the 1950s.*

Sydenham Park Road (*c.*1846) was intended for his son Horton. Shanklin Villa, no. 20 Sydenham Park Road, was built in 1855 by another son, Thomas Harrild.

Thomas Hunt, the second main developer, was the Sydenham Road builder, timber merchant, and brickmaker (*see p.*40). Park Terrace, the present 3 to 25 Sydenham Park, was built by him on his own land between 1842 and 1851. The present 3 and 5 were the first houses completed on the reservoir estate. There may have been a business connection between Hunt and William Henry Whittle, the third developer, who was another brickmaker, with extensive fields and kilns on the south side of London Road. Co-operation between the two men is suggested by the fact that the large houses built in 1843 on Whittle's land on the south-east side of Sydenham Park (now the site of Whittell Gardens, etc.) were soon afterwards owned by Hunt.

The fourth of the main early developers is the most interesting. George Allen (1798-1847) was an architect who specialised in warehouses and other commercial buildings, but is also known to have designed various villas and churches. Among the official appointments he enjoyed were those of Surveyor to the Parish of St Nicholas Deptford, to the Haberdashers' Company (major landowners at New Cross), and to the Deptford Creek Bridge Company. He had offices in Tooley Street, Southwark, but his burial at St Bartholomew's in

Sydenham suggests a close connection with the area at the time of his death. His principal landholding on the reservoir estate was in and around Park End, the cul-de-sac section of Sydenham Park that later led to the railway footbridge. He bought the land in 1841, created Park End, began the ornamental plantation intended to screen his development from the railway, and re-sold the property in small building plots, with suggestions for styles and layout, in 1842. The surviving 68 and 70 Sydenham Park and the demolished Park End House (no. 72) were built before Allen's death in 1847, and may well have been designed by him.

102. *Park End House, Sydenham Park, c.1900, with part of the surviving no. 70 on the right.*

103. Park Cottage, 59 Sydenham Park Road, in 1991.

It is even more likely that Allen was the architect of Park Cottage, 59 Sydenham Park Road, which was built in 1843, the year in which he sold the property to Edward Hinton, the first occupant.

There is the intriguing possibility that these four principal landowners were working in co-operation. A plutocrat, a brickmaker, a builder, and an architect would offer an ideal combination of talents for such a venture. Development on the reservoir estate proceeded briskly throughout the 1840s and '50s. Two houses were built c.1842, thirteen in 1843, and some sixteen more by 1847. In 1849 the total number was over fifty, and by 1851 over seventy. The likely role of George Allen as designer of some of the houses has already been mentioned. Another architect who may have been involved is Edwin Nash, who lived at the demolished 53 Sydenham Park (in Park End) from 1849 until 1857, when he moved to the Red House, Border Road, which he had built for himself on the Lawrie Park estate. This was a trend of the late 1850s, as Sydenham Park lost fashion and status to this new rival.

The growth of Sydenham and Forest Hill before and after the opening of the railway line can be measured fairly accurately. The 1818 and 1837 ratebooks include 231 and 461 houses, the 1841 census gives 576, the 1849 ratebook 753, and the 1851 census 870. An average of twelve new houses were being built each year in the first twenty years or so after the enclosure of the common, the figure had nearly doubled to twenty-three or four in the late 1830s and during most of the '40s, and by the end of the decade the rate of additions had risen to more than fifty. Throughout the period the great majority of these new houses were built on the former common, including the old canal reservoir. Before 1840 most were cottages and shops intended for working people earning a living in the Sydenham area. The three hundred added between 1841 and 1851 were chiefly houses of varying degrees of smartness intended for the commuting middle classes. Some 75 were built on the Sydenham Park reservoir estate alone. The population of Sydenham and Forest Hill was 2,900 in 1841 and 4,501 in 1851.

THE GOODWINS

Major figures in the development of Sydenham and Forest Hill during the 1840s and '50s were the Goodwin family. John Goodwin, who came from Abingdon in Berkshire, established himself in Lewisham c.1830, as a bricklayer. He lived next door to the Lion and Lamb public house in the High Street, and had a yard adjoining the pond of the Riverdale Mill. From 1840 he was heavily involved in the first substantial lower middle class housing scheme in the village, the creation of Avenue Road and its offshoots on what is now the site of the Lewisham Centre. This was a major landmark on Lewisham's road from Kentish village to London suburb.

John Goodwin had built up a large workforce (one hundred men in 1851) while engaged with Avenue Road. As opportunities on that estate declined he evidently cast his eyes towards Sydenham and Forest Hill, where the new railway had made the district suddenly attractive to City men. Like many another builder Goodwin found his ambition growing with his resources. His Avenue Road houses had scarcely required the services of an architect, but the middle class clients he hoped to attract at Sydenham and Forest Hill would have to be lured by individual features and modish touches in what was a very competitive market. It was common for upwardly mobile builders to educate a son to be an architect. Goodwin went one better by choosing that profession for his eldest and youngest sons, Edward and George, while William was trained to carry on the building business. He also established a connection with a rising young architect named Henry Edward Buckmaster Coe (1825-85), a pupil of Sir George Gilbert Scott. Although he was only a few years older Coe may have superintended the professional education of Edward and George Goodwin. One of them certainly entered into partnership with him.

104. Westwood Hill c.1915, showing the Church Meadow houses between St Bartholomew's and Jew's Walk.

LONDON ROAD AND CHURCH MEADOW

The first results of the Goodwins' arrangement with Coe were seen in London Road, Forest Hill, where they became involved during the late 1840s with the building of Prospect Villas on John Forster's land. The name 'Prospect Villas' was later extended to include fifteen houses on the south side of London Road, seven of them on land controlled by William Whittle, but it originally applied only to the four semi-detached pairs closest to the Dartmouth Road corner. Of these nos. 5 and 9 survive in tatters. John Goodwin built at least four of these eight substantial houses, and it seems almost certain that they were designed by Edward Goodwin and Henry Coe, for the two young architects were living in 5 and 6 Prospect Villas (later 9 and 11 London Road) in 1849, while the houses were still being built. No. 6 had been commissioned by a solicitor, Samuel Cotton of Lothbury, who moved in before the spring of 1851.

The Goodwins were outstripped here in Forest Hill by William Henry Whittle, who has already been encountered in Sydenham Park. By the mid-1830s he had bought four and a half acres on London Road from two beneficiaries of the enclosure, and had leased nearly twenty acres more from the Earl of St Germans and Thomas Watson

Parker, the Lewisham solicitor. The great brickfields Whittle established provided first the materials and then the site for nos. 29 to 87 London Road and the whole of the Queen's Road (Taymount Rise) estate. There were only six or seven houses in London Road when the Dartmouth Arms (Forest Hill) station opened in 1839. By 1851 there were thirty.

An architect who may have been employed in this development was one Stokes (possibly Montague Stokes), who was living at Gothic Cottage, now the site of 89/91 London Road, in 1851. Thomas Roger Smith (1830-1903), a far more eminent architect, must also have been involved in the growth of London Road, where he lived from 1858 until 1871. His house, which he presumably designed himself, was Laurel Bank, no. 92. It stood well back from the building line between the Horniman Gardens and Honor Oak Road. Smith lived here in the early part of his career, when local commissions must have been welcome. He went on to found and edit *The Architect*, and to design many important buildings in England and India. His son and partner, Professor Ravenscroft Elsey Smith (1859-1930), was born at Laurel Bank.

Whittle's large estate limited the opportunities

105. The former Prospect House and The Acacias, London Road, in 1991. They have long been combined as the flats now numbered 79.

of the Goodwin family in London Road, but they soon found new scope for their energies in Sydenham. Church Meadow, which comprised most of the land between Westwood Hill, Jew's Walk, Kirkdale, and St Bartholomew's Church, was made available for building by Samuel Forster in the late 1840s. John Goodwin took a lease and began work in 1850. Two houses, nos.26 and 28 Westwood Hill, were occupied by the spring of 1851, and nos.14 and 16 were also completed by John and William Goodwin before September of that year. The designs were presumably supplied by Henry Coe or one of the Goodwin brothers. Although the building firm seems to have withdrawn from the Church Meadow development in 1852 the similarity in style between 14 to 28 Westwood Hill, 1 to 13 Jew's Walk, and 180 to 186 Kirkdale suggests that the same architect was responsible for all these early 1850s houses.

Church Meadow was the last substantial result of the railway boom. As W.S.Clarke wrote in 1881:

"The opening of the Croydon (now Brighton) Railway in 1839, with a station at Sydenham, produced the buildings on the northern side of the road between the Greyhound and the corner of Wells-road and High-street, with the collateral branches of private residences; and the fashion set in among London tradesmen to live in Sydenham. These purchased large spaces for their private residences, giving the district its high reputation; which it has retained by its merit ever since, for it is one of the most delightful of suburban retreats."

The Church Meadow houses attracted several eminent residents in their early years, including Sir George Grove, Sir August Manns, and Henry Wyndham Phillips, the portrait painter.

PALACE MANIA

The railway boom was running at a rate of about fifty houses a year when the news broke in 1852 that the Crystal Palace was to be re-erected on Sydenham Hill. Judged in terms of the numbers of houses the effect was to double the speed of development. The increase in investment was far greater, because land prices had exploded, and the average house built in the 1850s was far larger than that of the 1840s. In 1851, twelve years after the coming of the railway, there were 870 houses in Sydenham and Forest Hill. By 1861 the number had leapt to 1,803, by 1863 it had reached 1,880, and in 1871 the total was a staggering 3,514. All these figures exclude Sydenham outside the Lewisham parish boundaries. This makes hardly any difference in 1851, but by 1861, with the development of Lawrie Park, Sydenham Hill, and Newlands Park, the Sydenham houses in Beckenham and Dulwich push the total increase in the decade to more than a thousand. Between 1861 and 1871 it was over one thousand seven hundred. The population was 10,718 in 1861 and 19,065 in 1871.

As early as 1858 a local writer was able to view this process with a degree of detachment and perspective.

"The great event in the history of Sydenham was the selection of the hill above it as the site for the Crystal Palace, the first column of which was raised on the 5th of August, 1852. Magnificent, and at first, alas! too visionary, were the anticipations of the promoters of this grand enterprise. The Crystal Palace was to be the nucleus of a new metropolis. Here, in fact, was to be new London; - that Old London, viewed seven miles away from the summit of the hill, was to be venerated as a relic of the past; it was to become again Londinium, more worthy of an antiquary's pilgrimage than Chester, Dover, or Winchester. These vague expectations wrought their own cure; they set a fancied value on the land, and building, which had commenced with spirit, received a severe but temporary check. More reasonable ideas, however, soon prevailed, and the result of the steady progress which then set in has been, that its steadiness is now almost forgotten, and the transition from the Sydenham of 1852, to the Sydenham of 1858, appears to have been effected by the stroke of an enchanter's wand."

The huge numbers of houses built in Sydenham and Forest Hill during the two decades of the Crystal Palace boom mean that only the most significant developments can be described here.

LAWRIE PARK

The Goodwin family apparently withdrew from the development of Church Meadow to pursue the greater prizes offered by Lawrie Park on the other side of Westwood Hill. Its closeness to the new wonder made this the most valuable site in Sydenham when the Crystal Palace Company found that it was surplus to requirements. As the 1858 writer described it:

"Having enclosed their Park, and reserved sufficient for the spacious roads which traverse the district, nearly all the remaining land between the Park and Westwood Hill was sold to Mr. George Wythes, at an increased price, for building purposes. Mr. Wythes was a sufferer from the depression or stagnation which ensued; but we are happy to say that he is now in a fair way to reap the reward of his spirit and enterprise. He has carried on, under the superintendence of his agent, Mr. West, a large manufacture of bricks on the upper part of this land; whilst below, between the church and the branch railway bridge, he has laid out roads rivalling those formed by the Company, and has erected, and is erecting, a number of elegant and spacious villas, letting at from £150 to £200, and even £250 a-year, and instead of seeking tenants as formerly, is now scarcely able to build rapidly enough to meet the demand. These villas are each provided with ample garden-ground, and are tastefully designed and substantially built. Some of the designs were furnished by Messrs. Banks and Barry, and serve to show that the refined taste of Sir Charles Barry, in the application of the Italian style, will not become extinct with himself. The new neighbourhood has been termed Lawrie Park, the land being part of that originally purchased from Mr. Lawrie."

The brickworks run by William West were in the angle of Westwood Hill and Crystal Palace Park Road. Charleville Circus was built across the site in the 1880s, as the final stage in this thirty-year process of development.

George Wythes (1811-1883) was the financier and planner behind the Lawrie Park estate, and in the first year or two he employed builders directly. Woodville and Elm Bank, the present 74 and 76 Lawrie Park Road, are an example of this method. Thomas Searles of Evelyn Street, Deptford, built

106. *Florian, formerly St Germains, Lawrie Park Avenue, in the 1890s. It was built by William Henry Goodwin in 1859, and demolished in the early 1950s.*

this pair for Wythes in 1856. But financial pressures soon forced him to adopt the safer method of granting building leases, and by 1857 the Goodwins had become the principal builders of the estate. William Henry Goodwin had taken over from his father, and he soon moved the business to Lawrie Park. In 1861 he built himself a fine mansion there, which survives as Cecil House, 191 Lawrie Park Gardens. William Goodwin shared it with his brother George, one of the two family architects, and it is reasonable to suppose that he provided the designs for many of the Goodwin houses built between 1857 and 1866. The firm are known to have been responsible for at least half of the fifty or so houses that appeared on the estate during that period, and it is probable that they built three quarters or more.

As W.S. Clarke recalled thirty years later:

107. *Cecil House, 191 Lawrie Park Gardens (William Goodwin's own residence) in 1992.*

108. *The Haven, formerly Willoughby House, no. 42 Crystal Palace Park Road, a Lawrie Park house built in 1860 and destroyed in the 1970s.*

"The transfer of the Palace produced little less than a craze in the public mind. The neighbouring proprietors were soon convinced by the sanguine promoters of that magnificent enterprise that their time had come; and hence the first idea of erecting the Palace on the Dulwich-road grew, until it seemed as if half Kent would be wanted to make a new heaven and a new earth. Mr Schuster made his very good bargain, and so did Mr Lawrie, by selling their entire estates to the Company; and the great grounds of the Palace were enclosed, a road was formed, now called Crystal Palace Park-road, which cut through the

109. *Lichfield House, 79 Lawrie Park Road, in 1991.*

Westwood and Lawrie Park Estates, and the off-ground was purchased by Mr George Wythes, the well-known contractor, who created Bickley and many other places. He put it into saleable form, made Avenue-road, Westwood-road, Lawrie Park-road, Border-road, and little fancy ins-and-outs; planted on them houses, some with two or three acres, and all with large grounds; these command rents from £120 to £300 and are let. He is the proprietor of most of them, and was well-nigh losing a lot of money when the fever went down; however, by holding on, a splendid property was secured... This part of Sydenham is very attractive from its retirement, its excellent conformation, and well-made roads."

Lawrie Park soon became the focus of a school of Sydenham architects, for there was much for them to do in this rich and growing suburb. At their head stood Charles Barry (1823-1900), President of the Royal Institute of British Architects, and the eldest son of Sir Charles Barry, the designer of the Palace of Westminster. Both men were surveyors to Dulwich College; the rapid development of its estate after 1852 made it convenient for the son to live in Sydenham, where he had relations, and that naturally produced local commissions. The part taken by Charles Barry and his partner Robert Banks in the design of the Lawrie Park houses has already been noted. Barry may have lived in Sydenham Park or Honor Oak Road c.1855 – the ratebook for that year lists a 'Charles Barry' in each. He was certainly at Lapsewood on Sydenham Hill throughout the 1860s and '70s, and in the 1890s he moved to Stanley House, 112 London Road, one of the properties that was demolished to enlarge the Horniman Gardens.

Second in importance was Henry Currey (1820-1900), a Vice-President of the RIBA, the architect of many public buildings, including St Thomas's Hospital on the Albert Embankment, and the man responsible for the design of Eastbourne. His known local works were the lych-gate at St Bartholomew's, which was built as a memorial to Mayow Wynell Adams, and (in conjunction with his son Percivall) the Sydenham Public Halls at the corner of Jew's Walk and Kirkdale. Henry and Percivall Currey came to live in Lawrie Park during the 1880s, the father at The Chestnuts in what is now Hall Drive, and the son at Pen Bryn in Border Crescent.

Locally, the most active of the group was Edwin Nash (1814-1884), a competent all-round architect who designed a number of buildings in Sydenham, including St Philip's Church (now demolished) and St Michael's Schools. He built the Red House, Border Road, for himself in 1857 (after eight years in Sydenham Park) and remained there at the centre of Lawrie Park for the rest of his life. It is unlikely that he designed any other houses on the estate, where the Red House stood out as a lonely Gothic rock in an Italianate sea.

A fourth member of the group was the Dublin-born engineer and architect, Joseph Fogerty (*c.*1832-1899). It is significant that when he became a fellow of the RIBA in 1880 his three proposers were Henry Currey, Edwin Nash, and Charles Barry. Fogerty lived at Ashbourne, the present 10 Lawrie Park Gardens *c.*1866 to 1889, and at Enderby, 7 Lawrie Park Road, during his last decade. This was one of the 24 houses built over the garden of the Old Cedars after its sale in 1888. (Under its later name of St Andrews, 7 Lawrie Park Road was occupied by W.G. Grace during his ten years in Sydenham.) The fact that Fogerty moved into one of these new houses suggests the possibility that he was the architect employed by Edward Van Vliet, the developer. Fogerty's chief local work was almost certainly Horner Grange, now the Sydenham High School for Girls, which was built in the early 1880s, next door to Ashbourne. Unfortunately the direct evidence only proves that he designed the stables, the winter garden, and other outbuildings in 1889.

Two more architects who lived on the Lawrie Park estate were John Norton and James Tolley, senior. Norton was the man responsible for the extraordinary series of houses on the south side of Crystal Palace Park Road (*see p.106*). While he was planning that great enterprise in the late 1860s and early '70s he was conveniently placed at Lichfield House, now 79 Lawrie Park Road. By 1876 he had moved to one of his own creations, St Helens, 55 Crystal Palace Park Road, now replaced by garages. Tolley, who was district surveyor, designed several shops and other premises in Kirkdale, including the London and South Western Bank. It was built in 1875, and closed by Barclays in 1998. After living in Westwood Hill during the earlier '70s, Tolley moved to The Chestnuts, Hall Drive, a house later occupied by Henry Currey.

110. *Longton Grove in 1964, shortly before all the houses on the right were demolished. The view is eastwards from an upper window of no. 64, which was also doomed. The shadow of the distinctive turret of no. 66 can be seen in the foreground.*

111. Rosslyn Villa, 1 Longton Grove, at the corner of Jew's Walk, another house that was demolished in the 1960s.

THE FORSTER FARM ESTATE

The news about the Crystal Palace was the signal to Major Forster of Southend Hall that his family's patient wait was over. The greater part of their Sydenham Common farm land was immediately offered for sale on 99-year building leases. The most valuable section, because it was the closest to the Palace, was the West Hill Estate, consisting of Longton Grove, Longton Avenue, and parts of Westwood Hill and Jew's Walk. Here the new roads were laid out by Forster's surveyor, Francis Sadleir Brereton (1838-1911), who also provided model designs for the quality of houses expected. Nearly all of the early development on this estate was undertaken by a firm of Paddington builders, Charles and Frederick Sewell of Charles Street, Westbourne Terrace. Their first houses were completed in 1854.

The 1858 commentator described the early results of their efforts:

> "Above the Jew's Walk the hill is termed West Hill, or Westwood-Hill, and on the right hand is occupied by a number of newly-built villas of great variety of design, erected by the late Mr. Sewell, the owner of the land, and leading upwards to the Longton Hotel, a very superior and admirably conducted establishment, also erected by Mr. Sewell, and carried on by his brother, Mr. C.E. Sewell. In ordinary phrase we may say that this extensive hotel is replete with every convenience, and externally it has all the appearance of an elegant private residence.
>
> Forming a crescent-like curve from the Longton Hotel, we have a fine road, planted with limes, and descending at the back of the hill into the Jew's Walk; and here are a number of detached villas, also erected by the spirit and enterprise of

Mr. Sewell. A great amount of taste and fancy is displayed in the villas and other buildings in this neighbourhood. The Tudor or Old English Style prevails in most of them – walls of red brick or stone, with mullioned windows and ornamental dressings – towers, turrets, slated gables, and ridge-tiles meet the eye in every direction. Variety is occasionally carried too far into irregularity; but, upon the whole, the effect is already highly satisfactory, and will be still more so when time shall have toned down (as it will do, even in the pure atmosphere of Sydenham) the dazzling whiteness of some portions of the stonework."

SYDENHAM HILL

Eight houses already existed on the eastern side of Sydenham Hill, in the parish of Lewisham, when the new Crystal Palace was opened. Nearly all the landowners were spurred into immediate action and by 1860 development was practically complete, with only St Mary's, the house designed in 1852 by Father Frederick Faber (1814-1863) as a country retreat for the Brompton Oratory, offering any resistance to the process. For nearly a century after 1860 activity on this side of the road was practically confined to the odd rebuilding of a single house.

Almost the whole of the western side of Sydenham Hill, in the parish of Camberwell, was occupied by Dulwich Wood, the property of Dulwich College. Before 1852 the only house here was Holly Brow, the present no. 135, which had its origin in the cottage attached to an Admiralty signalling station at the summit of the hill. The coming of the Crystal Palace spurred the college Governors into action, and during the late 1850s and early '60s such advertisements as this were regular features of local publications:

112. The garden front of Beechgrove, 111 Sydenham Hill, one of the lavish houses built in Dulwich Wood in the 1860s.

"DULWICH WOOD, BUILDING LAND - Eligible plots of land for building villas upon this property, in the immediate neighbourhood of the Crystal Palace, and of the Gipsy Hill Station, on the West End Railway, may now be obtained."

The Governors had an unusual extra inducement to offer. The growing reputation of Dulwich College after its reform in 1857 had resulted in a waiting list for admission, and Charles Barry, the Surveyor, was authorised to offer guaranteed places to the sons of those commissioning villas on the Dulwich Wood estate.

Progress was slow during the 1850s, but faster in the next decade. Ten houses on the west side of Sydenham Hill were occupied in 1862, 17 in 1864, and 24 in 1869. That was the end of large-scale development, for the total had only risen to 34 by the end of the century. The resulting houses, very few of which survive, were large and ostentatious. Lapsewood is the one to be most regretted, as it was presumably designed by Charles Barry, the first occupant.

THE TWO EARLS IN FOREST HILL
The most prominent luxury development in Forest Hill was Dartmouth Park, the present Sunderland Road, Westbourne Drive, Waldram Park Road, Church Rise, and South Road. The estate was built over Pickthorns, the sixty acres of half-year land (semi-common) that became the freehold property of the Earl of Dartmouth after the enclosure. The contractor William Colson took a lease of Pickthorns in the 1840s, and was probably the practical man behind the layout of the estate. He was certainly making bricks here in the 1850s, and was one of the first five Dartmouth Park residents. Another important figure in this development, as in many others in Forest Hill, was Robert James Chaplin of Stanstead Road. Five houses had been completed by 1854, and at least 25 were occupied only four years later. Early residents included the tea-importing Tetley brothers, Edward and John, who lived in adjoining houses in Sunderland Road.

Dartmouth Park was given focus by the prominent sacred and profane buildings that occupied the highest ground. Christ Church (designed by Ewan Christian) was the exact contemporary of the new Crystal Palace, for the foundation stone was laid in 1852 and the consecration was in 1854. Lord Dartmouth had given the site, moved by piety, no doubt, but also by the common Victorian belief that a church was the essential first ingredient for a successful new suburb. Until the spire was completed in 1885 Christ Church was not the most

prominent building on the top of the hill, for directly opposite stood Red Hall (later known as Tudor Hall, *ill. 135*), which was first occupied in 1855 by one Matilda Murray. This was possibly the Hon. Amelia Matilda Murray (1795-1884), the slavery abolitionist, who was maid of honour to Queen Victoria from 1837 until 1856. She returned from her American tour in October 1855.

Lewisham's other noble landowner, the Earl of St Germans, was also busy in Forest Hill in the 1850s, when he named two developments in his own honour. Eliot Bank still recalls the earl's family name, but the more important 'St Germans Park' did not last long. After spells as The Drive and Semaphore Hill the new road became Honor Oak Park. The man behind this estate was the architect and surveyor Richard James Woodcock, who took part of Telegraph Field on a building lease in 1850. He proceeded to make bricks on the land, for which he paid the earl a royalty of one shilling per thousand. The first six houses were built in 1856.

Observatory House, the largest, stood at the top of the hill, where its gates still survive opposite the convent. It brought an influential new figure into the picture, for the engineer and astronomer Edwin Clark (1814-1894) probably built it for himself, as a place from which to make the observations of comets that he communicated to the Royal Astronomical Society. He used a telescope bought with a legacy of £2000 left to him by Robert Stephenson. Clark soon took over the whole development from Woodcock, and eventually built many houses in Honor Oak Park. Another architect involved was William Morphew, later of Sevenoaks, who was living here by 1857, in one of the large semi-detached houses on the northern side. In 1859 Morphew took the building lease that resulted in Fawley Lodge, one of the largest houses, and he probably designed others.

SOUTH SYDENHAM PARK
The last major development during the Crystal Palace boom years transformed the northern part of the Mayow estate. Alexander Gordon Hennell (1838-1915), an architect with offices in Chancery Lane, had moved to Sydenham from Wandsworth in 1863. He lived first at Rothsay Villa, Park End (the cul-de-sac section of Sydenham Park, leading down to the railway), and gazing across the tracks to the farmland opposite perhaps suggested the idea of a development opportunity. 'South Sydenham Park', the thoroughly inaccurate name he gave to the new estate, seems to indicate such an association in his mind, as does the prominent

part he played in establishing the footbridge between the two areas.

Hennell quickly came to terms with the Wynell Mayow and Dacres Adams owners of the land, and set about the creation of the roads named after them. As the writer of his obituary recalled fifty years later:

> "Hennell became actively engaged in the work of developing South Sydenham-park, now bordered by the railway, the recreation ground in Mayow-road, and Perry Vale, and designed practically all the large houses and mansions which have been erected on the estate, which, when Mr Hennell first came to live in the neighbourhood, was simply fields and meadow land".

In 1863 nothing had been done towards the creation of South Sydenham Park. By 1867 27 houses were occupied in Wynell Road, and at the northern ends of Dacres Road and Mayow Road. Hennell built a house for himself, Oakwood, no. 16 Mayow Road (later part of St Winefride's Convent), in 1868, and lived there until his death. Development continued at a more leisurely pace after 1870, with the creation of Inglemere Road and Bampton Road to open up the interior of the estate. Most of the houses in these two roads were built by Andrew Black of Perry Vale, beginning in 1875. Hennell educated his son Alexander Robert as an architect, and by the end of the century they were working in partnership. The Hennells were not the only South Sydenham Park architects. Saratoga in Dacres Road was the home of Thomas Aldwinckle (1843/4-1920), who designed two prominent public buildings in Dartmouth Road, the Forest Hill Baths in 1884-5 and Louise House, the Girls' Industrial Home, in 1890-91.

DINOSAURS

The Crystal Palace boom might be said to end with the 1860s. The population and the number of houses more than doubled between 1851 and 1861, and nearly doubled from 1861 to 1871. In the next decade the rate of growth was far less dramatic, largely because fresh building land on the former common was becoming scarce. When development picked up again in the 1880s and '90s it included far more small houses, often built over the grounds of demolished mansions in Lower Sydenham. In 1881 the population was 26,054, and the number of houses 4,920. By 1891 the figures were 34,162 and 6,485.

The production of large houses did not cease after 1870. Some of the area's most extravagant

113. *For the purpose of this impression, published in 1873, John Norton brought together three of his mansions from different parts of Crystal Palace Park Road. The houses, all viewed from the garden and park side, were (from left to right) 29, 69 and 51. No. 69 is the only survivor.*

mansions were built towards the end of the nineteenth century, but only in Dacres Road, Silverdale and Crystal Palace Park Road were significant numbers of them on fresh sites. The plutocrats who settled in Upper Sydenham in the 1880s and '90s stamped their personalities on the district – unattractive personalities to judge them on their results – by rebuilding houses on a greatly enlarged scale. Westwood House (1881), Burnage Court, Lawrie

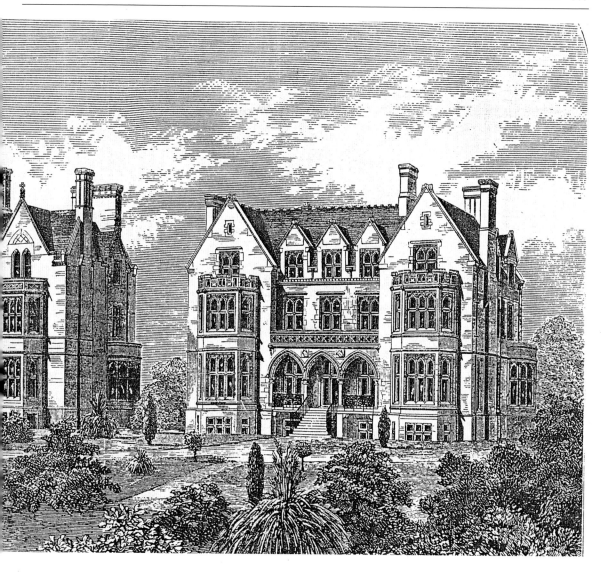

Park Avenue (1888), and Castlebar (1879) and The Cedars (1898) in Sydenham Hill, were all examples of this trend. Most of these dinosaurs passed into institutional use after the deaths of their creators, for the few men wealthy enough to buy them could equally well afford to pursue their own fantasies.

During this period the most important new initiative in the field of quality housing was the development of the south side of Crystal Palace Park Road, principally in the 1870s. The Company had not intended to build here, but the financial problems of the Palace forced the hand of the directors. In 1868 they evidently decided that if there had to be houses around the park they would at least be exceptional houses, and John Norton (1823-1904) found himself with a commission that might be any architect's dream. His job was to design dozens of lavish mansions in a continuous sequence ranged along half a mile of rising and gently curving road. The houses were to exhibit a general uniformity of style, Gothic and fantastic, but within that framework Norton was free to employ infinite variety of external detail and internal planning. Even after the ravages of bomb damage and post-war demolition the surviving houses are one of the outstanding features of the Sydenham area.

A PARK TOO FAR

The fortunes made, or suspected, in Lawrie Park, Westwood Hill, and other favoured areas during the Crystal Palace boom, were the cause of much jealousy in Lower Sydenham, where the Crystal Palace Gas Company's works threatened to have a very different effect on land values. Some proprietors made a realistic assessment of their prospects. Paxton Park, a cheap and cheerless group of 1850s artisan terraces, was an example of this. Its nominal tribute to the Palace's creator was distinctly maladroit. But closer to Bell Green, encouraged by the opening of Lower Sydenham station in 1857, several landowners were determined to struggle for a larger share of the bonanza.

One scheme brought a famous architect into brief and unhappy association with Sydenham. Sir James Knowles (1831-1908), who went on to a second career as the brilliant editor of *The Nineteenth Century*, was hired in 1861 by a shady developer named William Woodgate, to design the Champion Park estate. Woodgate had bought The Lawn, one of the great houses of Sydenham Road (*see p.25*), "as a Building Speculation".

The Lawn was immediately demolished to allow what is now Champion Road to be formed across its site. In 1862 it was replaced in a slightly different position by an equally large mansion that was called Champion Hall. Knowles may possibly have been the architect of that fine house, which was built by Piper and Wheeler of Bishopsgate Street. It later became the Sydenham Children's Hospital. Knowles undoubtedly designed the Church of St Michael and All Angels, which was built in 1863 as the intended centrepiece of this prestige estate. The kind of resident Woodgate hoped to attract is indicated by his calculation that he would rapidly recoup the £4000 spent on the church out of his share of the pew rents. In the event not a single builder was prepared to speculate in the quality of houses Woodgate and Knowles had in mind, and it was not until the 1870s that a few modest terraces began to appear. By that time Knowles had withdrawn in disgust, and probably unpaid, and Octavius Hansard (1826-97)

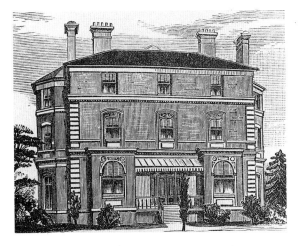

114. Champion Hall shortly after it became the Sydenham Home and Infirmary for Sick Children in 1885.

had taken his place. Thirty years after the building of the church the Champion Park estate, even on this reduced scale, was only half completed, and as late as 1908 the pew rents amounted to a mere £9 per annum.

Another example of ambitious failure in Lower Sydenham is provided by Fairlawn Park, which was named and laid out in a style usually associated with far larger houses than are found there. The discrepancy arose because the churchwardens of St Olave's, Southwark, the trustees of the land, had decided to build as early as 1843, and set out the basic road pattern not long afterwards. In 1869 they agreed with a developer to the construction of eighty houses at a cost of £400 each. He completed the roads and sewers, but could find no clients for houses of that size – now that the gas company was making its distinctive contribution to the quality of life at Bell Green – and had built none by 1880. He then asked for modified terms and was allowed to build a larger number of houses at a cost of £250 each. Work began at once, and eventually about 165 houses and shops were squeezed in.

115. *The Crystal Palace in 1854. The north transept, in the centre of the print, was destroyed in the fire of December 1866.*

Musical and Social Life 1850-1900

THE PALACE OF MUSIC

When a memorial concert of the music of Sir Arthur Sullivan, who had died on 22 November 1900, was given at the Crystal Palace on the 8th of December, it was also a symbolic farewell to the great days of Sydenham, with which Sullivan had been so closely associated. Thirty-eight years earlier the same conductor and orchestra, in the same building, had won overnight fame for the young composer by their performance of his *Tempest* music. In 1900 few of Sullivan's local friends survived to mourn him. The most devoted of them all, Sir George Grove, had died six months before his famous protégé. The conductor, Sir August Manns, was about to retire from his post at the Crystal Palace, and had only seven years to live. The

Saturday Orchestra, which he had raised to international renown, was being disbanded, and the Palace was sinking into terminal decline, taking Sydenham and its other satellite suburbs with it. The vivacity of the music can have done little to lighten the gloom of the occasion.

It was a sad contrast to the boundless hopes that George Grove had brought to Sydenham in 1852, on his appointment as Secretary to the rebuilt Crystal Palace. In those exciting early years the directors of the new marvel believed that it was destined to lead the world in every branch of art and science. That music should be the field in which their dreams came closest to realisation was a mere accident, and the more unlikely in that the provision of a band had been nearly overlooked in their initial planning. It was only the imminence of the opening ceremony in 1854 that opened the eyes of Samuel Laing and his colleagues to the omission. An extraordinary collection of 62 brass instruments, one piccolo, and two clarinets was hastily scraped together, and Herr Schallehn, the bandmaster of the 17th Lancers, was appointed conductor on a casual royal recommendation. From

116. *August Manns c.1861.*

117. *Sir George Grove.*

this unpromising origin sprang the finest orchestra the country had ever known.

Schallehn made only one contribution to the success of the Crystal Palace music, but it was decisive. As his assistant he appointed another German military bandmaster, August Manns (1825-1907). The fact that Schallehn almost immediately stole one of Manns's compositions for publication under his own name, and then sacked his subordinate for daring to complain, was only a temporary setback. A year later, in October 1855, Schallehn was dismissed and Manns recalled to replace him. A week after his return he mounted his first concert, of which one half featured a string orchestra, made up of the more versatile wind players and some reinforcements from London. In February 1856 he was able to give the first British performance of Schumann's fourth symphony, and in April that of Schubert's great C minor, then considered an almost impossibly difficult work for even the most experienced orchestra.

George Grove (1820-1900) was largely responsible for the recall of Manns, and it was the stimulating, if not always entirely harmonious, relationship between them that made the Saturday concerts so outstanding. Manns provided the musical contacts and the genius for orchestral training, Grove the ideas, enthusiasm, and social skills that attracted an influential audience to Sydenham. Friction arose because Manns sometimes thought that Grove was gaining more than his fair share of the credit for the glories of the Crystal Palace music.

Grove was an engineer by training, and at one time worked as assistant to Edwin Clark, later of Honor Oak Park (*see p.103*). But a lack of rapid advancement in his profession led him to accept the post of secretary to the Society of Arts, as successor to John Scott Russell, and the involvement of the Society with the planning of the Exhibition of 1851 gave him an important role in that great event. When the Crystal Palace Company was formed to move the exhibition building from Hyde Park to Sydenham Hill, Grove was offered the secretaryship at a minimum salary of £600 per annum. That was in May 1852. By October he was established in his new home at 1 Church Meadow, now 14 Westwood Hill. Manns lived mostly at various addresses in Norwood, but for a time in the 1860s he settled just around the corner at Athol Lodge, the present 174 Kirkdale.

London was starved of good music in the second quarter of the nineteenth century. The Philharmonic Society's concerts were exclusive and expensive, and Jullien's Promenade Concerts at the Surrey Gardens had rather the format of music hall performances, and were not many notches above their level in quality. The standard programme featured a large number of short orchestral, instrumental, and vocal items, with a heavy emphasis on ballads sung by the favourite soloists of the day. Manns and his orchestra provided similar fare in their weekday entertainment of visitors to the Palace. On Saturdays, although the directors, and even Grove at first, were dubious, Manns decided to break the mould by presenting the best of recent and contemporary music with an enlarged orchestra, and his enterprise met with an enthusiastic welcome. As a critic recalled in 1908:

"One must go back a long way thoroughly to understand what a boon the Saturday Concerts were to amateurs who hungered and thirsted after better things than could be found in town. Orchestral concerts in London through the winter were like the proverbial visits of angels.... This state of things sufficiently accounted for the

Saturday rushes to Sydenham, not only of cultivated amateurs, but of professionals also ... All that was great in the London musical world might have been seen at Victoria Station on the winter Saturdays as the special trains were backing to the departure platforms.... It was not a company of many opinions, but a band of worshippers, having one faith and one soul."

The cheapness of the Crystal Palace concerts should not be exaggerated. They were very reasonable for the middle class Sydenham and Forest Hill residents, many of whom were season ticket holders, or subscribers to the series, but less so for the poor music lover travelling from town. As Bernard Shaw calculated it in 1885: "These concerts are not cheap enough for the people. A Crystal Palace Saturday Popular, taking place on a half-crown day, with an extra charge for admission to the concert room, a sixpenny programme, and a railway journey makes a larger hole in half a sovereign than many amateurs care to make in five shillings." The sixpenny programmes were an essential expense, because the notes written by Sir George Grove were one of the most celebrated features of the Saturday concerts, and a vital el-

118. *Even more popular than the Saturday concerts were the three-day Handel festivals held in the great central transept, and they continued after the disbandment of the Saturday orchestra. This view of one of the Edwardian festivals shows the orchestra, the choir, and the Great Handel Organ.*

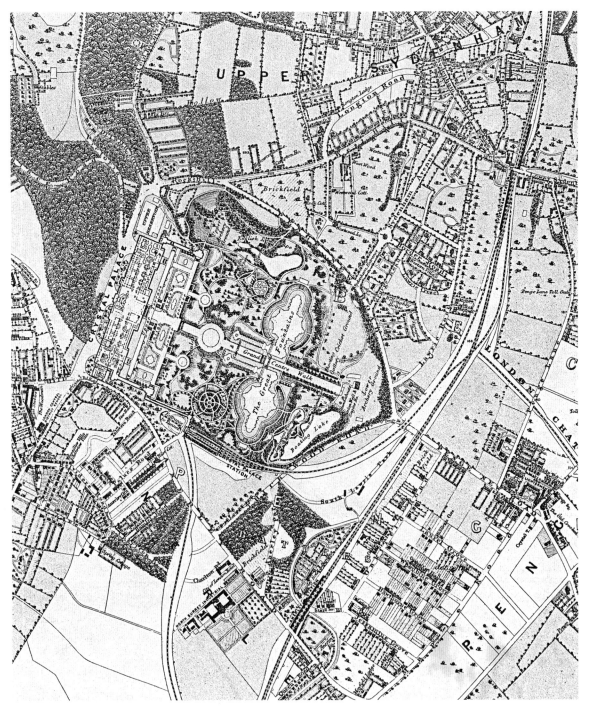

119. *The Crystal Palace and Upper Sydenham in the late 1850s. Westwood Lodge is marked. Peak Hill Lodge is below the 'M' of SYDENHAM*

ement in their mission to create a public for the best music. Grove's famous *Dictionary of Music and Musicians*, still the standard authority in the field, began merely as an extension and expansion of these notes.

A great parade of continental composers and performers came to the Palace at the invitation of Manns, many of them to conduct their own works. Meyerbeer was the first, in 1859, followed by Clara Schumann, who was to be a regular soloist, Joseph Joachim, Gounod, Bruckner, who gave organ recitals, Anton Rubenstein, Max Bruch, Massenet, Saint-Saëns, Dvorak, Liszt, and Paderewski. To see and hear these legendary musicians, and to absorb new works by Brahms, Wagner, Berlioz, Strauss, and many others, was an unprecedented opportunity for young British aspirants, and helped prepare the national revival at the end of the century. For those sufficiently determined, far more serious difficulties than the ones mentioned by Shaw proved no deterrent when such riches were on offer. One English composer recalled:

> "I lived 120 miles from London. I rose at six, walked a mile to the railway station, the train left at seven; arrived at Paddington about eleven, underground to Victoria, on to the Palace arriving in time for the last three quarters of an hour of the rehearsal; if fortune smiled this piece of rehearsal included a work desired to be heard, but fortune rarely smiled and more often than not the principal item was over. Lunch, concert at three. At five a rush to Victoria, then to Paddington, on to Worcester, arriving at 10.30. A strenuous day indeed; but a new work had been heard and another treasure added to a life's experience."

Who was this enthusiast? Edward Elgar, who later spent some months living within a stone's throw of the Palace, and devouring all the rehearsals and concerts.

The provincial Elgar, the greatest of them all, was the only significant British composer of the period overlooked by August Manns. With this serious exception, the German conductor was a wonderfully generous and discerning promoter of the music of his adopted country. For the first twenty years of the Saturday concerts the chief hopes of serious British music rested on the shoulders of young Arthur Sullivan (1842-1900), who was the most important native talent introduced to the public by Grove and Manns.

MUSICAL FAMILIES

Sullivan was a part of the Crystal Palace music from the beginning, for as a young chorister he sang in the opening ceremony of 1854, and he also performed in the first of the immensely popular Handel festivals, in 1857. Grove and he met in 1861, shortly after Sullivan's return from his studies in Leipzig. His graduation piece had been incidental music to *The Tempest*, written in imitation of Mendelssohn's *Midsummer Night's Dream*. Grove and Manns liked the work, and decided to make it the centrepiece of a Saturday concert on 5 April 1862, when Sullivan was still only nineteen. The success was immediate. "At the conclusion there was a loud call for 'the composer' who, being led forward by Herr Manns, was greeted with the heartiest applause on all sides." Sullivan's name was made, and the Grove/Manns policy of fostering native talent established.

Sullivan became more closely associated with the Palace than any living composer. Not only was his music frequently performed there – his symphony and cello concerto were premiered in 1866 – but he acted as accompanist at vocal recitals, and was professor of pianoforte and ballad singing at the Crystal Palace School of Art, Science, and

120. Arthur Sullivan in 1864.

Literature. Once or twice, when Manns was ill, Sullivan conducted a Saturday concert, and late in life he became a director of the Crystal Palace Company. During the 1860s Sydenham was his second home. For long periods he stayed as a guest at the house near Bell Green to which Grove had moved in 1860, and while writing his *Sapphire Necklace* in 1862-3 "he took rooms over a shop in Sydenham Road, to be near his kind friend Grove, at whose house he almost lived".

Grove's social talents and influential position had made his home the centre of intellectual life in the district, even when he lived in the comparatively small house in Westwood Hill. At Lower Sydenham he had much more space, and soon began to entertain the many famous men and women who came to perform at the Crystal Palace, or to swell the audience. Young, handsome, charming, and famous, Sullivan became the most popular figure in this circle, especially with the ladies. Even Grove's chilly wife loved him. Writing many years later to one of his Royal College of Music students, Grove recalled the impact that Sullivan had on his own mind and spirit:

"To me he is always what he was in 1863, when I first knew him – the same simple, good, gay creature that he was then. That was the second youth of my life. Everything budded and blossomed to me, and for the first time, though then forty-three, I understood poetry, music – all the world, and Sullivan is bound up with it..."

The Crystal Palace boom brought many cultivated people into the area, but à certain snobbery maintained the distinction between them and the families that arrived during the railway boom. Those ten or fifteen years were equivalent to a social gulf. One of the most prominent of the 'old' families was that of Robert von Glehn, a German

121. Peak Hill Lodge before 1886.

merchant who moved to a house in Sydenham Road (*see p.37*) *c.*1840, and soon afterwards took a sixty-year lease of Peak Hill Lodge. Louise Creighton, one of his daughters, later recalled the Sydenham social scene in the years around 1860:

"In Sydenham itself my parents had a small and select circle of friends consisting of the old inhabitants of the place, the 'first families' who always kept themselves very distinct from the suburban population which in time grew up in Sydenham ... My parents, with the Rowlands, Davidsons and Scott Russells, met weekly during the winter at one anothers' houses for what was called a reading party, when some book was read aloud and discussed. These reading parties were given up as the young people grew up, but the families remained on terms of close intimacy till death. The Rowlands and Davidsons had no children, but the Scott Russells had three daughters, beautiful and brilliant girls, and one son, who were close friends and companions of my elder brothers and sisters. Among other Sydenham friends were Henry Philips, the artist, and his wife, and probably chief of all, George Grove, the secretary of the Crystal Palace, who settled at Sydenham in 1852. Mr Grove delighted in my mother's talk and as the years went on, his intimacy with the family only deepened, his friendship with my sister Mimi was the closest. In the days of my girlhood he used to call every morning at our house on his way to the Crystal Palace and sometimes in the evening also, and would often stay for a long talk."

Charles Davidson and David Rowland, a barrister and a solicitor, lived next door to one another at the Old Grange and the Cottage in Sydenham Hill. Henry Wyndham Phillips (1820-68), the artist, lived at 24 Westwood Hill in the late 1850s, while George Grove, whose portrait he painted, was at no.14. For the last six or seven years of his life Phillips moved to the much larger Hollow Coomb, near the top of Westwood Hill. John Scott Russell (1808-82), the naval architect and engineer, was one of several original directors of the Crystal Palace Company who were established in Sydenham before the Great Exhibition. He lived at Bounds Cottage, at the corner of Kirkdale and Charlecote Grove, *c.*1847 to 1852, and then at Westwood Lodge, a house that he built between Crystal Palace Park Road and Westwood Hill, on land leased from the Company. In the 1850s the other prominent house was Rockhills, where Sir Joseph Paxton frequently entertained the Duke of Devonshire.

122. John Scott Russell c.1850.

EMOTIONAL ENTANGLEMENTS

Arthur Sullivan soon became as intimate with the von Glehns and the Scott Russells as he was with the Groves. "Sullivan was in and out of these three homes as an ever welcome guest, for he had a charm that was irresistible." One of the von Glehn daughters recalled that:

"we used to indulge a good deal in private theatricals ... and on a few occasions Sullivan would act with us – but the memorable occasion was the first (or nearly the first) performance of 'Box and Cox' at our house, in which Sullivan played Box, Fred Clay, Cox and Norman Scott Russell, Bouncer; while Franklin Taylor officiated as orchestra. Both Sullivan and Clay had voices of great beauty, and this delightful operetta went with a charm and go which I don't think has been equalled by any other performers since."

Freddie Clay, a popular composer of songs and ballads, was Sullivan's closest friend, and the pianist Franklin Taylor had been his fellow student in Leipzig.

The von Glehns and Scott Russells were musical families, and attended all the Saturday concerts, rallying round the enthusiastic figure of George Grove in his seat in the gallery. Grove's ambition was "to keep a boy's heart to the end of life". Afterwards there were delightfully intricate walks in which the young people could lose themselves on their way back to Westwood Lodge or Peak Hill. Soon Freddie Clay paired off with Alice Scott Russell, and Sullivan with her sister Rachel. She was intensely earnest, and used all her influence to persuade Sullivan to be a serious composer, and not to waste his talents on anything frivolous like operetta.

The von Glehn and Scott Russell sisters were not the heiresses that their opulent homes may have suggested. Robert von Glehn's mercantile house was in gradual decline, and John Scott Russell was never far from the bankruptcy courts. The girls' parents, and especially Mrs Scott Russell, were therefore anxious to see them make prudent marriages. Freddie Clay, a wealthy dilettante composer, and the son of a fashionable MP, was an acceptable suitor, but this was not the case with Sullivan. He had only his wits to live on, and his father was an Irish bandsman. He and Rachel planned to marry when he had "any *settled* thing like a conductorship", but three years of waiting put a great strain on their emotions, especially as Rachel could never be confident of what the inconstant Sullivan was up to in London. How was she to make sure of him? In 1867 the couple became lovers in the modern as well as the Victorian sense. And then Mrs Scott Russell learned the truth, and Sullivan was expelled from Westwood Lodge.

The affair dragged on for three more years in defiance of parental authority, but as Sullivan's opportunities for seeing Rachel declined and his opportunities for meeting other women increased,

123. Westwood Lodge c.1913.

relations became more and more strained. In 1868 the eldest sister, Louise, became involved as go-between and mediator and fell in love with Sullivan herself. He was willing enough to encourage her; but Sullivan could not confine himself even to the two sisters. Louise was quickly disillusioned, and by 1870 even Rachel was reconciled to her loss. Freddie Clay, whose engagement with Alice Scott Russell had been entered into under the influence of his domineering friend, also backed out, and Alice consoled herself with other admirers, including John Millais, for whom she posed. The musical idyll of Westwood Lodge was ending on a sour note.

The middle aged Grove, unhappy in his marriage, and devastated by the death of his daughter Lucy in 1863, was also caught up in the emotional turbulence. At first he had been attracted to Louise Scott Russell, and his friends had to warn him of the dangers of his visits to Westwood Lodge, his 'daily transit of Venus'. But in 1863 he transferred his interest to Mimi von Glehn, a pianist of outstanding gifts, and this relationship continued to be the absorbing personal interest of his life until the 1880s.

> "The first real moment in my life came when I was 43 years old, when my Lucy died, and I became madly in love with Mimi von Glehn. *There* was a passion! It lasted twenty years and more – till her death, and with it came my first real insight into music, poetry, nature – everything."

It will be noticed that Grove associated this 1860s awakening equally with Mimi von Glehn and Arthur Sullivan (*see p.112, col.1*).

In the 1870s the emphasis of intellectual life in Sydenham began to change from music to literature. Grove had become editor of *Macmillan's Magazine* in 1868, and in 1873 he resigned as Secretary to the Crystal Palace. Although he joined the board and continued to write the programme notes for the Saturday Concerts, his new responsibilities and contacts meant that his parties at Lower Sydenham were now attended by as many writers as musicians. A curate of St Bartholomew's recalled his introduction to this society in 1869:

> "There was no pretence about anything: no starch or stiffness, no dulness. After dinner we all went out into the garden. We talked, and smoked, and had tea. There were endless stories, and endless jokes, Sir George taking the lead, but just as good a listener as he was a talker, till at length came eleven o'clock – what might be described as 'closing time' on Saturday evenings at Lower Sydenham – when the Londoners had to

leave in order to catch the 11.22 train to Victoria. Each party, nay each individual if he went alone, was accompanied to the gate by our host – a parting word on his lips for everybody. I can see him now:- to those he was fondest of, his usual valediction, seizing one's hand in both of his, was – 'good-bye, good-bye, God bless you!'... Many were the distinguished people I met – Arthur Sullivan, John Hullah, Henry Leslie, Joachim, L.Straus, Stockhausen, Gounod, Ferdinand Hiller, W.H.Lecky, F.W.Myers, Holman Hunt, to speak of no others prominent in art, science, and literature."

Some visitors not included in this list were Browning, Arthur Penrhyn Stanley, Hubert Parry, and Anton Rubenstein, who destroyed Grove's piano by the violence of his playing.

At Peak Hill Lodge the composers were succeeded by the historians. Louise Creighton, who came to the fore in the late 1860s, was less musical than her elder sisters, and more intellectual. The Rev. John Richard Green, author of *A Short History of the English People* remembered "the steady right-mindedness of a certain Louise von Glehn, moving amidst that sceptical self-indulgent circle, with her resolute spirit of love and duty". Green first visited Peak Hill Lodge when he was in his late twenties, and Louise thirteen. Many years later she wrote that:

> "He had great sympathy with young girls and soon won my unbounded devotion. He talked to me about my reading and my studies, told me books to read and gave me much wise advice and showed me much affection. The nature of the friendship changed a little as I grew up. Mr Green liked tender relations with young women and during the long years of his friendship with our family, his friendship with Olga, Mimi and me passed through many phases. I remember at one time being afraid that it was going further than I desired and drawing back a little..."

Green began a correspondence with Louise and her sister Olga, and the contrast between his letters to each is remarkable. To Louise he was always didactic, to Olga playful and flippant. One of his few serious letters to Olga was written to oppose the idea that Louise should visit Oxford:

> "Of course your mother will whistle Miss L's plans of 'a year at Oxford' down the wind. As to 'studying' there are a thousandfold better lectures to be got in London than in Oxford, and the society of Peak Hill is of a healthier intellectual type, because of a far broader intellectual type... Deutsch is a greater scholar, Haweis a

124. Mandell Creighton.

greater wit, and George Grove a more accomplished person than any three men she could meet at Oxford..."

Green's instinct was right, if not his information. Louise did go to Oxford, and there she met a better historian, and a more mature man. The Rev. Mandell Creighton, who went on to write the *History of the Papacy*, joined the Peak Hill set, cut out Green, and married Louise at St Bartholomew's in 1872. He rose to be Bishop of London, and would almost certainly have been Archbishop of Canterbury had he not died so young.

THE DECLINE OF SYDENHAM'S MUSICAL LIFE

The musical life of Sydenham was intermittent and seasonal. Earlier in the century the village had been a summer retreat for rich people whose main home was in town. Now that it had been fully integrated into London by the railway system the rich made Sydenham their base, but deserted it during the summer for long continental tours. Until the 1870s the Saturday concert season at the Crystal Palace ran only during the winter and spring, and private musical parties in the houses

of the district tended not to last much longer. A gloomy article in the local paper, under the heading 'A Deserted Village', shows the impecunious music lover's plight during the Sydenham summers.

"Meanwhile those whom business, or poverty, or imperative claims of pursuits or family, keep at home, are friendless. Is anything more depressing than to pass a house usually ablaze with cheerful light in the evening time, and from whose windows cheering strains of music come, inviting you with irresistible enticements to enter and join the friends who will welcome you so gladly, but which is now dark and silent and gloomy. Yes, there is a more depressing experience we know of, connected with the annual exodus; it is to enter a house with the host as he calls on his road from town to his chosen temporary retreat. The outside of the house is dreary, but desolation reigns within. The books glare at you from behind glass, as at an intruder, shapeless masses of covered furniture and heaps of curtains wrapped in holland, offer themseves to obstruct your path and hurt your shins - your host moderates his breath and speaks in whispers, and you imitate his example. A pyramid of newspaper covers and conceals the pile of music you know so well and have played or sung from with such pleasure. The piano is dumb, and is apparently of calico not wood. How different to the last time you were in the house, when the newest operetta was on the music desk, and the hours flew in laughter and enjoyment. You are glad to get away."

Already in 1876 Grove was expressing nostalgic regret for "our good old days when we brought out a Reformation Symphony or *Rosamunde* music every two or three months and all was electric and the air full of Schubert". London concert managers were overwhelming the Crystal Palace with the sincerest form of flattery, and by the early 1880s the decline of Sydenham's brilliant musical and social life was becoming obvious to all. Grove's appointment as first director of the Royal College of Music in 1882, and his resignation as editor of *Macmillan's Magazine* in the following year, greatly reduced his spare time for entertaining, and limited the flow of famous literary visitors to Sydenham. It was no longer such a pleasant place to visit. In 1891 Grove wrote to a friend that his house "is quiet too – so far – but a high road close in front, and cottages crowded round somewhat militate against more than a *degree* of it". Death was breaking up the Scott Russell and von Glehn circles, as Grove's biographer explained:

"time had made many gaps in that bright coterie which had its focus at Peak Hill. Mr von Glehn had since his wife's death sunk into a state of profound melancholy, and his daughter Mimi, who for the last four years had been obliged to winter at Cannes or Davos, was literally dying by inches of consumption. The delightful Sunday afternoons, with Mimi von Glehn at the piano and Stockhausen, with unwearied voice and unflagging enthusiasm, singing Schubert, Schumann, Bach, and Brahms, or with Canon Ainger or Grove reading poetry aloud in the garden in summer, or round the fire in winter, were already a thing of the past."

At the funeral service for Mimi von Glehn, who died in 1886, Sir Charles Stanford made his farewell to Sydenham by playing the organ at St Bartholomew's. He had been another regular visitor to Peak Hill Lodge, which was sold in that year.

The last great triumphs in Sydenham's musical history were achieved by a newcomer who was regarded as a vulgar upstart by the Grove set. Henry Littleton (1823-1888) rose from very humble origins to become the proprietor of Novello and Company, which he built into the largest music publishing firm in the world. In 1874 he bought Westwood House, and employed the fashionable architect John Loughborough Pearson to remodel it as a Renaissance fantasy palace, with a magnificent music room as the centrepiece. The work was not completed until 1881, so Littleton only enjoyed his grand home for seven years, but he crowded much excitement into them. Grove attended one of his lavish entertainments:

"I was at a great masked party given by old H. Littleton at his house in Upper Sydenham. I have an African chief's robe – very full, dark blue, with lovely embroidery on the front. I put on also a red fez with a turban round it, and you may imagine it made me rather unrecognizable... I found old L. (one of the vulgarest old snobs imaginable) sitting in his hall to receive his guests, with a large visitors' book on the table by him. I walked up to him and began, 'O great sage I have come from the ends of the earth to enjoy your hospitality and taste the flavour of your wisdom, deign to utter a few words of welcome to your slave' I never saw a man look so bewildered. 'Oh, shut up, shut up,' said he, 'tell us 'oo you are', on which I took up the pen and fortunately recollected Persian enough to write a long name in the book."

Both Dvorak and Liszt stayed at Westwood House during their visits to the Crystal Palace, and Liszt gave one of his last piano recitals in Littleton's music room in April 1886.

125. *The main front of Westwood House c.1905, when it was the Passmore Edwards Teachers' Orphanage.*

126. Edward Miall.

A LONDON ROAD ELITE

Forest Hill had its own intellectual society in the 1860s and '70s, distinct from the Sydenham musical set, and with a bias towards political economy and antiquarian pursuits. A number of its leading figures lived in London Road. Edward Miall (1809-81), who was MP for Rochdale 1852-7 and Bradford 1869-74, lived at Welland House, now Kings Garth, no. 29, between 1864 and 1881. The first tenant of the house next door – Prospect Villa, now Princes Garth, no. 31 – was Augustus Mongrédien (1807-88), the economist. He lived there from the early 1850s until the late '70s, and afterwards at 31 Waldram Park Road, where he died.

Miall, after whom a road is named at Bell Green, was one of the most radical parliamentary politicians of his day, a bigoted Nonconformist, and constant advocate for the disestablishment of the Church of England. Most of his books inhabited the borderlands of religion and politics. He moved to Welland House at the age of 55 because "nothing could have been so congenial to his natural disposition as to have withdrawn altogether from public life, and to spend his later years in rural

seclusion. The best compromise within his reach, committed as he was to the responsibility of newspaper editing, and to a full share of the burden of directing the policy of the Liberation Society, was a small house with a well-sheltered garden at Forest Hill, which he took upon a long lease, hoping that the strain of mental work would in future be so far lightened as to allow of some relaxation in the contemplative study of natural objects, and in his favourite pursuit of reading."

Augustus Mongrédien, the son of a French refugee, was of the same political school as his neighbour, with whom he also shared a love of music and gardening. Mongrédien wrote several books about the cultivation of trees and shrubs, and was the first president of the Sydenham Horticultural Society, which he founded in 1860. Other interests of this versatile man included chess, languages, of which he spoke seven fluently, and above all political economy. His many authoritative works on the subject, written from a Liberal, free-trade standpoint, earned him a civil list pension on the recommendation of Gladstone. Both Miall and Mongrédien were great patrons of radical movements in the Sydenham district, so it was natural that when Mongrédien wanted to entertain his friends in 1867 he should do so at the radical headquarters, the Lecture Hall in Kirkdale:

"On Thursday evening one of the most brilliant and gay events that has occurred in the village of Sydenham took place in the Lecture Hall, – viz., a grand private *bal masqué,* given by A. Mongredian Esq., of Forest Hill, to a circle of about 200 friends. The hall, that has been frequently decorated, never assumed so grand an aspect as on this occasion, the sides and ends being filled with exotics, ferns, and flowers... Several splendid oil paintings gave an additional charm to the hall. The refreshment-room was also finely arranged with prints, candelabra, and plants of different descriptions. The supper-room ... contained every delicacy of the season, including the best and choicest wines, various portions of the pastry being most artistically displayed. The costume of the ladies was most brilliant, comprising the classical, heroic, and fantastical. The gentlemen appeared as sailors, soldiers, philosophers, and poets, Turks, Prussians, Greeks, and Russians. Most of the dresses assumed dated from the reign of Elizabeth, but there were several in the costume of Charles II. The splendid dresses of the company, seen under the brilliant display of gas lights, was one of the most effective and dazzling scenes ever witnessed in this locality."

Two other London Road celebrities lived at Rose Hill, a house demolished early in the twentieth century for the enlargement of the Horniman Gardens. Thomas Farncomb, a founder of the London and Westminster Bank, and Lord Mayor in 1849/50, died there in 1865. Sir John Kaye (1814-76), head of the Political Department at the India Office, and a voluminous writer on Indian history, also spent the last few years of his life at Rose Hill. Frederick Horniman, the founder of the museum, lived at four addresses in Forest Hill, including two in London Road, and the Tetley brothers were equally devoted to the district. These were the most famous of the many tea merchants who settled here.

The local antiquaries were headed by Dr Charles Rogers (1825-90), a cantankerous Scotsman who swept through life in a cloud of controversy, making fervent friends and bitter enemies wherever he settled. For about ten years from 1873 this was in Forest Hill, where his admirers built him a house that he called Grampion Lodge, in what was then Westwood Park, now Horniman Drive. He was a minister of the Presbyterian church, but devoted the better part of his life to antiquarian research. During most of his Forest Hill years he was Secretary to the Royal Historical Society, which he claimed to have founded. He was eventually accused of embezzling the society's funds – not an isolated event in his career – and was forced to resign.

127. *Grampion Lodge, c.1875.*

Local historians tend to be far more dull and respectable. One who lived in the area, but sadly failed to write about Sydenham or Forest Hill, was William Rendle (1811-93), the author of *Old Southwark and Its People* (1878), and, with Philip Norman, of *The Inns of Old Southwark and Their Associations* (1888). Rendle, who practised medicine in Southwark for nearly fifty years, and was Medical Officer of Health for St George's in the Borough, lived at Treverbyn, 111 Sunderland Road, which was built for one of his family in the late 1860s. Perrymount Primary School is now on its site.

The most distinguished of the Forest Hill artists was William Powell Frith (1818-1909), the painter of extraordinary crowd scenes like *Ramsgate Sands* and *Derby Day*. His private life was equally crowded, for he had twelve children by his first wife, two by his mistress Mary Alford, and five more by her after she became his second wife. Between 1889 and 1896 Frith moved his extended family to Ashenhurst, 7 Sydenham Rise. The five Alfords living with him in 1891 were described as his stepsons.

LITTLE GERMANY

Sydenham, Forest Hill, and the other Crystal Palace suburbs housed one of the major German communities of London. It was predominantly middle class, and at various points overlapped the intellectual and musical society that clustered around Sir George Grove. The conductor of the Crystal Palace orchestra was a German, and so were many of the players. Others set up in the area as teachers of music, or of languages, and there were several German schools. The majority of the immigrants were merchants or clerks, but often they were also amateur musicians or lovers of music who had been induced to settle here by the fame of the Saturday concerts. The existence of this large potential congregation led to the foundation of the German Evangelical Church in temporary accommodation at Sydenham in 1875, and that in turn attracted more settlers. The Dacres Road church was built in 1883.

The German community was complex. The responses of the settlers to British life were as various as their motives for leaving home. Some of the incomers remained eternally alien, their eyes forever fixed on the longed-for return to the Fatherland. Others tried to become more English than the English, and their children rapidly merged with the native population, even though they themselves might fail to adapt. Typical of this type was Robert von Glehn, whose thoroughly English children thought of his sentimentality and lack of humour as Germanic:

A RESPECTABLE SUBURB

It was a characteristic of wealthy Victorian suburbs that their populations were overwhelmingly feminine, while the working class districts compensated by harbouring more men than women. This was mainly because the big houses drew a huge maiden tribute from the slums in the form of cooks, nurses, and other domestic servants. Sydenham and Forest Hill were advanced examples of this trend throughout the nineteenth century, and in 1891 the area housed 14,451 males and 19,711 females. Their distribution was very uneven. In such areas as Lawrie Park, Sydenham Hill, and Honor Oak Road the men were outnumbered by more than two to one, but in Wells Park Road and at Bell Green there was a small male majority. The true disparity was even greater than the quoted figures suggest, because they exclude the predominantly wealthy parts of Sydenham and Forest Hill outside the parish of Lewisham.

The solid middle class families of merchants, civil servants, and professional men that populated this feminine world produced many children who were to make an impact on the twentieth century, long after Sydenham and Forest Hill had sunk back into obscurity. Woodthorpe in Kirkdale was the teenage home of Thomas Sturge Moore (1870-1944), the poet, and of his brother George Edward Moore (1873-1958), one of the most distinguished of modern philosophers. Clifton Cottage, the present 28 Kirkdale, was the birthplace of Douglas Cockerell (1870-1945), the great bookbinder, and the childhood home of his brother Sir Sydney Cockerell (1867-1962), the director of the Fitzwilliam Museum. They were the grandsons of Sir John Bennett, the clockmaker, who lived at The Orchard, Mount Gardens (*see pp.90 and 127*).

The novelist Horace Annesley Vachell (1861-1955) was born in Sydenham, and the sublime cartoonist Henry Bateman (1887-1970) was educated at Forest Hill House School (*see p.66*). Sir Ernest Shackleton (1874-1922) was brought to live at 12 Westwood Hill when he was ten, and his father, Dr Henry Shackleton, had his practice there for more than thirty years. One of his less successful cases was that of Eleanor Marx, daughter of Karl, who lived at 7 Jew's Walk from 1895 until her suicide three years later. A more unexpected figure to emerge from these middle class suburbs was George Lansbury (1859-1940), who was leader of the Labour Party before Attlee. He spent part of his early childhood in Sydenham, where his father worked as a railway sub-contractor.

When the nearly bankrupt Crystal Palace Company dissolved its professional orchestra in 1900 it turned to sport as a last desperate resource. W.G. Grace had been engaged the year before to organ-

128. *The German church in Dacres Road, c.1900.*

"We never felt him as a play fellow; his German nature I think made it difficult for him to unbend. I never saw him play the fool, and I think he was always puzzled at English jokes, particularly when older people talked nonsense."

There is another example in Louis Behrens of Weisbaden, a Brazil merchant of Liberal views who came to England after the Franco-Prussian War, married an Englishwoman, and settled in Forest Hill. He sent his daughter to Roedean and his eldest son to Clifton College and the Royal Military Academy at Woolwich, but Louis Behrens never quite transformed himself into an English gentleman. His correspondence with his son's masters reveals a tragi-comic inability to understand the public school tradition and ethos; and the movement for the emancipation of women, regarded humorously by most Englishmen, filled him with gloom. "That franchise vampyre", he called it, because it was sucking the pleasure from his domestic life.

129. *The six-foot-four-inch Sir Philip Dawson dominates this group. "On the outbreak of the European War in 1914, he joined the local Voluntary Force, and, by reason of some outstanding qualities, was soon chosen as Commandant of a body that, before recognition by the War Office, uniformed and to some extent armed itself, so that later, after full recognition, he was gazetted Major in command of what became the 3rd Volunteer Battalion, 'The Queen's Own', Royal West Kent Regiment."*

ise and captain a London County Cricket Club, and he lived for a decade at 7 Lawrie Park Road while trying unsuccessfully to get his team accepted into the county championship. In the end even the minor counties rejected the new club. At least the Crystal Palace Indoor Bowling Club, which Grace also founded, continues to flourish – in Anerley.

Lawrie Park remained fashionable for longer than the rest of Sydenham, and Grace was not the only distinguished Edwardian resident of those charming avenues and crescents. Frederick Greenwood (1830-1909), who was successively editor of *The Cornhill Magazine*, *The Pall Mall Gazette* and *The St James's Gazette*, spent his last years at Rothay, 6 Border Crescent, and Sir Philip Dawson, MP for West Lewisham from 1921 until his death in 1938, lived for 36 years at Maybourne in Springfield Road.

Suburban Amenities

SHOPS, PUBS, AND ENTERTAINMENTS

Sydenham was not in the position of its neighbour and rival Norwood, where the whole supporting apparatus of suburban life had to be created after the enclosure of the common at the beginning of the nineteenth century. Sydenham was an ancient village that already provided a firm, if narrow, base for the growth of the community. Shops, inns, schools, a church, coach services, and a busy social life of balls and dinner parties were firmly established features of Sydenham before the enclosure of 1810 began the fresh period of growth. Forest Hill did have to start from nothing, but in those early days it would be wrong to regard Forest Hill as an independent place. It was only the establishment of the railway station in 1836, and its renaming as Forest Hill in 1845, that began to give the area any sense of a separate identity. In 1847 it was described dismissively as "a pleasantly situated hamlet of detached villa residences", and as late as 1853 a directory included Forest Hill

merely as a road in Sydenham. Any real independence had to wait until Christ Church was made a parish in 1855.

Because Sydenham was already so well established in 1810 many aspects of suburban development required merely the multiplication of existing amenities. The shops in the village at that time, probably no more than ten, were all either at Bell Green, or in the central section of Sydenham Road, close to the Dolphin and the Golden Lion. The number grew to twenty in 1826, thirty in 1832, seventy in 1839, and eighty in 1847. In 1853, just before the arrival of the Crystal Palace, there were about 140 shops, and in 1864 270. By then the great majority were no longer in Sydenham Road, but in the High Street (the area around the junction of Kirkdale and Dartmouth Road), in Lawrie Place, the fashionable terrace later absorbed by the growing Cobb's department store, and at the northern end of Dartmouth Road, which was sometimes called Forest Hill High Street.

Public houses had existed in Sydenham from the early eighteenth century, if not before, and by the 1860s every grade from the smart hotel to the disreputable beershop was well represented. There were four in 1810 – the Greyhound, Dolphin, Golden Lion, and Two Brewers – which was three fewer than the village had boasted fifty years earlier. The

130. *Alexander Robert Hennell's impression of his first design for the interior of the Sydenham Public Halls, on which he collaborated with his father, Alexander Gordon Hennell. At this stage it was intended to build the Halls in Newlands Park.*

131. *Aberdeen House, between the station and the Dartmouth Arms, was one of the oldest butcher's shops in Forest Hill. Frederick Chalk acquired it c.1885. The photograph was taken in the 1890s.*

132. *The building on the right of this 1972 photograph has been the Foresters' Arms, under its variant names, since the early 1850s, but the pub was probably founded in 1847 in the building on the left. It subsequently became the Armoury, the headquarters of the Sydenham Rifle Corps, a volunteer force established in 1858.*

number had risen to six by 1830, to twenty by 1850, after the first impact of the railway, and to forty or so by 1870, at the end of the Crystal Palace boom. The total remained about the same for the rest of the century, despite further development.

Two of the public houses, the Golden Lion in Sydenham Road, and the Talma in Wells Park Road, contributed to Sydenham's amusement with music hall performances. Other entertainments tended to be in the hands of the churches or working men's institutes, and were generally less lively, but the amateur variety concerts given at the Lecture Hall during the 1870s were an exception. "When", asked the local paper, "did Sydenham and Forest Hill before see fifty men rushing wildly through its streets, armed with sticks, at ten at night, a terror to all? Yet this exhibition was the outcome of our so called Public Readings."

After 1854 the dominance of the Crystal Palace discouraged any other expensive attempts to amuse the public. Even as late as 1897, with the Palace in serious decline, the Sydenham Public Halls, built at the corner of Kirkdale and Jew's Walk by a limited company, proved an instant failure. The district continued to rely on the Palace for nearly all its entertainments until the first three cinemas were opened in 1910. The earliest and smartest, in Silverdale, had begun life in the previous year as a roller skating rink. The provision of parks in Upper Sydenham was also discouraged by the Palace, and for its only example, Wells Park, it had to wait until 1901. Lower Sydenham did better. The Recreation Ground (Mayow Park) was opened in 1878 and Home Park in 1901.

133. *The fields that were about to become Wells Park, sketched in 1898. The two churches, both now demolished, were St Philip's in Taylor's Lane, and St Matthew's in Panmure Road.*

SCHOOLS AND POLITICS

There had been private schools in Sydenham since the middle of the eighteenth century, so this was another local amenity that had only to grow with the suburb. The four or five that were the average number between 1810 and 1840 more than doubled in the next decade, and remained close to ten throughout the 1850s. Half of these schools were in Sydenham Park, and only one or two in Forest Hill. Although the numbers remained fairly stable the names and addresses of the schools were constantly changing, and very few became lasting institutions. The best were identified in the 1862 directory:

> "The Sydenham College, of which the Rev. W.T. Jones, M.A., is the principal, will bear favourable comparison with the best classical and commercial schools in the south of England; and the Ladies' College, on Peak Hill, of which Mrs Parker is the lady principal, and Mrs Todd's Establishment at Perry Hill, well deserve the high esteem in which they are held."

The Rev. William Taylor Jones's school was in Sydenham Park Road. Mrs Todd's academy, which was about to move to Tudor Hall in Dartmouth Park, is still flourishing, though not, alas, in Forest Hill.

134. *The Rev. Dr John Wood Todd, minister of the Sydenham Baptist Chapel, Dartmouth road, Forest Hill, and co-proprietor of the Tudor Hall School.*

135. Tudor Hall School, South Road, c.1880. Dr Todd, husband of the Principal, is the central figure. Only the wing to the right survives. The main body of the house was demolished in the 1950s. (See p.103)

By 1870 the total number of private schools was approaching thirty, of which nearly two thirds were in the rapidly growing Forest Hill. That trend was to continue: in the 1880s only fifteen of the forty private schools in the area were in Sydenham. By this time there were fewer boarding schools, and the most common type was the day school for girls. Sydenham High School, founded in 1887, is the surviving example. Many boys from Sydenham and Forest Hill were sent away to public schools, and a number attended Dulwich College. The 1870 Education Act, which was to devastate the country's private schools, initially had little impact in these wealthy suburbs. The total number rose from 27 to forty between 1869 and 1884, and had only declined to 38 in 1894.

Schools for the poor were fewer and of much later growth. Mary Mayow's Church of England infant school in Sydenham Road, founded in 1815, was the first. The Anglicans maintained their educational dominance in the area by attaching a National School to most of their new parishes: St Bartholomew's School was opened in 1832, Christ Church in 1859, St Michael and All Angels' in 1872, St Philip's in 1873, and Holy Trinity in 1874. The other denominations could not match this, although a Non-conformist British School was founded in Sydenham Road in 1851, and moved to larger premises in Kirkdale ten years later, while the Roman Catholics set up their school in Sydenham Road, in connection with the church of Our Lady and St Philip Neri, in 1875. There was also a school attached to the Methodist church in Dartmouth Road, but it did not long survive the Education Act.

136. *The St Bartholomew's National Schools as rebuilt in 1862-3, to the designs of Edwin Nash.*

Suncroft Place is now on the site.

The School Board for London, set up under the Act of 1870, was the creation of a Liberal government, and therefore not opposed by the Non-conformists, who soon transferred most of their schools into its keeping. The Anglicans and Roman Catholics were united in abhorrence of the Board and all its ungodly works, and the church schools established in the 1870s show how hard they strove to keep it at bay. But even in wealthy and conservative Sydenham and Forest Hill they could not create enough new places to succeed absolutely. The Board's first local school was built in 1874, and suitably placed in West Kent Park, one of the poorest areas in Forest Hill, at the corner of Dalmain Road (then Grove Road) and Brockley Rise. Its first foothold in wealthy Upper Sydenham was provided by the British School in Kirkdale, which it took over in 1875, and greatly enlarged in the next year. At Bell Green, Sydenham's worst slum, the Church of England tried to keep the neighbourhood "free from the interference of that uncertain and ever changing body, the London School Board", as the vicar put it, by several enlargements of the St Michael's Schools, but the rapid growth of the population soon proved overwhelming. The temporary Haseltine Road Board School, the last in the area during the nineteenth century, was opened in 1882, and the permanent building was completed in 1885.

The British School in Kirkdale was housed in part of the Sydenham Lecture Hall. This superior working men's institute, based on a design by Sir Joseph Paxton, and opened by him in 1861, became the centre of radical politics in the area, and an object of suspicion to the conservative majority. Kirkdale was the field of most political action in Sydenham at this time, and there the Liberals had occupied the high ground. During general election campaigns the Conservatives had their headquarters at the Greyhound, which was covered with the party's orange handbills, and the Liberals set up camp at the blue-placarded Fox and Hounds, where the hustings were usually erected. "Dear old Mr Mayow Adams stood at one side of the entrance gates exhorting all and sundry to vote Conservative; leaders of the other party on the other side, did the same." The schoolchildren predictably took part in the contest, the 'British Brats' at the top of the hill on the Liberal side, and the 'National Brats' at the bottom in support of the Conservatives. There were several battles between them before the masters were forced to intervene.

The main local issue of the period, the campaign against the continued levying of church rates, was also organised from the Lecture Hall after 1861, and before that from even higher reaches of Kirkdale and Sydenham Hill. While the vestries were still the centres of local government the Anglican churches were clearly public buildings which it

was not unreasonable to expect the public to maintain. When the Boards of Works were set up in 1855 the position changed, and the Non-conformists were no longer willing to pay for buildings used solely for Church of England services. The struggle began in 1857 under the leadership of George Cockerell, the coal merchant, of the Manor House, Sydenham Hill, and John Bennett, later Sir John (1814-97), the celebrated Cheapside clockmaker, who lived at The Orchard, Mount Gardens. The dispute continued to divide Sydenham into bitterly hostile camps until the appointment of the conciliatory Augustus Legge as Vicar of St Bartholomew's in 1867.

Even then there was a bizarre postlude in the form of the Taylor's Lane riots. Richard Beall, a wealthy silk warehouseman, moved in 1867 from Elm Grove to Longton Hall, formerly a hydropathic hotel and later the first home of the Sydenham High School. He immediately decided to increase his privacy by blocking the upper portion of Taylor's

137. Mayow Wynell Adams (1808-98).

138. Longton Hall c.1900, when it had become the Sydenham High School for Girls.

Lane, between Longton Avenue and Westwood Hill. Beale was a strong churchman, and one of the chief supporters of St Philip's, and as a result the mob decided that this was a sinister move in the church rates controversy. As often as the fences and walls were set up they were smashed to pieces:

"On Thursday the crowd was immense, people coming from the surrounding localities on purpose to be eye witnesses of the exciting scene... At 8 o'clock the signal was given, when the men marched with axes, etc. – the police giving way to the movement – to the fixture erected at the top of Taylor's-lane, and soon the place resounded with heavy blows, amidst deafening cheers; numbers of torches throwing a fiery glare over the thousands who were present. Mr Beall was occasionally seen hurrying about in the midst of the din and uproar; still the work of demolition gradually progressed; board after board being split into hundreds of pieces; huge gaps being made in the work, amidst the loud hurrahs of the people; a right of way was cleared in about 30 minutes, when the throng marched through to the waving of torches and tremendous cheering. On arriving at the entrance to Longton-grove, similar destruction took place, attended by some noise and excitement; after which, the large assembly quietly dispersed. On Friday, strong impediments were again erected, and at night were hewn to pieces and scattered in all directions. On Saturday, Mr Beall discontinued his efforts to stop the thoroughfare... Taylor's-lane presents a most extraordinary spectacle, large pieces of splintered timber, thousands of bricks scattered about, large mounds of earth thrown up in different parts, and *debris* of all descriptions, gives it the appearance of a place that has undergone the bombardment of artillery."

Taylor's Lane remained open and Mr Beale went mad. Was the decision to put up the fences a symptom of approaching insanity, or was the breakdown caused by the violent opposition? History cannot provide an answer. With Longton Grove offering such an easy alternative, the public inconvenience from Mr Beale's plan would not have been serious. There were no riots at the town hall when that same part of Taylor's Lane was abolished in the 1970s.

The Sydenham Working Men's Association moved its headquarters to the Lecture Hall, and mounted a programme of talks by such local celebrities as Paxton and John Scott Russell, the president of the institute. It organised penny readings, concerts, classes in practical subjects, a reading room, and reference and lending libraries, all for four shillings a year. This was not the only source of cheap reading for the poor. There was the Perry Hill Public Lending Library, run on similar lines, which many years later became the first publicly funded library in Lewisham, and at least two of the Anglican churches – St Bartholomew's and Christ Church – had parochial libraries. For the middle classes there were numerous commercial circulating libraries, and the excellent reading room at the Crystal Palace.

CHURCHES

The only old church in the district, the chapel in Sydenham Road, was wrested from the Dissenters in 1794, and used thereafter by the Anglicans. The dislodged congregation resorted to open air meetings on the common, near Peak Hill, and later made use of a tent, until a chapel was built in Sydenham Road (*see pp.39 and 40*) in 1819. (In 1850 this was replaced by the Park Chapel, which still exists at the Kirkdale end of Sydenham Park, and in 1867 that too was abandoned in favour of the Congregational Church in Jew's Walk, the Church-in-the-Grove.) The Anglican reply was St Bartholomew's, which was built largely from public

139. *A sketch for St Bartholomew's church by the architect, Lewis Vulliamy. Building work began in 1827, but was not completed until 1832, because of the many disputes that disrupted the project.*

140. *Sydenham Parsonage in Westwood Hill, later known as the Vicarage, was built for the Rev. Charles English in 1848-9.*

141. *The foundation stone of St Matthew's Panmure Road, being laid in 1879 by the Rev. Huyshe W. Yeatman, Vicar of St Bartholomew's. He changed his name to Yeatman-Biggs, married the Earl of Dartmouth's daughter, and became Bishop of Southwark.*

funds between 1827 and 1832. The only other churches in Sydenham by 1851 were both built in 1849. One was a short-lived Congregational chapel in Wells Park Road, and the other the Dartmouth Road Wesleyan church, the site of which is opposite Sydenham School. In 1851 there were no churches in Forest Hill.

By 1901 the number of churches in the district had risen to more than thirty, half of them in Forest Hill, with almost every denomination and shade of doctrine represented. As William Pett Ridge remarked in 1927, "few joys in this world equal that of staying away from church. Sydenham has more trouble in doing this than many neighbourhoods. If missed by the Parish Church, in West-hill, there are many waiting to catch, in the slips." Most were built from local contributions, providing striking proof of the wealth and piety of the district during those fifty years of its prime. The building funds were not always narrowly sectarian. In 1882 the subscription list for the German Lutheran church in Dacres Road featured clergymen of various denominations, and almost as many English as German names.

TRANSPORT

Coach services had played an important part in Sydenham life since it began to be a wealthy commuter suburb at the end of the eighteenth century, and they enjoyed a monopoly of local public transport until 1839, when the two stations were opened. The coach proprietors had no hope of competing with the railway, which was no more expensive, and infinitely faster. Services advertised in 1826, "coaches to London from Sydenham at 8, 9, 9.30 a.m.", and in 1832, "coaches to London from Golden Lion and Greyhound, every morning at 8.45", had been withdrawn by 1839.

Sydenham and Forest Hill were well served by the Victorian railway companies, with eleven stations opened in or immediately adjoining the two suburbs during the fifty years of their prime. Only seven still survive. Provision began in 1839, when the opening of Sydenham and the Dartmouth Arms (Forest Hill) stations on the London and Croydon line gave the first boost to local development. The Crystal Palace had a great influence on railway planning – was indeed largely promoted by railway owners. The Low Level station was opened in 1854, at first only as a loop from Sydenham, but extended two years later to provide a direct link with the West End. Lower Sydenham on the Mid Kent Line followed in 1857 – it was moved to its present site, further from Bell Green, in 1906 – and Sydenham Hill and Penge East in 1863. The Crystal Palace and South London Junction Railway, which opened in 1865, immediately added three stations, Honor Oak, Lordship Lane, and Crystal Palace High Level, and eventually a fourth when Upper Sydenham was added in 1884. The line was never a great success, and was finally closed in 1944. The last of the local stations was Honor Oak Park, opened in 1886. As Pett Ridge put it: "The residents find nothing perplexing in the number of railway stations; the visitor will nevertheless do well to make his choice warily, lest he should find himself remote from his actual objective."

The earliest recorded Sydenham omnibus service had been established by 1845. It left the Dolphin daily at a quarter to nine, and returned at six in the evening. By 1852 the terminus had been moved to the Dartmouth Arms at Forest Hill and the frequency increased, but three years later no London buses were advertised. The only service was then from the Greyhound at Sydenham to Bromley, four times a day. The omnibus and the coach clearly found it equally hard to compete with the London

142. *Forest Hill station in 1862, showing the dangerously narrow centre platforms in use. On the left is the booking hall of 1854, which was superseded in 1883, but survived to be destroyed by the 1944 flying bomb that also shattered its successor.*

and Croydon Railway on any but short, cross-country routes. Later in the century the most important of these were provided by the leading independent bus operator, Thomas Tilling, who lived locally at Perry Hill Farm.

Trams were not well adapted to the social or physical geography of these rich and hilly suburbs, and they never penetrated into Sydenham. There was a proposal for a service along Sydenham Road in 1914, but it was abandoned at the outbreak of war. Forest Hill was reached in 1908, when an extension was opened from Dulwich to the end of London Road, opposite the station. In 1911 trams began to run from Brockley Cross to the Perry Vale entrance to the station, and in 1913 tracks were laid along the eastern portion of Stanstead Road to provide a direct link with Catford. The final piece of the Forest Hill tram system was added in 1915, when track was laid between London Road and Waldram Park Road. This involved demolishing the shop at the corner of London Road and Devonshire Road, to ease the bend, and deepening the road under the railway bridge.

UTILITIES

A Sydenham writer complained in 1862 that "the wealthy town of to-day has merged from amidst the simple obscurity of the past in a transit of confusion – no order, no controlling power." This was not absolutely true, but the great Crystal Palace boom did come at a time of transition in local government, when neither the moribund old authorities nor the uncertain new ones were able to give firm guidance.

The huge growth in building and population made the construction of effective sewers the vital task of the 1850s. In the first half of the decade the responsibility lay with the Metropolitan Commissioners of Sewers, a remote and unaccountable body, despite the fact that its chairman, Edward Vitruvius Lawes, lived in Kirkdale. The sewers built in the village under his direction, planned before the Great Exhibition, and still incomplete when it became known that the Crystal Palace would be moved to Sydenham Hill, proved quite inadequate to the new situation. Lawes may himself have been one of the victims of the unhealthy environment he helped to create, for he died in 1852 at the age of 35, shortly after the early deaths of several of his colleagues.

Worried Sydenham residents formed an Anti-Aggression Association to remedy the situation. One member claimed that "before the Commission came here, the old parish drains acted well, but now they had been taken out of the hands of the parish and received no attention at all". Another,

Dr William Roberts, reported in 1853 that "a patient whom he was attending ... died in 72 hours from direct poison arising from the foul state of the sewers, and it was the very worst case of fever he had ever seen. Should an unhealthy season or very hot weather set in, he was of opinion that many of the inhabitants would be victims". It was only after 1856, when the Lewisham Board of Works took control of the local sewers, that substantial, and very expensive, improvements were made.

Water supply was a closely linked problem. Until the village grew so rapidly in the 1840s streams and wells had satisfied the demand, although the distance of Upper Sydenham from the Pool River and the depth to which wells had to be sunk greatly reduced the pace of building development on the common between 1810 and 1840. Water rights were of great importance and were often set out at length in property deeds. A Peak Hill lease of 1812 gave a new tenant the right to the "passage of William By's garden between 8 and 9 in the morning and 4 and 5 in the afternoon" to collect water from a pond.

The subsequent history of Sydenham's water supply was well summarised by a local paper in 1870:

"When Sydenham was a pretty rural village, with good fishing in the canal ... the inhabitants obtained good water from the Pool River, Lady Well, and the canal; in addition to the chalybeate springs all over the neighbourhood. But the railway disposed of the canal, sewage rendered the Pool River no longer available for consumption, and other sources of supply were eagerly sought for.

Among the landowners of Sydenham is the Leathersellers' Company, and upon their estate at Peak Hill they sunk a deep well some forty years ago for the supply of the houses occupied by their tenants. The water from this well is of excellent quality, it is raised from a depth of about 500 feet... In 1844 the Peak Hill well was leased to the present proprietor, Mr Carter, who expended a considerable sum in erecting machinery, laying mains, and substituting steam power for hand labour. As the other sources of supply we have named failed, the Peak Hill water was in great request, and in addition to the direct supply to a number of houses, the carts of many a perambulating purveyor of water were filled and re-filled at the Peak Hill well.

Presently the Crystal Palace Company took Sydenham by storm, and the conditions of the water question were entirely changed. At one time it was hoped that the Company would utilise the Peak Hill well for the supply of the Crystal

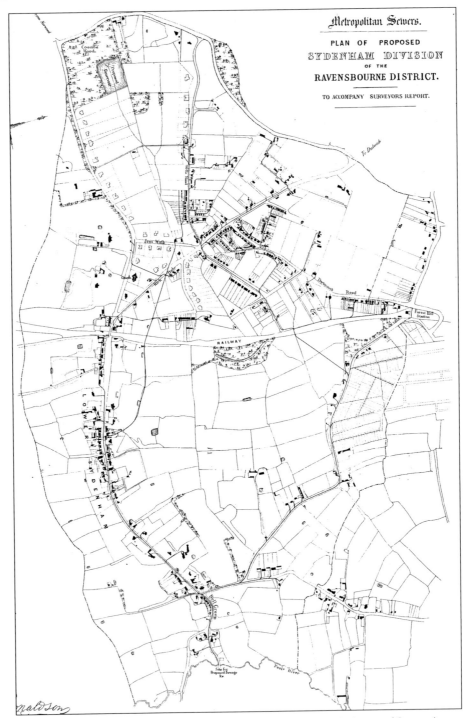

143. *The drainage proposals put forward by the Metropolitan Commissioners of Sewers in 1849. Their map gives an excellent idea of Sydenham, and part of Forest Hill, at the height of the railway boom. Existing buildings are shown in black, planned buildings in outline. Not all the developments were carried out exactly as envisaged.*

Palace and the whole neighbourhood; but this project was rejected in favour of an artesian well at the foot of the hill on which the Palace stands... The well sunk by the Crystal Palace Company going below that of Peak Hill somewhat lessened the productiveness of the latter source of supply, and at a time when, owing to the rapid increase of the neighbourhood, the capabilities of Mr Carter's works were taxed to the uttermost.

The Lambeth Company at length determined to extend their business to Sydenham, and, at a cost of nearly a quarter of a million sterling, carried their mains to the summit of Sydenham Hill, and undertook the water supply of the neighbourhood."

Gas was one of the many amenities that the district owed to the Crystal Palace. The potential suppliers had concluded in the late 1840s that the Sydenham area did not offer a promising field for investment, but enterprising capitalists were quick to anticipate the explosion of building that the great news of 1852 would produce. Two companies founded in that and the following year to supply all the expected new houses amalgamated as the Crystal Palace District Gas Company in 1854. The first two gasholders were on the south side of Southend Lane, but the company (later known as the South Suburban) soon expanded across the road onto the site it still partially occupies.

The prestige of the Crystal Palace also gave the district early access to electric power. In 1891 the leaders of the young industry decided to hold a major exhibition to begin on the 9th of January in the following year, and the Palace was the only suitable venue. But an electrical exhibition could not take place without power, and so the Crystal Palace District Electric Light and Supply Company was formed to provide it. An old brewery in Springfield, off Wells Park Road, was purchased, and in just over four months a power station was built and the laying of the cables completed with only an hour or two to spare before the opening of the exhibition. The company then turned its attention to supplying the domestic needs of this wealthy area, where there were any number of potential clients for the new luxury, and very soon

it had laid fifty miles of mains. A fatal explosion in 1900, that flung a six-ton boiler thirty feet into the air and destroyed much of the Springfield works, prevented the company from reaping the rewards of its enterprise, but the public did not suffer from these financial setbacks and the amalgamations that followed.

Gas and electricity added to the risks of fire, but the district did little to protect itself during the nineteenth century. As in so many other fields it tended to rely on the Crystal Palace, the brigade attached to which was regularly described as 'most efficient' until it failed so miserably to deal with the fire at the Palace in 1866. Sydenham had a self-service fire reel and hose – "its action requires no skill" – at the Bricklayers' Arms in Dartmouth Road, and there was a fire engine manned by volunteers housed in London Road; but it was not until 1901 that the district enjoyed a professional London County Council fire brigade at the station in Perry Vale.

With the Board of Works so hard pressed to cope with its sewerage duties, and with new utilities producing constant digging and disruption, the district's roads were a cause of bitter complaint throughout the Victorian period. The Board was slow to accept extra responsibilities by adopting any new roads, and in the meantime they all became impassable whenever it rained. Even the main streets were in an appalling condition, and ladies complained that they had to go to the West End for their shopping, as it was impossible to walk down Sydenham Road. In 1862 a local rhymer sprang to their defence:

> "With boots enveloped in mud,
> With splashes all up the skirt,
> The ladies of Sydenham are forced to walk
> In the untouched Sydenham dirt,
> Mud, mud, mud,
> In the town and over the hill,
> To have it removed one must trust to a flood,
> For the scavenger's hand it is still."

But even with this eloquent advocacy it was decades before any great improvement was achieved.

Change, Stagnation and Decay

Most of the important events in the history of Sydenham and Forest Hill occurred in the nineteenth century. All before that was the prelude, and everything since has been the anticlimax. The prelude has been described in some detail because it is necessary to the understanding of the great days, but I have no heart to linger over the epilogue. Until Thomas Campbell came to Sydenham in 1804 the village was hardly known to the world in general, which was apt to confuse it with Dulwich if it thought about it at all. Over the next century Sydenham and Forest Hill touched national, and even international, life at various points. Now they are forgotten again.

Suburbs are essentially dynamic, and having reached the heights of wealth and fashion in the 1860s and '70s Sydenham and Forest Hill had nowhere to go but down. The decline was not dramatic. The physical characteristics of the area give it some natural protection against wholesale change, and even today its hills and valleys shelter much that is delightful. Nevertheless, the theme of the last one hundred and twenty years is the relentless destruction of what was good in architecture and town planning, and the creation of what is at best mediocre. It would be hard to find any twentieth-century building in Sydenham or Forest Hill that is better to look at than the Georgian or Victorian work it has displaced. From the aesthetic point of view the interest of the modern suburb centres almost entirely on what has been saved from the wreckage of its prime.

The 29th of November 1877 was a significant date in Sydenham's history. It was then that the heirs of William Smith, who had died the year before, sold the Newlands estate to the British Land Company for intensive redevelopment. The many small houses built in Venner Road and its offshoots in the following years altered the nature of this smart end of Sydenham Road, and ensured that the other big houses would also be demolished as soon as they fell vacant. The division between rich and poor Sydenham, which had been creeping up the hill from Bell Green, now leapt to the railway line. When funds were being collected for the building of All Saints' church at the beginning of the twentieth century, the vicar urged that:

144. Country club Forest Hill in the 1920s. The Queen's Tennis Club was named after Queen's Road, later Taymount Rise, the road on the left. The club's headquarters was the house called Taymount, seen in the foreground. The courts ran down the hill to London Road. When the flats called Taymount Grange replaced the house in the 1930s the courts became amenities for the tenants.

"There will need to be much greater self-denial and generosity on the part of the parishioners of Christ Church, and very much less real dependence upon the rich folk of Upper Sydenham, if any headway is to be made in material additions to the building fund. Our friends over the bridge will do more for us when they see that we ourselves are putting our shoulders to the wheel."

Here the population was changing from upper to lower middle class, and the process was patchy, running through many gradations from the terraces of Knighton Park Road to the substantial houses of the Thorpe Estate and Trewsbury Road. At Bell Green events were more dramatic. In 1881 alone hundreds of little houses were built in Dillwyn Road, Miall Road, Porthcawe Road, Maddin Road, etc., over the grounds of Home Park Lodge and The Lawn, two of Sydenham's largest mansions. These streets, occupied mainly by gas workers and other labourers, rapidly degenerated into one of Lewisham's worst slums.

In Upper Sydenham the change during the 1880s was more subtle, but equally significant. The houses built during that decade, in Charleville Circus, Hillcrest Road, and upper Westwood Hill, were tall, ugly buildings, squeezed on to plots that were small by the standards of this wealthy area. They contrasted unfavourably with the spacious layout of Lawrie Park, Jew's Walk, Longton Avenue, Sydenham Hill, and other estates of the 1850s and '60s.

That landlords were finding it harder to obtain tenants for the big houses of Sydenham and Forest Hill is indicated by the many that fell into institutional use during the last decades of the nineteenth century. There had never been an absolute bar on private schools, but teachers now found it easier to get a footing in the best roads. Such establishments as the homes for unmarried mothers in Sydenham Hill, and for inebriate ladies in Silverdale, would not have been welcome anywhere in Sydenham while the landlords felt able to discriminate between prospective tenants.

Between 1880 and 1914 the main area of growth was Forest Hill, where the acres of painfully dull streets between Stanstead Road and Perry Hill, and to the west of Brockley Rise were built in tight patterns of scarcely differentiated terraces. By the 1920s there was little virgin land left in the district, except for the water meadows in the Pool valley, where numerous cricket clubs had their grounds

Between the wars, with the sharp decline in demand for the large Victorian houses that were the speciality of Upper Sydenham and western Forest Hill, the district tried to promote itself as a convenient residence for the single business man

or woman, or the young married couple. In 1933 it was boasted that "the very splendid service of electric trains on the Southern Railway enables the journey to be made in speed and comfort, while the season ticket rates, or daily return fares, are exceedingly moderate." In 1927 William Pett Ridge commented:

"Sydenham has always, within my knowledge, been ready to meet the views of young people who want to leave home. Many a business girl, having, so to speak, lost her parents – either by her own fault or theirs – and having reached her Independence Day, has found in Sydenham some motherly woman to provide a bed-sitting room, with breakfast on week-days, and, on Sundays, a mid-day meal."

The lodgings and houses converted into flats that satisfied this demand in the decade after the Great War were challenged in the 'thirties by luxury flats on the West End model, advertised as the perfect solution to the servant problem. One in Taymount Rise was planned almost as a country club, with a swimming pool and an array of tennis courts. The nearby Dorrell Estate in London Road, which had pioneered flat-dwelling in Forest Hill in the first years of the twentieth century, also had a tenants' sports club with tennis and croquet lawns.

This trend in private housing might have dominated the area's future, but it was halted by the Second World War, and Sydenham and Forest Hill had few purpose-built blocks of private flats until the 1950s. The most prominent pre-war example in Sydenham is the present Denham Court in Kirkdale, which was built, as Sydenham Court, in 1934.

The new Forest Hill flat dwellers of the 1930s helped to slow the economic decline of the area, which had been badly hit by the loss of the wealthy merchants who favoured it until 1914. In 1930 a shopkeeper gave this gloomy verdict:

"I am very much afraid that Forest Hill, which means London-road and Dartmouth-road, will never become the shopping and market centre so eagerly desired by some of the tradesmen. Unfortunately the closing down of Messrs. C.F. Mayo & Co.[the London Road department store] has brought to an end any hope that had existed. There is no question but what Catford and Rye-lane, Peckham, has taken what little trade was ever done... A certain prominent trader recently said to me, 'It's no use flogging a dead horse. When the German colony left Forest Hill it became useless for business purposes...'"

145. *The restricted lives of several generations of the Bell Green poor are encapsulated in this view of Maddin Road waiting to be demolished in 1960. An example of the 1880s and '90s terraces in which they lived is on the right, and their corner shop appears on the left. Haseltine Road Board School, in which most were taught, is behind the houses, and one of the holders at the gasworks, where so many were employed, can be seen in the distance.*

When Mayo & Co. closed in 1930 Joshua Allder tried to tempt the Forest Hill shoppers to Catford with the offer of Mayo's bankrupt stock at bargain prices.

Lewisham had very little council housing before the Second World War, and Kent House Buildings was the only example in Sydenham or Forest Hill. The estates in Lewisham and Grove Park featured houses. Here at Bell Green, "having regard to the very congested conditions now prevailing in this part of the Borough", it was decided to build sixty flats instead of the 48 houses that could have been squeezed onto the site. The five blocks, three in Kent House Lane and two in Winchfield Road, were built in 1930-31. They were designed by H.J. Higgins, Chief Architectural Assistant to the Borough Surveyor, who received one hundred guineas for his trouble. A glance at these depressing tenements suggests that he was grossly overpaid.

There were plenty of new jobs available in Lower Sydenham. Throughout the 1930s the industrial estate built in and around Worsley Bridge Road and Kangley Bridge Road was growing rapidly.

The two factories listed in 1931 had grown to sixteen by 1939, and in 1951 there were more than twenty. Light industry was the theme here, and such firms as Baird Television Ltd. in Worsley Bridge Road contributed to social change by offering employment to many married women. The Baird factory, which was connected with the pioneer broadcasting operation at the Crystal Palace, also introduced the excitement of industrial espionage into the area.

Any optimism raised by the influx of a younger flat-dwelling population into Forest Hill, and by the new employment opportunities in Lower Sydenham, was deflated by the fire that destroyed the Crystal Palace on the 30th of November 1936. The practical importance of Paxton's great building to its satellite suburbs had been declining for fifty years, but it still had immense symbolic significance. It had called great parts of Sydenham and Forest Hill into existence, and now they were left to find a new role in the world.

△ *Horniman's Museum in Forest Hill, London.*

The terrible sum straggled down the page; a hopeless trail of soft-pencilled figures died into a last desperate smudge, where a licked and

and then richly hung with pods. Now, dry and scrawky, autumn-nibbled, the spiral-ling stems looked like basket cane. The top class girls had made baskets last year

THIS
A Column

146. *The Oxford Works in Worsley Bridge Road, seen here in 1999, is the best of the surviving 'thirties factories on the Lower Sydenham industrial estate. It was built in 1939 for John Bell, Hills and Lucas Ltd, wholesale druggists.*

147. *The Horniman Museum, c.1906.*

THE HORNIMAN MUSEUM

As the dying Crystal Palace struggled for profit and survival part of its educational role had been taken over by the Horniman Museum. Frederick John Horniman (1835-1906), may well have been inspired to begin his collection of artefacts and natural curiosities from around the world by the example of the early Crystal Palace, with its courts evoking the great civilizations of history. It was the marvel of his youth. Horniman, a wealthy tea merchant and Liberal MP, whose business duties involved extensive travel, began the collection as a private hobby, but by the 1880s it had grown so large as to fill his London Road home, Surrey House. It was then, according to legend, that his wife issued an ultimatum: either the collection would have to go, or she would. In the event, the collection stayed while the whole family moved up the hill to Surrey Mount.

The amazing array of primitive weapons, musical instruments, stuffed animals, fossils, etc., etc., had long been shown to parties of friends and distinguished visitors. In 1890 Horniman threw it open to the public, and it soon became one of the most popular attractions not only of Forest Hill, but of south London in general. As the collection and the numbers of visitors continued to grow, plans were made to replace Surrey House. The new museum created by the distinguished architect Harrison Townsend is the most important modern building in the borough of Lewisham, but although modern in spirit, it was entirely Victorian in design and construction. Work began in 1897, and the doors were opened in 1901.

Horniman gave the building and collection to the public, and showed equal munificence in adding Surrey Mount and its gardens as a park, the only one indisputably in Forest Hill. His great generosity, and that of his family in continuing to support and extend the museum after his death, have been among the brightest features of the district's history during the twentieth century.

A POST WAR BLITZ

Sydenham and Forest Hill were heavily bombed during the Second World War, but no more heavily than the rest of south Lewisham or the other neighbouring suburbs. The houses, though, probably began the war in worse condition, because numbers of the big ones were empty, or in institutional use, and others had been clumsily divided into flats. It was very hard to maintain big houses during the war, and those that fell empty were requisitioned or earmarked for redevelopment. During and immediately after the war the combination of bomb sites, derelict houses, overgrown gardens, and woods bereft of gamekeepers turned Upper Sydenham, and especially Sydenham Hill and Westwood Hill, into an endless, glorious adventure playground for children. But it could not last. Soon came the time when every unexploited fraction of an acre was an offence to the utilitarian spirit of the age.

Lewisham Council had 2,700 requisitioned houses under its control at the end of the war, was actively acquiring more, and was extremely reluctant to release any of these properties, a disproportionate number of which were in Sydenham and Forest Hill. This was '1984', so queues of humble petitioners attended each meeting of the housing committee to plead that they needed their own homes to shelter their own families. Nearly all were sent packing with a curt refusal. There were still over two thousand of these requisitioned houses in 1955, and some were not finally torn from the hands of the bawling councillors until 1960. By that time their casual division into flats, to accommodate several families, had become hard to reverse.

As they were the least densely occupied areas of the borough it was upon Blackheath, Sydenham, and Forest Hill that the new Lewisham Council, the first ever controlled by the Labour Party, concentrated its attention in 1946, when the subject of new council estates began to be seriously discussed.

About a third of the housing schemes undertaken between 1946 and 1961 were in Sydenham and Forest Hill, and the proportion was higher in the immediate post-war years. Among the earliest blocks were Byron Close at Bell Green, Sunderland Mount in Sunderland Road, and Shackleton Close in Thorpewood Avenue, all built in 1948-9. Close behind came three estates completed in 1950, Perystreete in Perry Vale, Pikethorne in South Road, and the flats between Burghill Road and Addington Grove. The huge Valentine Court in Perry Vale was built in 1951-2.

The blocks of flats continued to appear with little respite through the 1950s and '60s, some built by Lewisham council and others by the LCC, and compulsory purchase powers were more and more widely used. It was not only the wealthy parts of the district that suffered. The old-established and tightly-knit community of Wells Park Road and its offshoots was almost entirely swept away in a wave of clearances between the late 1950s and the mid 1970s. In 1966 Hazel Grove in Lower Sydenham was chosen as the council's experimental laboratory for the testing of the cheap industrialised building system, which used factory-made concrete sections. Ten years later the blocks were falling apart, and the repair bill was twice the original building cost.

The growing unease about such developments found a voice in 1972 with the creation of the Sydenham Society. Its first public meeting was addressed by Rolf Harris, then a Sydenham resident. The event was publicised with a handbill entitled 'SOS – SAVE OUR SYDENHAM', which stated that:

> "The fact that Compulsary Purchase Orders have been placed on selected areas in Sydenham without prior consultation has brought home to residents of all political opinions that there is a real need for an Organisation to safeguard the interests of everyone who lives in Sydenham. It is known that there are other far-reaching plans that will effect our district. YOUR ROAD COULD BE THE NEXT TO BE THREATENED BY LEWISHAM COUNCIL"

The society has been hanging on the rear of the car of Juggernaut ever since, without noticeably impeding its progress.

The fate of most suburbs is sad: they are found to have completed a long journey from obscurity to absurdity. Sydenham and Forest Hill have done rather better. If they are now a little disorientated after their trek from Kent to London they can claim to have been somewhere on the way. That is no mean achievement, at least in the eyes of history.

148. An artist's impression of Shackleton Close, the council flats built off Thorpewood Avenue in 1948-9.

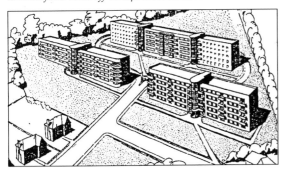

Further Reading

Adams, Jad: *A History of Kings and Princes Garth and Forest Hill* (1993).

Adams, Mayow Wynell: *Sydenham* (1878).

Bates, William: *The Maclise Portrait Gallery* (1898).

Beattie, William: *The Life and Letters of Thomas Campbell* (1849).

Bevan, Arthur H: *James and Horace Smith* (1899).

Bury, Lady Charlotte: *The Diary of a Lady-in-Waiting*, ed. A. Francis Steuart (1908).

(Clarke, W.S.): *The Suburban Homes of London, a Residential Guide* (1881).

Coulter, John & John Seaman: *Sydenham and Forest Hill*: Archive Photographs Series (2nd edn. 1995).

Creighton, Louise: *Life and Letters of Mandell Creighton* (1904).

Creighton, Louise: *Memoir of a Victorian Woman: Reflections of Louise Creighton*, ed. James Thayne Covert (1994).

Creighton, Louise: *A Victorian Family as Seen through the Letters of Louise Creighton to Her Mother 1872-1880*, ed. James Thayne Covert (1998).

Drake, Henry H.: *Hasted's History of Kent, Corrected, Enlarged and Continued; part I: The Hundred of Blackheath* (1886).

Emmerson, George S: *John Scott Russell* (1977).

Farington, Joseph: *Diary*, ed. Kenneth Garlick *et al* (1978-98).

Graves, Charles L: *The Life and Letters of Sir George Grove* (1903).

Green, John Richard: *Letters*, ed. Leslie Stephen (1902).

Hall, S.C: *A Book of Memories of Great Men and Women of the Age* (2nd edn. 1877).

Jacobs, Arthur: *Arthur Sullivan, a Victorian Musician* (1984).

Markham, Violet R: *Paxton and the Bachelor Duke* (1935).

Miall, Arthur: *Life of Edward Miall* (1884).

Musgrave, Michael: *The Musical Life of the Crystal Palace* (1995).

Prockter, Adrian: *Forest Hill and Sydenham* (1987).

Pullen, Doris: *Sydenham* (1975).

Pullen, Doris: *Forest Hill* (1979).

Raymond, J.G: *The Life of Thomas Dermody* (1806).

Redding, Cyrus: *Literary Reminiscences and Memoirs of Thomas Campbell* (1860).

Rogers, Charles: *Leaves from My Autobiography* (1876)

Spurgeon, Darrell: *Discover Sydenham and Catford* (1999).

Wolfson, John: *Sullivan and the Scott Russells* (1984).

Wyndham, H. Saxe: *August Manns and the Saturday Concerts* (1909).

Young, Percy M: *George Grove* (1980).

Young, Percy M: *Sir Arthur Sullivan* (1971).

Acknowledgements

Many individuals and institutions have helped in the preparation of this book. I would like to thank particularly Miss Nancy Campbell, Mrs Barbara Harrington, and Miss Valerie Langfield; Messrs Anthony Ashby and W.G.J. Baker; Professor James Thayne Covert; and Messrs Steve Grindlay, John S. Hillyer OBE, Geoff Hine, John Kenworthy-Browne, John Minnis, Jonathan Oates, Stephen Moreton Prichard, Keith Rooksby, John Seaman, Godfrey Smith, Darrell Spurgeon, and Richard Taylor. Also the Lewisham Local Studies Centre, the Department of Prints and Maps at the Guildhall Library, the Centre for Kentish Studies, Croydon Local Studies Library, Lambeth Archives Department, the London Metropolitan Archives, the British Library, and the Trustees of Dr Williams's Library.

The Illustrations

We would like to thank the following for permission to reproduce most of the illustrations in this book.

British Library: *85, 99*
Bromley Local Studies Library: *60*
Miss Nancy Campbell: *123*
Centre for Kentish Studies: *16, 17, 30, 44*
Croydon Local Studies Library: *77*
Guildhall Library, London, Department of Prints and Maps: *5, 81, 84*
Mrs Barbara Harrington: *101*
John S. Hillyer: *12*
Geoff Hine: *129, 144*
John Kenworthy-Browne: *49*
Lambeth Archives Department: *78*
Lewisham Local Studies Centre: *2, 4, 6, 8, 9, 10, 11, 15, 20, 21, 22, 24, 25, 26, 28, 29, 31, 36, 38, 40, 42, 43, 46, 47, 50, 52, 53, 54, 61, 64, 66, 67, 76, 79, 83, 86, 90, 91, 95, 97, 98, 100, 102, 106, 110, 111, 112, 114, 117, 121, 122, 130, 131, 132, 133, 134, 135, 136, 137, 139, 141, 143, 145, 148*
London Metropolitan Archives: *69*
John Minnis: *142*
Private Collections: *34, 39*
John Seaman: *68, 104, 108, 125, 128, 138, 147*
The Trustees of Dr Williams's Trust and the National Portrait Gallery: *48*

All other illustrations are from the author's collection

INDEX

Illustrations or captions (given by page not caption number) are indicated by an asterisk

ABBEY'S (OR ABBOT'S) FARM 59
Abel, John 7-8
Aberdeen House 122-3*
Acacia Grove 30
Acacias, The 98*
Adams, Mayow Wynell 47, 48, 79, 85-6, 87, 100, 104, 126, 127*
Adams, Robert 66
Adams, William Dacres 19, 69-70, 69*, 87
Addington Grove 26, 138
Addis, John & William 26
Ainger, Alfred 116
Aislibie, Benjamin 47
Albert Road 94
Aldwinkle, Thomas 104
Alford, Mary 118
Alford, Mr 44
All Saints' Church 37, 134
Allen, George 94, 94*, 95-6
Allen, Henry 25
Allingham, Adam 41
Allsop, Mrs 43
Alpine Cottage 94-5
Anderson, Edmund 25-26
Anderson, John 25, 25*, 62
Andrews, George 56
Andrews, William 39
Annesley, Bryan 61
Architects 43, 64, 95-8, 99, 100-104, 106, 137
Arden Cottage 46*, 47, 47*
Ardley Close 17
Armitage, George 56
Armoury 123*
Arundel Cottage 28
Ashbarry, Joseph 64
Ashberry Cottage 64
Ashbourne 101
Ashby, Frederick 24
Ashdale 84-5*
Ashenhurst 118
Ashtree Cottage 90, 90*
Asquith, Mr 26
Athol Lodge 108
Atkins, Charles 91
Atkins, John 26
Atkinson, Samuel 63, 64
Aubrey, Dr William 9-10, 68
Avenue Road, Lewisham 9

BACON, SIR EDMUND 24
Baird Television Ltd. 136
Bampton Road 104
Banks, Robert 100
Banks & Barry 99
Barber family 26, 29
Barclays Bank, Kirkdale 101
Barefield 52
Bargrove, Richard 48
Baring, Sir Francis 86-7
Barnes, John 72
Barrett family 35
Barron, Mr 37
Barry, Sir Charles 99, 100
Barry, Charles 100, 101, 103
Bascombe family 41
Batard, Thomas Bearda 25, 26, 43
Bateman, Henry 119
Batt family 13-14, 22, 23, 24, 25, 34, 55, 58
Baukham, Oliver 58
Bay House 66, 66*

Bay Riddons 55
Beadnell, George & Maria 41
Beall, Richard Preston 43, 127-8
Bear, William 86
Beaton, Andrew 48
Beechgrove 102*
Behrens, Louis 119
Belbin, Charles 37
Bell alehouse 20, 20*
Bell Green 13, 19-20, 19*, 20*, 21, 22, 22*, 24, 26, 54, 106, 119, 121, 126, 134, 135, 136
Bell Green Cottage 25
Bell Green Lane 19-20, 22
Bell Orchard 20*
Bell public house 19, 20
Bellevue 90-91
Bennett, Sir John 119, 127
Benson Road 66
Bermondsey Abbey 59
Berryman's Lane 29, 30, 34
Bevington, John Wheeley 47
Bickley 100
Bill, Charles 29
Billiter, Henry 56
Bird's Cottages 18, 18*
Black, Andrew 104
Black Horse public house 31
Blackheath 86-7
Bond, Mr 49
Border Crescent 100
Border Road 96, 100
Bounds Cottage 112
Bowdler, Thomas 57, 85
Bowles, Jane & Sarah 51
Boxall, Thomas 31-2
Boyle, Charles 26
Bradley, Michael 63
Brereton, Francis Sadleir 102
Brick & tile kilns 10, 11, 62
Bricklayers' Arms public house 133
Bridge, The (house) 43, 47, 52*, 81*
Bridgell, John 41
Bridgland, William 39
British Land Company 48, 134
British School 38*, 40, 126
Broadway Parade 26
Brockley 14, 86
Brockley Rise & Road 75, 126, 135
Brongers 13, 14
Brooke family 11, 12, 13, 15, 56
Brookhouse family 11, 49-50
Brookehouse Farm 49-50
Brookville 66
Brown, Edmund 36
Brown, John Dudin 40*, 47
Browning, Robert 114
Browning, William 24
Bruch, Max 111
Bruckner, Anton 111
Bryges, Francis & Edward 9
Buckstone, John Baldwin 25, 55*, 56, 56*, 57
Bulcock, James 85
Bulkeley family 10
Bulls public house 29
Bunce, Sarah 51
Burghill Road 138
Burke, Edmund 82-3*
Burnage Court 104-5
Burrell family 22
Bury, Lady Charlotte see Campbell
Butt Lane 75
Buxton, Richard 14
By, William 131
Byron, George, Lord 71
Byron Close 23, 138

CALEDONIAN COTTAGE 48

Calton, Thomas & Margaret 61
Campbell, Lady Charlotte 60, 72, 72*
Campbell, Matilda 70, 81, 85
Campbell, Thomas 35, 37, 43, 54*, 55*, 56, 57, 60, 69, 70-71, 70*, 80-1, 85, 86, 134
Canonbie Road 65
Capps (or Cupp), John 62
Carlton House 64
Caroline, Queen 72
Carter, Joseph 57, 131
Cast lands 16
Castlands Road 13, 16, 16*
Castle, Christian 12
Castlebar 105
Catford 7-8
Catford, Manor of 7-8
Cecil House 99, 99*
Cedar Lodge 66, 67*
Cedars Cottage (or The Cedars) 39, 41, 43
Cedars, The 91, 105
Chalet, The 90, 90*
Chalk, Frederick 122-3*
Chamber, Richard 9
Champion Hall 25, 62, 106, 106*
Champion Park estate 106
Champion Road 25, 106
Chaplin, Robert James 103
Charles Street (Charlecote Grove) 45, 88, 90, 112
Charleville Circus 99, 135
Cheseman family 8
Cheseman Street 88
Chestnuts, The 100, 101
Chevall, William 61
Chilton, George 31, 41
Chilton, Henry Charles 41
Christ Church, Forest Hill 103, 121, 125, 128
Christ Church, Sydenham 37, 135
Christian, Ewan 103
Christian Fellowship Centre 66
Christmas, Edward 18
Church in the Grove 128
Church Meadow 87*, 97*, 98, 108
Church Rise 103
Churches 128-9
Cinemas 41, 44, 123
Clare Lodge 15, 16
Claremont 17, 17*
Clark, Edwin 103, 108
Clark, Elizabeth 15
Clark, John 29
Clarke, W.S. 98, 99-100
Clay, Frederick 113-14
Clerk, John 23
Clifford, Thomas 36
Clifton Cottage 119
Clifton Villa 26
Clowder's Farm 14
Clune House 31, 31*, 41
Coach services 93, 130
Coates, John 47
Cobb, Hewitt 31
Cobb, Walter 21, 121
Cobb's Corner 21
Cockerell, Douglas & Sir Sydney 119
Cockerell, George 127
Coe, Henry E.B. 96-8
Coleridge, Samuel Taylor 71
Coleson's Coppice 50, 57, 61-3, 75
Colfe, Abraham 10, 14, 16, 55, 77
Colson, William 103
Colville, Edward Dod 26
Constable, Joseph 26
Cookesley, John Keen 35-6, 37, 43
Cooper, George 48

Cooper, John 48
Cooper, Ralph 47
Cooper, William 29
Cooper's Wood 57-60, 62, 75
Corbould, Francis 35
Cotsumes 13
Cottage, The (Sydenham Road) 50*, 52*, 53
Cottage, The (Sydenham Hill) 91, 112
Cotton, Samuel 97
Council housing 136, 138
Courtenay, Henry 69
Courtenay, Thomas Peregrine 69
Cousen, John 23
Cousins, George 30
Cousin's Cottages 30, 30*
Covell family 35, 44
Covell's Cottages 34*, 35, 35*
Cowan, Sir John & Sophia 66
Cowburn, George 23-4
Crabbe, George 71
Creeland Grove 12
Creighton, Louise 112
Creighton, Mandell 115, 115*
Cricket 39, 119-20, 135
Crime 85
Crofton Park 14
Cromer House 35
Crooked Billet 14
Croydon Canal 52*, 55, 74-5*, 79, 81, 81*, 84-5*, 85, 88, 93, 131
Crystal Palace 21, 29, 40, 60, 98-9, 100, 102, 104, 106, 107-116, 109*, 110*, 123, 128, 130, 131, 133, 136
Crystal Palace & South London Junction Railway 130
Crystal Palace Company 19, 58, 60, 99, 108, 112, 119, 131
Crystal Palace District Electric Light & Supply Company 133
Crystal Palace District Gas Company 19, 20, 24, 106, 133
Crystal Palace Indoor Bowling Club 120
Crystal Palace Low & High Level stations 130
Crystal Palace Park Road 99, 100, 100*, 101, 104, 104-5*, 105,112
Crystal Palace Saturday Orchestra 107-113
Crystal Palace School of Art, Science, & Literature 111-12
Cupp see Capps
Currey, Henry & Percivall 100, 101
Cusack family 30

DACRES ROAD 104, 129
D'Aguilar, Baron 43, 47
Dalmain Road 126
Daniel, John 33
Dartmouth Arms public house 86, 90, 122*, 130
Dartmouth Arms station 93, 93*, 97, 130
Dartmouth, Earls of 17-18, 35, 48, 81-2, 86, 103, 129*
Dartmouth Lodge 18
Dartmouth Park 103
Dartmouth Place 89*, 90
Dartmouth Road 61, 88, 89*, 90, 104, 121, 124*, 125, 129, 133
Dartmouth Road Wesleyan Chapel 30
Datchet Road 13, 14, 16
Davidson, Charles 112
Davis, William 57
Dawson, Sir Philip 120, 120*
Dawson, William Henry 39
Dawson's Cottages 39

De Paiba see Pabia
Defoe, Daniel 78
Dence, Charlotte & John 43
Denham Court 135
Deptford 74-5, 95
Dermody, Thomas 18, 34, 68, 68*
Deskene, Abraham & James 61
Deutsch, Emanuel 114
Devonshire, sixth duke of 91, 112
Devonshire Road 61, 63, 66, 131
Dickens, Charles 41, 64
Dillwyn Road 135
Disraeli, Benjamin 66
Dog Kennel Houses 50*, 56, 81, 83
Dolman, Father 24
Dolphin public house 18, 31-3, 32-
   3*, 34*, 38*, 50*, 121, 130
Donald, James 29
Doo, Henry 53, 85
Doo's Wharf 40*, 52*, 53, 85
Dornford, Josiah 59
Dorrell Estate 135
Dowse, John 31
Drive, The 103
Dubois, Edward 72
Dudin, Henry 29, 63, 81
Dulwich College 43, 100, 102-3, 125
Dulwich Wells 78
Dulwich Wood 83, 102-3
Dunoon Road 61, 65, 66
Dvorak, Antonin 111, 116
Dyteman, Thomas 37

EARLE, GEORGE 23
Eastridden 24
Edgelar, James 31, 49
Edgson, John 62
Edmonds family 8-11
Edmondson & Sons 52
Edney family 30
Edney Street 30
Edney's Cottages 30
Edward VI 74
Edwards, Joseph 57
Electricity 133
Elgar, Sir Edward 111
Eliot see St Germans
Eliot Bank 103
Elizabeth I 9, 10, 74
Ellesmere House 45-6, 46*, 68
Elm Bank 99
Elm Cottage 57
Elm Grove 41, 42*, 43, 44, 47, 127
Elm Lane 9
Elms, The (Elm Lane) 12, 12*
Elms, The (Sydenham Hill) 91, 92*
Enclosure 86-7
Enderby 101
English, Charles 129*
Entertainments 123
Evans, Adrian 25
Evans, Mary 57
Ewelme Road 61, 66

FABER, FREDERICK 102
Fairlawn 65, 65*
Fairlawn Park 24, 26, 106
Fairlawn School 65
Fairs 60, 83-5
Farar, Samuel 43, 47
Farington, Joseph 68
Farncomb, Thomas 118
Fawley Lodge 103
Fenner, William 45
Fenner estate & family 44-8, 58
Fiander, Miss 26
Field, Barron 72
Fielding, John Crossley 67
Fire Brigades 133
Firs, The 35-6, 36*, 43

Flats 135-6
Florian 99*
Flynn, Mr 31
Fogerty, Joseph 101
Fonthill Lodge 65
Ford, Edmund 8
Forest, Adam atte 14
Forest Hill 50, 61, 61*, 63, 67, 93,
   121, 124, 125, 129, 131, 134, 135
Forest Hill Baths 104
Forest Hill High Street 121
Forest Hill House School 66, 66*,
   119
Forest Hill Road 65, 67
Forest Hill station 93, 93*, 97, 130,
   130*
Forest Place 63
Foresters' Arms 123*
Forster family 12, 86, 91, 92*, 97, 102
Fortnum, John 26
Foster, Richard 8
Fox, Charles James 82-3*
Fox & Hounds public house (1)
   55*, 81
Fox & Hounds public house (2) 81,
   87*, 126
Frederic Place 94
French, Hugh 28, 37
French, Pinkston Arundel 15, 28,
   36, 37, 44
Frith, William Powell 118
Fuller, Robert 47

GALTON, SIR FRANCIS 61
Gardiner, Sir Thomas 61
Garrard family 59
Gas 133
Genand Crofte 13
George III 79, 82-3*, 83
German community 118-19
German Evangelical Church 118,
   119*, 129
Ghent Abbey 74
Gipsies 85
Gipsy Hill station 103
Girling, Harriet 45
Girls' Industrial Home 104
Girton Road 39, 40, 41
Glehn, von, family 31, 37, 44, 57,
   112-16, 118-19
Glover, Thomas (1) 41
Glover, Thomas (2) 14
Godden family 47
Golden Lion public house 37-9,
   38*, 39*, 41, 121, 123, 130
Goodwin family 96-8, 99, 99*
Gothic Cottage, London Road 97
Gothic Cottage, Sydenham Road 22
Grace, W.G. 101, 119-20
Grammar School 36
Grampion Lodge 118, 118*
Granada Cinema 41
Grange, The (Honor Oak Road) 66-7
Grange, The (Sydenham Road) 26
Great Handel Organ 108
Great North Wood 22, 74, 85
Green, John Richard 114-5
Green Dragon 77*, 79
Green Man public house 56
Greenwood, Frederick 120
Greyhound public house 29, 35,
   36, 48, 49*, 50*, 52, 53, 53*, 54,
   56, 57, 58, 79, 79*, 81, 86, 121,
   126, 130
Griffith, John 33
Grimett, William 11, 12
Grogan, Marie 47
Grote family 25
Grove, Sir George 24, 24*, 25, 26,
   98, 107-116, 108*

Grove Cottage 44, 44*, 45*
Grove Road 126
Guitton, John 23, 25
Gwilt, George 19*

HALFHIDE, GEORGE 15
Halford, Mr 44
Haliwell Priory 61
Hall Drive 58, 100
Hambly, Peter 59
Hamborough, John 22
Hamilton Lodge 30, 30*
Handel Festivals 109*, 111
Hanover Lodge 26
Hansard, Octavius 106
Harding, John 44
Hardy, Josiah 26
Hardy, Susannah 39
Harrild, Horton & Thomas 95
Harrild, Robert 93*, 94-6, 95*
Harris, Rolf 138
Hartshorne, John 49
Haseltine Road School 126, 136*
Havelock House 64-5
Haven, The 100*
Haweis, Hugh R. 114
Hawker, Col. 43
Hawkhurst Lodge 41, 43
Hayne, William Burgess 37
Hazel Grove 29, 30, 35*, 138
Helps, Frederick A.W.M. 91
Henman, Abraham 47
Hennell, Alexander Gordon 103-
   4, 121*
Hennell, Alexander Robert 104, 121*
Henry VIII 57, 61, 74
Hermitage, The 63
Hewes, John 23
Higgins, H.J. 41
High Street 21, 88, 90, 121
Highfield 54, 56
Highfield House 55-6
Hill, Thomas 28, 71-2, 71*
Hill (or Hilton) Cottage 89*
Hill House 29, 63-4, 64*, 81
Hillcrest Road 135
Hiller, Ferdinand 114
Hinton, Edward 96
Hodge, Edward & Maria 24, 43, 70
Hodsdon family 25, 26, 30, 31, 33,
   49-51, 55, 56, 61, 62, 68
Hogg, James 53
Holden (or Holding), John 58
Holland, William 15
Hollow Coomb 112
Holness, William 57
Holy Trinity Church 37, 95
Holy Trinity School 125
Home Cottage 89*, 90
Home Park Lodge 22, 23-24, 135
Home Park Recreation Ground 24,
   123
Homewood, John 29
Hone, Nathaniel 58, 68
Honor Oak Hill 10
Honor Oak Park 84-5*, 108
Honor Oak Park station 130
Honor Oak Road 37, 43, 61-7, 61*,
   90, 100, 119
Honor Oak station 130
Honor Oak Wood 61
Hook, Theodore 72
Hope Lodge 22
Horne, Octavius 24
Horner Grange 91, 101
Horniman, Frederick 118, 137, 137*
Horniman Drive 61, 118
Horniman Gardens 100
House, Thomas 45
Howis, Edward 66-7

Howland, Jeffrey 10
Howlet, Richard 8-9
Hudson, John 62
Hughes, Thomas 70
Hull, Walter 16
Hullah, John 114
Hunloke, Lady 91
Hunt, Frederick Knight 64
Hunt, Holman 114
Hunt, James 90
Hunt, John & Leigh 72
Hunt, Thomas 40, 94-6
Hunt & Winton 35, 40
Hunting 53, 56, 63-4, 81-3
Hurst, William 43
Hutton, Thomas Palmer 37
Hyde, Joseph 53
Hyde, William 12

ION (OR I'ON), WILLIAM
   FREDERICK 35
Irving, Washington 71
Ivy House 46*, 47
Ivy Wall 16

JAMES I 77
Jew's Walk 37, 57, 97*, 98, 100,
   102, 102*, 119, 123, 128, 135
Joachim, Joseph 114
John Bell, Hills, & Lucas Ltd. 137*
Jones, William Taylor 124
Jordan, Dorothea 43, 64
Jordon, Lucy 43
Jorrocks, John 81

KALLYWELL SPRINGS 61
Kangley Bridge Road 136
Kaye, Sir John 118
Kemble, John Towgood 43
Kenman, Abraham 28
Kent House Farm 35
Kent House fields 85
Kent House Lane 20, 22, 37, 136
Kent House Road 21, 25, 33-4
Kent House Social Club 22
Kenton Cottage 24, 41, 43
Kerval, George Charles 56
King, Edward 15
King, Lucy 23
King Edward's Parade 26
Kings Garth 117
Kingsford, James 26
Kirkdale 40, 43, 48-9, 49*, 53, 53*,
   74-5*, 81, 87-8, 87*, 88*, 90, 91*,
   98, 100, 101, 108, 112, 119, 121,
   123, 125, 126, 128, 131
Kirtley Road 25
Knighton, William 29
Knighton Park Road 29, 35, 135
Knowles, Sir James 106

LADYWELL 131
Laing, Samuel 107
Lambeth Water Company 133
Lancaster, Joseph 29
Lance, James 28
Lance, William 34
Langford, William 45, 68
Lanier, Innocent 77
Lansbury, George 119
Lapsewood 100, 103
Larkbere Road 23, 25
Laurel Bank 97
Laurel Brook 16
Laurel Grove 30
Lawes, Edward Vitruvius 131
Lawn, The 23, 25, 43, 106, 135
Lawrence, Sir Thomas 69-70, 69*
Lawrie family 15, 28, 58-60, 100
Lawrie Park Avenue 59, 99*, 105

Lawrie Park estate 60, 98, 99-101, 119, 120, 135
Lawrie Park Gardens 57, 99, 99*, 101
Lawrie Park Road 100, 100*, 101, 120
Lawrie Place 121
Leathersellers' Company 14, 15, 55-7, 55*, 131
Lecky, William E.H. 114
Legge, Augustus 127
Legge, Edward 68
Legh (or Leigh), Nicholas 23
Leigh, Robert 22
Lekeux family 47
Lemaistre, John 44
Lepine, Mr 23
Leslie, Henry 114
Lethieullier family 20, 22, 23
Letts, Thomas 15
Lewisham Board of Works 131, 133
Lewisham Council 138
Lewisham House 11, 20, 23
Ligoe, Francis 62
Lime Tree Cottage 28*, 29
Linden Cottage 28, 71
Lindsay, Alexander 50
Liston, John 72
Liszt, Franz 111, 116
Litherland family 29
Little, William 91
Littleton, Henry 60, 116
London & Croydon Railway 84*, 130-31
London & South Western Bank 101
London County Council 138
London Road 61, 95, 97, 98, 98*, 100, 117, 118, 131, 133, 134*, 135, 137, 137*
Long, Captain Charles 26
Longton Avenue 102, 128, 135
Longton Grove 101*, 102, 102*, 128
Longton Hall 127
Longton Hotel 102, 127
Lordship Lane station 130
Louise House 104
Low Cross 79
Low Lane 20
Lower Sydenham industrial estate 136, 137*
Lower Sydenham station 130
Lowman, Christopher 24

MACHYN, HENRY 9
McPherson, Doughal 28
Maddin Road 135, 136*
Malin, Fanny 43
Mallam, James Crosland 60*
Malvern House 40*, 45*, 47, 70, 87
Man of Kent public house 30
Manchester House 44, 46*
Manning, William 22
Manns, Sir August 98, 107-11, 108*
Manor, The 65
Manor House, Honor Oak Road 65*, 66
Manor House, Perry Hill 15, 15*
Manor Lodge 65
Marriott family 15
Marryat family 28, 47, 57, 70, 86-7
Marsh, Samuel 36, 37
Marx, Eleanor 119
Mary Ann's Place 12
Massenet, Jules 111
Mathews, Charles 72
Matthew, Robert 61
Maybourne 120
Mayo & Co. 135-6
Mayow Cottages 33
Mayow family 17-18, 19, 26, 28, 31, 35, 47, 49-52, 55, 63, 68-71, 73, 79, 103-4, 125

Mayow Lodge 46*, 47
Mayow Park 123
Mayow Road 17, 19, 30, 31, 34*, 40, 104
Meadowcroft 17
Mello, William 26
Metropolitan Commissioners of Sewers 131, 132*
Miall, Edward 117, 117*
Miall Road 117, 135
Middleton, John 26
Mill Gardens 88, 89*, 90
Millais, Sir John 114
Miller, Frederick William 15
Milverton House 17
Milverton Lodge 90
Minson (or Minchin), John 25
Moncleare, William 23
Mongrédien, Augustus 117
Montague (or Montacute) Cottage 23, 23*
Moore, Edward 119
Moore, Thomas 71
Moore, Thomas Sturge 119
Morphew (or Morfee) family 34
Morphew, William 103
Morris, James 52
Morris, John 9
Morris, Sophia 22
Mortimer House 28*, 29
Moseley, Thomas 41
Mount Gardens 90, 90*, 119, 127
Murray, Amelia Matilda 103
Muscamp 61
Music hall 123
Myers, Frederick William 114
Myrtle Grove 30

NABORHOOD CINEMA (& CENTRE) 44
Nash, Edwin 96, 100, 101, 126*
Neale, Nicholas 25
Neville (shepherdess) 79-80
New King Street 75
Newlands 40*, 46*, 47-8, 73, 134
Newlands Park 40, 42*, 43, 44-5, 44*, 45*, 47, 98
Newport, Henry 75-7
Norman Cottage 43, 46*, 47, 47*
Norton, John 101, 104-5*, 105
Note, John 10
Nothard, Thomas 28
Novello & Co. 116
Nutgrove Hall 13

OAKFIELD 65-6
Oakley, William 66
Oakwood 104
Observatory House 103
Ogier, Peter 47
Ogilvy, John 31
Old Cedars 43, 48, 57, 58, 59*, 73, 74-5*, 85
Old Grange 91, 112
Old House 32, 47, 49-52, 50*, 51*, 55, 68-70
Old Surrey Hunt 81
Orchard, The 90, 90*, 119, 127
Orchard Cottages 16, 16*
Orchard House 16, 16*
Orger, William 15, 37
Our Lady and St Philip Neri Church 24, 26, 47-8, 125
Ouzman family 38*, 40
Oxford House 35

PABIA, MOSES 58
Padeerewski, Ignacy 111
Paget, Mr 47
Panmure Road 124*, 129*
Park Chapel 128

Park Cottage 96, 96*
Park End 94*, 95, 95*, 96, 103
Park End House 95, 95*
Park Road Cottage 95*
Park Terrace 95
Parker, Mrs 124
Parker, Sir Thomas 58
Parks, Ann & Hannah 44
Parry, Sir Hubert 114
Parsons, Samuel 41
Passmore Edwards Orphanage 60, 116*
Paulet (or Pawlet), Lord Giles 61
Pavott, Mr 12
Paxton, Sir Joseph 60, 91, 112, 126, 128
Paxton Lodge (or Cottage) 35
Paxton Park 30, 106
Peak Hill 40, 54-7, 57*, 72, 81, 83, 124, 128, 131-3
Peak Hill Lodge 44, 57, 112-16, 112*
Peake, Richard 31
Pearson, John Loughborough 116
Peckham Road 67
Pen Bryn 100
Penge 37, 44
Penge East station 130
Penge Lane 42*, 45*
Penge Wood 86
Percy Cottage 45
Perry, Richard 20
Perry Green 17
Perry Hill 8, 8*, 12, 13-17, 13*, 37, 56, 124, 135
Perry Hill Farm 14, 15, 16, 31, 131
Perry Hill House 15, 37, 124
Peak Hill Lodge 110*
Perry Hill Public Lending Library 128
Perry Rise 17, 22
Perry Slough 14, 17-19
Perry Street 13
Perry Vale 14, 17-19, 17*, 21, 22, 34, 50, 76*, 104, 131, 133, 138
Perry Vale Farm 18-19, 49
Perrymount House 19
Perrymount School 118
Perystreete 138
Pevril House 56
Phillips, Abraham 23
Phillips, Henry Wyndham 98, 112
Phillips, Joseph 26, 29, 30
Pickthorns 103
Pig Hill 54, 56
Pikethorne 138
Pillion, Thomas 25
Pitt, William 69, 81*
Place House 7-12, 21
Pool River 7, 9, 13, 16*, 19, 54, 131, 135
Pope, John 61
Population 96, 98, 119
Porthcawe Road 22, 23, 24, 135
Post Office 31, 39, 43
Pratt, Henry 37
Price, Sir Charles 53
Price, Ralph 40*, 50*, 53, 70, 73
Prichard, Selina 73
Priestfield Road 15*
Prince Alfred public house 25, 29
Princes Garth 117
Pringle, James 25, 74-5*
Pringle, William 25
Prior, George 23, 25, 26
Priory, The 35, 41, 43-4, 43*, 44, 47, 64
Priory Cottage 44, 44*, 45*
Priory Villa 44*
Priory Villas 43
Prospect House 98*
Prospect Villa 117

Prospect Villas 97
Public houses 121-2
Pugh family 15
Pulkinghorn, Thomas 53
Puplett family 58*, 59

QUEEN'S HALL CINEMA 44
Queen's Road 97, 134*
Queen's tennis club 134*
Quicke, Mrs 36-7
Quilter, Mary & Roger 47

RADCLIFFE 14
Railway Approach 53
Railway Tavern 53, 53*
Railways 93, 93*, 130, 130*
Raraty, Sarah 26
Rashlands (or Rastlands) 23
Ravensbourne River 7, 9, 13
Ray, Alfred S. 40
Raynes, Robert 77
Recreation Road 81
Red Hall 103
Red House 100-101
Redberry Grove 94
Redding, Cyrus 86
Redman family 48
Reeks, Charles Frederick 50
Rendle, William 118
Reservoir 85-6, 93
Reveley, George 41
Ridge, William Pett 129, 130, 135
Ridgway, Mark William 29, 35, 79*
Rivington family 41, 41*
Roads 133
Roberts, Alexander 77*
Roberts, William 47, 131
Robinson, James 26
Robinson, John 39
Robinson, William 12
Rock House 91
Rockhills 91, 112
Rocque, John 26, 27*, 37, 44
Rogers, Charles 118
Rogers, Foster 37
Rogers, Samuel 71
Rose Cottage, Mill Gardens 89*
Rose Cottage, Perry Vale 18, 18*
Rose Hill 118
Rose Retreat 78*
Rosedale 43, 44
Ross, Daniel 39
Rosslyn Villa 102*
Rothsay Villa 103
Round Hill 94
Round Hill House 90, 94
Rouselle Cottage 90*
Rowe, Herbert Mayow Fisher 52
Rowland, Alexander 67
Rowland, David 112
Royal College of Music 112, 115
Royal Historical Society 118
Royal Humane Society 86
Royal Oak public house 65
Royal West Kent Regiment 120*
Rubenstein, Anton 114
Rushey Green 76*
Russell, Edward 51, 52
Russell, John Scott & family 108, 113*, 128
Russell, William 48
Russell Street 88
Rutherford, James 66
Rutland public house 12
Ryle, Edward 10

SABIN FAMILY 12
St Andrew's 101
St Bartholomew's Church 7, 21, 87*, 93*, 95, 97*, 98, 116, 128-9, 128*, 129*

St Bartholomew's National Schools 125, 126*
St Bartholomew's Vicarage 129*
St Clement's Heights 91
St Germains 99*
St German's, Earls of 61, 87, 97, 103
St German's Park 103
St Helen's 101
St Mary's 102
St Matthew's Church 124*, 129*
St Michael & All Angels' Church 26, 37
St Michael's Schools 100, 125, 126
St Olave's, Southwark 106
St Philip's Church 100, 124*, 128
St Philip's Schools 125
St Saviour's, Southwark 20
St Winefride's 104
Saint-Saëns, Camille 111
Sanders, Misses 47
Sanderson, Rev.S 25
Sangwin, Mr 28
Saratoga 104
Saunders, Captain 26
Schallehn 107-8
School Board for London 126
School House 26
Schools 15-16, 22-23, 26, 29, 40, 43, 48, 56-7, 58, 60*, 91, 100, 18, 124-7
Schuster, Leo 100
Scilly, Samuel 34
Scott, Alexander 35
Scott, Sir George Gilbert 96
Scott, Sir Walter 70
Scudder family 24, 33, 35
Searles, Thomas 99
Secker, Mary 12
Second World War 135, 138
Selley family 34
Semaphore Hill 103
Sewell, Charles & Frederick 102
Sewers 131
Seymour Lodge 90, 91*
Shackleton, Sir Ernest & Henry 119
Shackleton Close 138, 138*
Shanklin Villa 95
Shaw, George Bernard 109, 111
Shawe, William 10
Shene Priory 74
Shenewood Estate 57, 59
Shepherd family 11
Sheppard, Thomas & Elizabeth 24, 26
Sheridan, Richard Brinsley 82-3*
Shops 26, 31, 121, 121-2*, 135-6
Shute, Richard 43, 70
Siddins, Sarah 71
Silverdale 40, 52-3, 81, 104, 123, 135
Sinkins, John 30
Sipa 7
Sippenham, Beatrici 13
Sitwell, William Hurt 26
Six Acre Field 26
Skeat, Walter W. 16
Skeet's Lane 88
Smith, Haskett 40*, 47, 73
Smith, James & Horace 71
Smith, Ravenscroft Elsie 97
Smith, Sydney 69
Smith, Thomas 23
Smith, Thomas Roger 97
Smith, William & Victoria 47-8, 134
Smiths Hills 62
Sneyd, Jeremiah 25
Society of Arts 108
South Bank 61
South Road 103, 138
South Suburban Gas Company 133
South Sydenham Park 103-4
Southend Lane 19, 19*, 20, 133
Southwark Cathedral 20

Spencer, William 12
Spring Hill 54
Springfield, Sydenham Road 35
Springfield, off Wells Park Road 88, 133
Springfield Road 120
Stanford, Sir Charles 116
Stanhope, George 62
Stanley, Arthur Penrhyn 114
Stanley Cottage 89*
Stanley House 100
Stanstead Road 75, 76*, 103, 131, 135
Staples, William 44
Station Parade 48
Steer, Abraham 53
Stephenson, Robert 103
Stevens, Charles 37
Stevens, John 41
Stevens estate 37-44
Stevens family (of Bell Green) 20
Still, Robert 53
Stocketts 24
Stockhausen, Julius 114, 116
Stollard, Timothy 86
Streetfield 26, 28, 29, 30
Stronach, Margaret 48
Strong, Edward 58, 59, 68
Style, Edmund 50
Style (or Stiles), John 25, 50, 55
Sullivan, Sir Arthur 69, 107, 111-14, 111*
Summerfield 37, 90
Suncroft Place 126
Sunderland Mount 138
Sunderland Road 103, 118, 138
Sunnydene Street 26
Surrey House & Mount 137
Sutton, John 35
Swanley 16
Swayn, Egidii 13, 54
Swaynesfeld 54
Swine Hill 54
Sydenham Albion Cricket Club 39
Sydenham Brewery 22, 22*
Sydenham Bridge 85
Sydenham Chapel 15, 36*, 36-7, 38*
Sydenham College 124
Sydenham Common 18, 35, 57-60, 74-92, 74-5*, 76*, 80*, 82-3*, 92*, 102
Sydenham Congregational Chapel 38*, 40
Sydenham Court 135
Sydenham Fair 60, 83-5
Sydenham Farm 19*, 20
Sydenham Green 19-20, 37
Sydenham Hall 58, 59, 60, 60*, 73, 74-5*
Sydenham High School 91, 101, 125, 127, 127*
Sydenham Hill 63, 74-5*, 76*, 91, 98, 100, 102-3, 102*, 105, 119, 126, 133, 135, 138
Sydenham Home & Infirmary for Sick Children 25, 95*, 106, 106*
Sydenham House Academy 56-7
Sydenham Lecture Hall 117, 123, 126, 128
Sydenham Library 24
Sydenham, Manor of 7-10
Sydenham New Town 63-7
Sydenham Park 40, 41, 93-6, 94*, 95*, 96*, 100, 101, 103, 124
Sydenham Park Road 94, 95, 96, 124
Sydenham Parsonage (Vicarage) 129*
Sydenham Place 37, 47, 48, 49*, 74-5*
Sydenham Public Hall 121*, 123
Sydenham Recreation Ground 123

Sydenham Rifle Corps 123*
Sydenham Rise 63, 118
Sydenham Road 13, 19, 20, 21-53, 21*, 27*, 121, 133, 134
Sydenham Road greens 40, 40*, 42*, 46*
Sydenham Society 138
Sydenham station 21, 93, 98, 130
Sydenham Wells 57, 78-9
Sydenham Working Men's Association 128
Sykes, Alfred 12
Symms, James 11

TAGGART, JAMES 40*, 41, 43
Tahourdin, Henry 23
Talma public house 123
Tanner's Hill 75
Tannsfeld Road 21, 43
Tappen, George 43, 64
Taylor, Franklin 113
Taylor, James & Thomas 12
Taylor's Lane 43, 78, 79, 88, 90, 124*, 127-8
Taylor's Lane riots 43, 127-8
Taymount & Taymount Grange 134*, 135
Taymount Rise 97, 134*, 135
Telegraph Field 103
Tetley, Edward & John 103, 118
Thomas, William 17
Thorne, James 16
Thornton, George 58
Thorpe estate 52, 135
Thorpewood Avenue 90, 138, 138*
Three Compasses public house 59, 79
Throckmorton family 9
Ticknor, George 71, 93
Tilling, Thomas 16, 131
Todd, John Wood & Mrs 15, 124, 124*, 125*
Todd, William 17
Toll gate 44-5
Toller, Charles 45
Tolley, James 101
Townsend, Harrison 137
Trams 131
Transport 130-31
Tredown Road 47
Trehearn family 12, 31, 33-4, 34*, 35, 39
Treswell, Ralph 21, 54, 63, 76*
Treverbyn 118
Trewsbury Road 37, 40, 135
Trinder, Thomas 66
Trinity Hospital 91
Tudor Hall 16, 103, 124, 124*, 125*
Tudor Lodge 90
Twiss, Horace 72
Two Brewers public house 12, 14, 14*, 121
Tyson, Ann 66
Tyson Road, Estate, & Gardens 66

UPPER SYDENHAM STATION 130

VALENTINE COURT 138
Van Vliet, Edward 101
Venables, Thomas 59
Venner Road 46*, 48, 134
Verey family 22
Verey's Lane 20
Verge, John 91
Vickers, Thomas 61
Vine Cottage 28*, 29
von Glehn see Glehn
Vulliamy, Lewis 128*

WAGHORN, WILLIAM 33

Wakers Croft 33
Waldram Park Road 103, 117, 131
Walker, Edward 49
Walker, Matthew Clement & Richard 24
Walmer 16
Ware, George 49, 53
Water supply 131-3
Watlington Grove 24, 25, 26
Welland House 117
Welles, Sir John 8
Wells, Rebecca 91
Wells Park 123, 124*
Wells (or Wells Park) Road 57, 78*, 88, 90, 91, 123, 129,133, 138
Westbourne Drive 103
Wesley Hall 28
West Hill estate 102
West Kent Hounds 81
West Kent Park 126
Westbourne Drive 18
Westmorland, Robert 29
Westwode, Theodici de 13
Westwood (or Westwode) 13, 54, 55, 74-7, 76*
Westwood Cottage 91
Westwood (or West) Hill 57-60, 74-5, 79, 85, 91, 97*, 98, 99, 108, 112, 128, 135, 138
Westwood House 58*, 59-60, 72, 73, 74-5, 104, 116, 116*
Westwood Lodge 110*, 112-14, 113*
Westwood Park 61, 63, 64, 118
Westwood Road 100
Whagow House 26
Wharton, Henry James 53
White Cottage 14
White Hart public house 14
White House 64, 64*
White House Farm 12
Whittell Gardens 95
Whittle, William Henry 94-5, 97
William IV 43, 64
Williams, John 37, 48*, 49, 68
Willoughby House 100*
Willow Walk 88, 88*
Wilson, Mr 52
Wilson, William 47
Wilson Place 28*, 29
Winchfield Road 136
Windemere Cottage (& Club) 31
Windmill 57
Winsford Road 15
Wissett, Robert 65
Wood, The 91, 92*
Wood, George 34
Wood Cottage 89*
Wood Minna Cottage 44*
Wood Vale 63
Woodcock, Richard James 103
Woodgate, William 106
Woodhouse, Mrs 62
Woodthorpe 90, 119
Woodville 99
Woodville Cottage 23, 23*
World's End public house 59
Worrell, Farefax 22
Worsley Bridge Road 136, 137*
Wright, William 29
Wunderbau 58
Wylde, William 50
Wythes, George 60, 99, 100

XIMENES, DAVID 60

YEATMAN-BIGGS, HUYSHE W. 129*
York House 28